Gothic Radicalism

Also by Andrew Smith

BRAM STOKER: HISTORY, PSYCHOANALYSIS AND THE GOTHIC *(co-editor with William Hughes)*

DRACULA AND THE CRITICS

Gothic Radicalism

Literature, Philosophy and Psychoanalysis in the Nineteenth Century

Andrew Smith
Lecturer in English
University of Glamorgan

First published in Great Britain 2000 by
MACMILLAN PRESS LTD
Houndmills, Basingstoke, Hampshire RG21 6XS and London
Companies and representatives throughout the world

A catalogue record for this book is available from the British Library.

ISBN 0–333–76035–2

 First published in the United States of America 2000 by
ST. MARTIN'S PRESS, INC.,
Scholarly and Reference Division,
175 Fifth Avenue, New York, N.Y. 10010

ISBN 0–312–23042–7

Library of Congress Cataloging-in-Publication Data
Smith, Andrew, 1964–
Gothic radicalism : literature, philosophy, and psychoanalysis in the nineteenth
century / Andrew Smith.
p. cm.
Includes bibliographical references (p.) and index.
ISBN 0–312–23042–7
1. English fiction–19th century—History and criticism. 2. Horror tales, English–
–History and criticism. 3. Psychoanalysis and literature—Great Britain–
–History—19th century. 4. Poe, Edgar Allan, 1809–1849—Fictional works.
5. Gothic revival (Literature) 6. Radicalism in literature. 7. Philosophy in
literature. I. Title.

PR868.T3 S59 1999
823'.0872909—dc21
                                      99–049747

This book is printed on paper suitable for recycling and made from fully managed and sustained
forest sources.

10   9   8   7   6   5   4   3   2   1
09 08 07 06 05 04 03 02 01 00

Printed and bound in Great Britain by
Antony Rowe Ltd, Chippenham, Wiltshire

For Joanne

Contents

Preface

The subject of this study is the Gothic rewriting of a tradition of idealist thought, one which begins with Burke and culminates in Freud. A range of critical methodologies are employed in order to draw out this Gothic history, one which inhabits a range of writings from Mary Shelley to Bram Stoker. Three interrelated histories are brought together here: a history of the sublime, Freudian psychoanalysis, and Gothic discourse. Such a history explains why psychoanalysis has been so fascinated with the Gothic, and why it is that the failings of psychoanalysis can be illuminated by a reading of the Gothic texts which it purports to analyse.

Acknowledgements

I would like to thank Andrew Clark, Helen Phillips and Jeff Wallace for their support of this project and for making time available in which to complete it. I would also like to thank the University of Glamorgan Research Development Fund for helping to finance the sabbatical in which this book was written. I am also grateful to Phil Cox and Michael Spitzer for their encouragement and support and for their detailed criticism of much of the final manuscript. I would also like to thank Paul Hamilton for his support for, and supervision of, this project in its earlier guise as a doctoral thesis at the University of Southampton. Thanks to William Hughes for his advice about the afterword, and to Jill Lake at Macmillan who responded to my anxieties over permissions with good grace and humour. I would also like to thank Charmian Hearne for her invaluable advice on how to structure the book. Joanne Benson painstakingly proofread the final draft and I owe her a debt for this and for her love, tolerance and support throughout the writing process.

I would also like to thank Johns Hopkins University Press for granting permission to quote from Thomas Weiskel's *The Romantic Sublime: Studies in the Structure and Psychology of Transcendence.*

Introduction

In many respects this study is a history of the ineffable. What is at issue is an exploration of a tradition of what I am going to refer to as idealist Gothic writing. My reading of a particular Gothic tradition which spans the nineteenth century is one which observes the mutations and developments in an idealist tradition of thought which has its roots in the eighteenth century and its terminus in the twentieth; in other words, the idealist tradition which extends from Burke's *Philosophical Enquiry* (1757) to Freud's 'The Uncanny' (1919). That such a tradition can be mapped is not controversial; Angela Leighton, for example, has identified a 'progressive internalisation of the eye' which began in the eighteenth century.[1] In this internalisation outward modes of perception were replaced by a new emphasis on introspection, the roots of which are to be found in Burke, and its culmination in Freud's account of the unconscious.

This tradition is reworked by the Gothic and a range of writing beginning with Mary Shelley, extending to Edgar Allan Poe, encompassing R.L. Stevenson and culminating with Bram Stoker, responds to this idealist presence. On the surface it might appear that some writers are more self-conscious about this tradition than others, and it is certainly unusual to position Stoker in relation to the sublime (although not so in relation to Freud). What is perhaps contentious is my claim that this disparate range of Gothic writings provides a meaningfully coherent critique of this idealist tradition, one which could plausibly be called radical. However, this is just the claim which I aim to substantiate.

One of the striking features of the Gothic is its analysis of the limits of rationality. The challenges posed to post-Enlightenment claims to certainty are developed within the Gothic as both an aesthetic feature (its fascination with narrative fragmentation), an ontology and, para-doxically, a kind of epistemology. The Gothic subject is a precarious being, always in danger of being subsumed by irrationality in all its guises – madness, desire, fear. But this strange being is invariably embedded in a narrative which self-consciously explores the rationality behind such irrational states. This oxymoronic process in the Gothic also points to the presence of a theorising about the nature of subjec-tivity which is one of its central themes.

There are parallels between this Gothic mode of subjectivity and the idealist tradition which it critiques. The Gothic subject on the edge of sanity/insanity, a subject threatened with some kind of mental col-lapse, is a subject to be found in accounts of the sublime *and* in Freud's version of the subject. In the Kantian sublime the subject feels this loss of self as a moment of transcendence, one in which a meaningful sense of a pure noumenal realm is intimated. It is, however, Burke's version of the sublime which is usually referred to in accounts of the Gothic as providing the source for a model of terror which the Gothic incorporates within its own modality of the terrifying. However, Kant is not to be overlooked, as terror might be pushed to the margins of his epistemology, but the initial fear felt by the subject in the sublime is a refinement of Burke's own notion of the fear of death as the principal basis of terror. It is this threatened dissolution of the subject which is explored in the Gothic's own fascination with liminal states.

Psychoanalysis has always played an important part in investigations into the Gothic. The reasons for this are quite clear. The Gothic seems to be a form of writing defined by its fascination with the illicit, espe-cially tabooed, desire and consequently it has been comparatively easy to make the Gothic conform to some kind of Freudian (or post-Freudian) topography of the unconscious.[2] However, the Gothic can also be understood in historical terms. The Gothic version of history is one which runs alongside the dominant history and it is by opening up the Gothic to such an historicist approach that the counter-cultural claims of the Gothic become clear. It is this which leads me to my central premise which is that the Gothic reads a particular history of idealist thought in such a way that it enables us to reinterpret that dominant history. I also attempt an explanation for the rise of psycho-analysis and, coincidentally, throw some light on why critics of the Gothic have been quick to see the form as a prescient quasi-Freudian discourse.

One critic in whose footsteps I tread is Rosemary Jackson's. Superficially this would seem to pose a problem for an historicist investigation such as mine, but I find that her attempts at theorising the subject psychoanalytically are to be found in earlier accounts of subjectivity such as Burke's and Kant's. The echoes between her identification of a Gothic subject and a sublime subject help to develop the debate that psychoanalytical readings of the Gothic are, historically speaking, determined by the history of the Gothic texts which they purport to analyse.

This exploration of the nineteenth-century Gothic inevitably rests on a repudiation of other histories of the sublime and the uncanny; histories which tend to unproblematically mark out a continuity between the literature and the theories themselves. Perhaps the most contentious area here is the provenance of the uncanny. Terry Castle in *The Female Thermometer* claims that the uncanny emerges in the eighteenth century.[3] Her argument is that in the eighteenth century a conscious belief in the supernatural is replaced by a more subtle sublimation of the supernatural, one which resituates it in the unconscious. Her analysis of Radcliffe's *The Mysteries of Udolpho* explores how characters refer to themselves and others, as being ghost-like entities, whereas ghosts are perceived as potentially having a life and reality of their own. This leads Castle to claim that 'We feel at home in Radcliffe's spectralized landscape, for its ghosts are our own – the symptomatic projections of modern psychic life' (p. 125). That is, Radcliffe's ghosts correspond to a Freudian version of the subject, one who uncannily sees the world as ghosted by a set of discrete presences which anticipate our own death but which soothe away our anxieties by giving us a vision of a 'life' to come. Castle sees in this the possibility of a reconsideration of the relationship between history and psychoanalysis; she writes, 'Seen in historical terms, as an offshoot of the radically introspective habit of mind initiated in the late eighteenth century, psychoanalysis seems both ·the most poignant critique of romantic consciousness to date, and its richest and most perverse elaboration' (p. 139).

Castle's view of the eighteenth century is in many ways a sophisticated and persuasive one but what is also of interest is what is omitted. One passing reference is made to Burke as one of the 'Writers on the imagination' (p. 134), and the only other reference is in an endnote referring to Burke's possible influence on Radcliffe's representation of pleasurable grief. There is no mention at all of Kant. In effect Castle can only come to her conclusion about the uncanny by pushing to one side the whole question of the sublime. It is this omission which I will put back into the Gothic tradition because it is one which accounts for both the emergence of the uncanny and the Gothic fascination with liminal states.

One study which deals in a sustained way with the relationship between sublimity and the Gothic is Vijay Mishra's *The Gothic Sublime*.[4] In some respects Mishra's book is crucial to an understanding of how the Gothic anticipates the uncanny. Part of Mishra's project is to account for the existence of some of the more formally repetitive elements to be found in early Gothic writings such as, for example, shared plots and the recycling of character names. The Gothic also recycles a range of core themes and issues and it is the presence of such repetition which structurally, for Mishra, refers to the uncanny in texts which also make explicit reference to the sublime. Mishra writes that:

> What marks off the various versions of the primary precursor text are levels of uncanny duplication at work in the Gothic. Read as the recognition that nothing ever happens, that all history has always already been played out and that the subject is simply locked into an incessant series of repetitions, the Gothic rewrites the sublime and prefigures its theorisation as the 'Uncanny'. (p. 71)

It is the nature of that rewriting which is problematic in Mishra's argument. This is partly because he wants to relate the Gothic fascination with fragmentation and the collapse of meaning to the postmodern, so that 'the rhetoric of the Gothic sublime may be seen as somehow anticipating the postmodern' (p. 20). Somehow indeed. It is history which is marginalised in this claim in what is otherwise a sophisticated attempt to explain the emergence of a Gothic version of the sublime. Mishra argues for the independence of the Gothic sublime from the Romantic sublime with which it has been more usually associated. To some degree David B. Morris's claims for a Gothic sublimity (which I comment on below) are Mishra's target here. There exists, however, a paradox in Mishra's championing of an independent sublime because Mishra also argues that the Gothic sublime's uncertainties are generated by the continuing influence of its Romantic variant. The Gothic therefore becomes characterised by its struggle with the orthodox philosophical tradition which it is trying to repudiate. This is because the sublime, for Mishra, is *a priori* a Gothic force. He writes:

> It is not that the word *Gothic* in the phrase *Gothic sublime* progressively assimilates the sublime into its own domain; on the contrary, it is the sublime that regressively colonizes its descriptor. In the final

analysis this is the terror of the sublime, the frighteningly contam-
inative force of the impossible idea itself. (p. 40)

This idea of a struggle at the centre of the Gothic is, according to
Mishra, subsequently replicated in the experience of the uncanny
where the subject feels this struggle as the defining characteristic of
modern identity. Mishra argues that, 'To read the Gothic is to understand the logic of the uncanny' (p. 63); the sublime becomes uncanny
and the uncanny becomes sublime in a relationship which meets its
most comprehensive expression in the postmodern.

Mishra's central interest is in observing how this Gothic sublime, formulated in the eighteenth century, lingers on into the present day. The
status of this Gothic sublime is not clear because it does seem as
though Mishra is prepared to entertain the idea that the sublime is
potentially already a Gothic force. It is, however, his problematic idea
concerning the existence of an independent Gothic sublime which I
will develop throughout this book, arguing that the Gothic reconstructs the Romantic sublime in order to pass comment on its failures
both as an ontology and as an epistemology. A history of metaphysics
becomes rewritten by the Gothic along the way.

I mentioned above that Mishra attempts to distance himself from
David B. Morris's contention that the Gothic sublime is a Romantic
variant (although Mishra repeats Morris's claims for a link between the
sublime and the uncanny). Morris's article 'Gothic Sublimity' was a
groundbreaking attempt at trying to identify and explain the influence
of the Gothic sublime, and I feel that Morris is correct in defining the
Gothic sublime as a form which exposes the central inadequacies to be
found within the philosophy itself. Morris writes that 'The Gothic
novel stands as an implicit critique of Burke – a testament to how
much he and his age were unable to explain the sublime.'[5] The incoherence of the sublime is exaggerated in the Gothic which highlights
the failures to be found within theories of the sublime in the first
place. In some sense this is also the basic premise of the first half of
this book (before I develop a similar critical position on Freud).

However, Morris perceives this Gothic sublime as a latent form of the
uncanny. He explores the early Gothic fascination with incest (his
main references are to Walpole) suggesting that this notion of desire
conforms to a model of repetition (within families) which echoes the
element of repetition associated with the uncanny. He also suggests
that what is left out of accounts of the sublime is desire. Burke may
posit fear as the principal source of the sublime but this, for Morris,

simply conceals the idea that at root it is desire which more properly generates the anxieties and confusions which are central to Burke's thesis, so that:

> Whereas Burke had founded his theory of the sublime on an irreconcilable split between terror and love, Walpole shows us how the intensest terror is located at the very origin of desire. In the Gothic novel, love and terror prove inextricable. (p. 306)

It is this omission which is subsequently developed by Freud in his account of the unconscious as the site where these anxieties are worked out. Morris therefore makes a direct correlation between the Gothic sublime and the uncanny, whereby Freud makes explicit what is only covertly present in the sublime. In this way the uncanny provides us with a critical reading of the specifically Burkean sublime, so that:

> The 'Uncanny' is especially relevant to the Gothic novel because it is not only a theory of the sublime but also, simultaneously, a theory of terror. The specific subclass of terror which Freud describes as the uncanny differs strikingly from the Burkean catalogue of wild, exotic, and overpowering dangers. (pp. 306–7)

In this way the uncanny provides us with an explanation for Burke's prevarications. Morris's version of the Gothic sublime is thus markedly different to Mishra's. Where Mishra considers the uncanny as a modification of the sublime, Morris sees the uncanny as exposing what the sublime hides. My own position is that the Burkean sublime needs to be explored historically. Freud may rewrite the sublime but the nature of that rewriting is also historically conditioned. Freud inherits, rather than exposes, many of the incoherences which characterise Burke's sublime. To understand why this happens requires a much closer analysis of Burke, Kant and Freud than that attempted by either Mishra or Morris.

The mutation of the sublime into the uncanny is played out in a peculiar way in the Gothic. Not only do certain writers such as Poe and Stevenson appear to anticipate Freud, but it is also the case that they provide a critique of Freudian ideas *avant la lettre*. What we find is that Poe, for example, looks back to the Romantics and forward to a culture of analysis.

That Poe is prescient in his Freudian anticipations is an argument that Clive Bloom makes in his important study *Reading Poe Reading*

Freud: the Romantic Imagination in Crisis. Bloom does not merely suggest that Poe anticipates Freudian analysis but also that Poe belongs to an intellectual tradition which makes Freud possible in the first place; this also, in part, explains why psychoanalysts, such as Bonaparte and Lacan, have been drawn to Poe's writings. Bloom explains the ground for this appeal:

> psychoanalysis' fascination with Poe is that Poe conceives of a world which is a mirror image of Freud's own. This world is one in which the conditions which allowed Freud to find a discourse of 'fact' allowed Poe to form from those conditions a certain type of fiction. This reversal of polarities allows us to see how Freudian concepts took form and yet also how that discourse requestions that conceptual process.[6]

Bloom proceeds to explore the complex interchanges between a range of psychoanalytical positions and how they reflect on Poe and how Poe can be used to reflect on them. However, although Bloom identifies Poe as part of an intellectual, certainly idealist, tradition, he does not reflect on the nature of that tradition. The sublime is here, as it is in Castle's reading of the eighteenth century, pushed to the margins. This present study is concerned with putting the sublime back and consequently I read Poe in a rather different way to Bloom, by shifting the focus back on to the sublime and away from the Freudian uncanny.

The Gothic does not merely anticipate the arrival of Freud, it also, as Bloom suggests, identifies the inconsistencies and incoherences which govern Freud's accounts of the unconscious and the uncanny. This is apparent, for example, in how Stevenson's *The Strange Case of Dr Jekyll and Mr Hyde* reworks the uncanny through the image of the double. In some respects the doubling appears to accord with the notion of repetition which is central to Freud's reading of Hoffmann's 'The Sandman'. Stevenson's novella, however, can only be made to conform to a crude Freudian investigation; what is of greater import is the way that it resists a Freudian reading because it both anticipates the uncanny and simultaneously undoes its ontology. The uncanny read via Stevenson becomes an arbitrary experience which rests on a false and unsustainable notion of a bipartite self riven with repression. What is often overlooked in readings of the novella is Jekyll's claim that the chemically produced Hyde is the product of a limited scientific knowledge. The self collapses into itself because it has not been properly separated so that Jekyll and Hyde contaminate each other as they meet. It is this conclusion which enables us to reconsider the problems to be found in Freud's own account of the uncanny which itself reduces everything to a condition of potential uncanniness. The Gothic thus constitutes a history of criticism of this idealist tradition which enables us to consider that tradition anew (and the Gothic's relationship to it).

The close scrutiny which I give to Burke, Kant and Freud in this study is designed to highlight the shared problems which exist between their respective metaphysics. In order to do this I relate the theoretical problems in their works to the Gothic of the time. The effect is to illustrate how the Gothic rewrites the sublime and the uncanny in such a way that it radically critiques the status of nature, language and subjectivity. In particular I look at how the relationship between the sublime and the uncanny needs to be reconsidered and how the relationship between the Gothic and a specifically Freudian psychoanalysis needs to be reinvestigated. This latter issue is to some degree implicit in my historicist arguments. If Burke's treatise supplies the eighteenth-century Gothic novelist with a template for fear then, at the end of the nineteenth century, it is the troubling desires associated with the Freudian unconscious which seem to capture the essence of the Gothic's new anxieties.

Theories of the sublime and how they correspond to a Gothic discourse require an historical analysis of subjectivity. That the Gothic self can be compared to the models of the self found in theories of the sublime and psychoanalysis is explored in Chapter 1. In addition I give a close reading of Longinus, Burke, Kant and Weiskel's *The Romantic Sublime*. Weiskel's acknowledgement that the sublime cannot be properly psychoanalytically examined underlines my central claim that psychoanalysis cannot explore the sublime because the sublime is itself a precursor of the Freudian unconscious. It is a reading of the Gothic which makes this clear and Chapter 2 explores how *Frankenstein* exposes the limitations inherent in Burke's model of sublimity through its attack of the privileged status which Burke accords to nature. I also plot Shelley's novel in relation to Foucault's claims concerning modernity. Foucault's notion that the arrival of modernity is characterised by the creation of 'man' as an object of knowledge is referenced through Victor's own construction of the creature. Such a reading helps to explain how, and why, the sublime becomes rewritten in the process. I also sketch a Kristevian reading of *Frankenstein* because there exist parallels between her account of subject formation and the creature's construction. More significantly this reading also exemplifies the Gothic anticipation of Freud (through its formulation of an analytical scene between Victor and the creature) and some of the more recent psycho-analytic practices.

Chapter 3 looks at how the early-nineteenth-century sublime is compromised by Romanticism's continued reliance on Classical thought. Mary Shelley develops this idea in two of her short stories: 'Valerius: the Reanimated Roman' and 'The Mortal Immortal: a Tale'. These stories reveal how the continued presence of the past undermines claims made for the ahistorical status of the sublime. Her tales also reveal how and explain why a pantheistic sublime becomes replaced with a more limited (somehow less transcendent) version of the secular sublime. Her tales therefore illustrate how the Gothic critiques the pantheistic sublime through its superior understanding of the sublime's incoherencies and failures.

The Romantic period also witnessed a change in emphasis from the importance accorded to individual experience to a new, greater, importance which is associated with communal life. The need for confession, such as Victor's to Walton, suggests the existence of a concern with society, a concern which transcends individual needs. Chapter 4 develops this notion by exploring how Poe refers to such issues in his novel *The Narrative of A. Gordon Pym*. Poe's novel uses images of communal life in order to refer to the complexities of urban experience. Crucially, Poe extends the narrative to include elements of the mystery story and in so doing he gestures towards the necessity of interpretation. In a wider sense this refers to the idea that urban spaces possess mysteries of their own, ones which in Poe's hands become associated with a reworking of the Kantian sublime.

This idea of the specifically urban mystery in need of interpretation is represented in Poe's detective tales through a modified version of Kant's model of the sublime. Chapter 5 explores the idea that the detective in Poe's tales occupies the same position towards a mystery that Kant's subject does to the sublime. What is at issue is the status and function of reason. For Kant a world of reason is associated with the sublime and Poe extends this Kantian intimation of the presence of reason into a fully developed attainment of it, one which is located within the mental world of the detective. Poe's tales, such as 'Mesmeric Revelation', also exploit Kant's idea of noumenal and phenomenal realms. Poe looks back to the Romantics and forward to Freudian analytical investigations of the self.

In Chapter 6 Stoker's *Dracula* is read through Foucault's account of Victorian sexuality in *The History of Sexuality*, vol. 1. The novel develops a specifically sexual version of the sublime which is related to the troublesome functions of the unconscious. The novel stops short of an investigation of the unconscious and in so doing the sublime's destabilising tendencies are never properly contained by the pseudo-scientific attempts at policing desire. This Gothic reworking of the sublime points towards a Freudian scene but in such a way that the claims made for scientific certainty are challenged.

That Freud rewrites a model of the sublime is clear from an investigation of his essay 'The Uncanny'. Chapter 7 argues that the continuation of the sublime in the guise of the Freudian uncanny is a destabilising presence which can also be found in *The Interpretation of Dreams* and *The Psychopathology of Everyday Life*. The incoherent nature of Freud's arguments concerning the uncanny and the unconscious can be illuminated by a reading of Stevenson's *The Strange Case of Dr Jekyll and Mr Hyde*. The novella's representation of a failed scientific practice provides us with a radical critique of Freud's model of subjectivity.

Throughout I emphasise how the Gothic critiques a tradition of idealist thought. That this idealist tradition possesses a neglected fecundity will, I hope, become clear. I have mentioned other works in this area and my stance towards them is awkwardly positioned somewhere between a repudiation and an acknowledgement for their help in mapping out particular elements of this history. What we will find is that this alternative Gothic tradition of the nineteenth century is central to any attempt at trying to grasp the limitations of the dominant intellectual culture of that century.

1
The Gothic and the Sublime

David B. Morris writes of the Gothic sublime that:

> In exploring the entanglements of love and terror, the Gothic novel
> pursues a version of the sublime utterly without transcendence. It is
> a vertiginous and plunging – not a soaring – sublime, which takes us
> deep within rather than far beyond the human sphere. The
> eighteenth-century sublime always implied (but managed to
> restrain) the threat of lost control. Gothic sublimity – by releasing
> into fiction images and desires long suppressed, deeply hidden,
> forced into silence – greatly intensifies the dangers of an uncontrol-
> lable release from restraint. (p. 306)

Although I take issue with Morris's claims that the Gothic sublime is
little more than a repressed version of the uncanny, I do acknowledge
that his identification of an inherent instability within the Gothic
sublime is a useful starting-point for our analysis. This idea of instability can also be extended to accounts of the Romantic sublime; an
analysis of which enables us to bring together a Gothic discourse and
certain Romantic philosophies.

In the sublime the subject is threatened with annihilation in ways
which directly correspond to how the Gothic subject is precariously
posed on thresholds between the human and inhuman, sanity and
insanity, and conscious and unconscious. The sublime is an important
register in the Gothic because it provides the Gothic with a philosophy
through which the world is both emotionally constructed and understood. As a philosophy it attempts to explain the emotional resonances
inherent in fear. The sublime is also much more than this, because in
an extended sense it is a theory which is centred on both language and

11

aesthetics as well as emotional states. Language and aesthetics often retain a problematic place in accounts of the sublime because of their 'unnatural' features. The cultural status of language and art suggests that the world is already mediated in such forms, and their respective status is the focus of considerable debate. This problematic also informs some of the very methodology to be found in accounts of the sublime which take on the ambivalence and vagueness which is supposedly inherent in the sublime itself. The sublime in its most basic form is a construct through which the world is endlessly interpreted, and also the nature of that construct is itself subject to continual re-interpretation; in this way the sublime always offers a series of provisional truth-claims whose status is subjected to further inquiry. To some degree this is to acknowledge the commonplace that philosophical inquiry is not a static affair, but it is also the role of the Gothic to enter into these debates and to offer resolutions to them, resolutions which often pre-empt these moments of self-reflective inquiry.

To understand the sublime it is necessary to explore its mutations, and to understand that these mutations occur because of theoretical incoherence. It is these sites of incoherence which the Gothic is focused upon and which provide the Gothic with its own particular sceptical vision. I am aware that so far this seems to imply that the Gothic is founded upon a paradox, that it moves away from the sublime only to re-encode an idealism of its own through a scepticism which never quite escapes its object of investigation. In this way, at a purely theoretical level, the impossibility of transcendence appears within an idealist debate. To make some of these issues clear we need to develop a mode of inquiry which parallels the development of the sublime with a theory of the Gothic.

One parallel area concerns the function of language in the sublime and the relationship which this language has to the subject. Language is a key strand in this discussion as it runs through a range of writings on the sublime and its investigating metadiscourse. Language and the problem of representation is also a key issue to be found in the Gothic, and in Freud's reading of a Gothic sublime in 'The Uncanny'.[1] Language is problematic in accounts of the sublime because it suggests that the cultural is inextricably linked to that which is non-linguistic (the sublime), which poses problems for the investigation of subjectivity. What we find is that this philosophical dilemma is repeated in the Gothic. Broadly speaking the fantastic is centred on the same problems of interpretation and admits the same difficulty in analysing states of mind that we find in accounts of the sublime. Rosemary Jackson in

Fantasy: the Literature of Subversion makes an important point concerning the way that the Gothic hero/protagonist is confronted by problems of what constitutes I/not-I, and it is this focus on the problems surrounding debates about identity which are also to be found in the sublime.[2] Jackson's is largely a psychoanalytical inquiry, and this is to some degree significant in this instance because the sublime will, historically speaking, mutate into the unconscious at the end of the nineteenth century. However, this is to get beyond ourselves as first it is necessary to look at, an admittedly selective, history of the sublime. In looking at philosophies of the sublime it is necessary that we subject them to a close and exact investigation, necessary in order to identify the precise areas of incoherence to be found in such accounts. What we will find is that it is often difficult to keep the two discourses, that of the Gothic and that of the sublime, apart. The reason for this is because this study is to some degree already reading these accounts in a Gothic manner.

The key areas in all of these accounts concern the relationship between language, representation and the sublime. To properly understand the complex interchanges between these registers we need to explore the mechanism behind these philosophies; we must examine how these arguments are constructed as much as what they have to say to us. Failures in method have ramifications for our understanding of the conceptual weaknesses in these accounts. We need to pay close attention to how these arguments are organised because they reveal to us how certain lines of inquiry are problemtically developed, especially those concerned with the status and function of language. One of the first accounts of the sublime is that of Longinus, and as his treatise on the sublime was influential on later philosophers it is worth reassessing his ideas before seeing how the sublime is plotted in the eighteenth century.

Longinus

Longinus' *Peri Hypsous* had an important influence on eighteenth-century accounts of the sublime due to the popularity of Boileau's French translation published in 1672. In his treatise Longinus identifies two types of the sublime: the natural and the rhetorical. The latter is found in an account of language and how language 'moves' (in certain circumstances) the listener to some higher plane. For Longinus, certain types of rhetoric can transport the reader (or listener) into a sublime state, and this is an idea which is integral to the relationship between Art and Nature. He writes that 'For art is ... perfect when it seems to be nature, and nature, again is most effective when pervaded by the unseen presence of art.'[3] This close relationship between Art and Nature is one which is ordained through God's presence; this means that for the reader/listener, 'the Sublime lifts him (*sic*) near to the great spirit of the Deity' (p. 69). This complex three-way relationship between Art, Nature and 'the Deity' gives the sublime a totalising power. So far the issue of the sublime seems clear, but this is something which is problematised because, elsewhere in his treatise, he fragments the concept of Art by emphasising the difference between poetic language and oratory. Longinus writes that the difference exists because 'in poetry, as I observed, a certain mythical exaggeration is allowable, transcending altogether mere logical credence. But the chief beauties of an oratorical image are its energy and reality' (p. 35). This reference is ambiguous. In oratorical writing is it the 'reality' of the image which gives life to the language, or is it that oratory should concern itself with 'real' (extra-linguistic) concerns? Basically the problem which Longinus has is in deciding whether language is figural or truly representative. Either way, trying to suggest a connection between the 'real' and language in oratory is undermined by what Longinus sees as the *sine qua non* of rhetoric. In rhetoric, 'an image lures us away from an argument: judgement is paralysed, matters of fact disappear from view, eclipsed by the superior blaze' (p. 36). Again, 'the use of figures has a peculiar tendency to rouse a suspicion of dishonesty' (p. 40). It is this concentration on 'figures' and images and their relationship to oratory which fails to properly separate oratory from poetic language; both are subsumed by the category of 'Art'.

From these examples it is possible to see how Longinus' account of the sublime is riven by problems of referencing. These problems are inherited by other philosophers of the sublime, and it is an area which constitutes a problematic for the Gothic itself. In the specifically Gothic discourse the subject is constructed through a variety of apparently uncategorisable impulses. This is manifested in an overt way through the Gothic's reliance upon nameless 'monsters' and spectral presences. Language disintegrates in front of an image which is more powerful than language can express. These presences also dramatise how the problematic status of language in relation to 'authentic' experiences is inherent in discourses on the sublime. This relates directly to the Gothic because there the idea of presence is established outside of cultural codes (outside the laws of the possible); the sublime itself is an experience beyond culture and the very attempt to analyse it makes the sublime disappear. In other words, the sublime appears to be a gap in thought itself and the act of trying to think about that gap makes the sublime slip away from experience. Likewise, the attempt to analyse the spectral is founded on the contradiction of an absent presence which disappears when confronted with the cultural authority which it seems to challenge. This idea of the *aporia* is thus present both in the Gothic and in Longinus in a way which brings them together.

As we saw, Longinus fails to separate oratory from poetic language. In failing to do so the sublime's transcendent status is questioned. That he acknowledges that language is the problem here is shown in his account of figurative language (a language also used in the Gothic). He argues that there is a problem with the figurative because it is closely linked to the possibility of deception. This problem is associated by Longinus with oratory rather than poetry. However, he tends to confuse the two terms (both are linked by him to 'Art') and their problematic relationship is restated rather than resolved. He writes that:

> To allay ... this distrust which attaches to the use of figures we must call in the powerful aid of sublimity and passion. For art, once associated with these great allies, will be overshadowed by their grandeur and beauty, and pass beyond the reach of suspicion. (p. 41)

Art is thus lost in the sublime moment. However, the implication is that the possibilities of deception in Art have merely been 'overshadowed' by the sublime. It does not mean that Art itself does not delude through its use of rhetorical ploys (its persuasive language). This means that the potential for deception in figurative language remains. Longinus attempts to resolve this problem by formulating a crude psychological theory to account for it:

> passion and grandeur of language, lying nearer to our souls by reason both of a certain natural affinity and of their radiance, always strike our mental eye before we become conscious of the figure, throwing its artificial character into the shade and hiding it as it were in a veil. (p. 4)

The peculiarity in this is that it implies that the sublime (as it here appears in language) does not necessarily accord with an idea of 'true' experience. Longinus attempts to account for this discontinuity by suggesting that the inner depths of the subject are correlated by the limits of representation. In this the 'passion and grandeur of language' are in harmony with authentic experience (as 'felt' by the subject).

This is a typically complicated and problematic point made by Longinus, but it is a process which he accounts for in two ways. Firstly, this is ratified through an idea of the soul: 'passion requires a certain disorder of language, imitating the agitation and commotion of the soul' (p. 44). Secondly, it is confirmed through how the mind functions: 'Indeed, we may say that with strict truth that beautiful words are the very light of thought' (p. 57). However, even here the problem of figurative language's deceptive possibilities has not been fully accounted for. This problem resurfaces when Longinus writes about 'excess' in such a way that it denies language the possibility of representing the sublime. He writes, 'That the use of figurative language, as of all other beauties of style, has a constant tendency towards excess, is an obvious truth which I need not dwell upon' (p. 61). There is a paradox here, one which is helpfully illustrated by Thomas Weiskel's notion of excess in the sublime. Weiskel writes that 'Any excess on the part of the object cancels the representational efficacy of the mind which can only turn, for its new object, to itself.'[4] The ramifications of this for Longinus are that where Longinus observes an excess of 'style' in figurative language, this has to be logically linked to an excess to be found in the subject. The reason why this occurs is because of the links he has established between figurative language, the soul and the mind. The effect of this is to imply that the mind can easily be deceived by the excessive and mendacious aspects of language. It is this position which prompts Longinus to review his earlier claim about language, made in an account of 'passionate frenzy'. This account has a somewhat revisionist air to it as he writes: 'For, as I am never tired of explaining, in actions and passions verging on frenzy there lies a kind of remission and palliation of any licence of language' (p. 73). It is therefore through the remission and palliation of language that its licence is effaced, meaning that the subject is now placed outside language and nature; as Longinus had written, 'it is from nature that man (*sic*) derives the faculty of speech' (p. 70). The subject is thus finally alienated from the sublime; the subject cannot escape the limits of language and as such the sublime cannot be properly represented, nor properly understood.

This problematic relationship between the subject and the sublime is implicit in Longinus' treatise, but it is to some degree revealed through the often tortuous attempts he makes to force the sublime to cohere with some rational explanation (and 'objective' representation). This confusion about the sublime is something which the early-nineteenth-century Gothic directly responds to, a point which will become apparent as our argument develops.

We have looked at Longinus in this way in order to highlight the inconsistencies and confusions which are to be found in accounts of the sublime; these sites of confusion are developed in the Gothic as a critique of the sublime project. Also, the problems to be found in Longinus are ones which are inherited by other theorists, whose direct influence on the Gothic has long been acknowledged (although rarely rigorously explored). The first of these is Edmund Burke.

Burke

Burke, in *A Philosophical Enquiry into our Ideas of the Sublime and the Beautiful* (1759), constructs a version of the sublime which is associated with terror.[5] His treatise provided the Gothic with a series of definitions of what terror is and where it can be found. This highly influential account is one which Mary Shelley takes issue with in *Frankenstein*, but before moving on to outline the nature of Shelley's critique we need to examine Burke's *Enquiry* with the same type of scrutiny which we applied to Longinus' treatise. The implicit influence of Longinus on Burke is clear, and one of the effects of this is that Burke inherits a series of problematics concerning language which are never properly resolved.

Burke's starting point in his *Enquiry* is nature. He argues that we can interpret nature, but provides a caveat concerning procedure: 'The characters of nature are legible it is true; but they are not plain enough to enable those who run, to read them. We must make use of a cautious, I had almost said, a timorous method of proceeding' (p. 4). Examining nature poses methodological problems, because the danger is that the observer's prejudgments will overshadow the object of investigation. Burke writes:

> For when we define, we seem in danger of circumscribing nature within the bounds of our own notions, which we often take up by hazard, or embrace on trust, or form out of a limited and partial consideration of the object before us, instead of extending our ideas to take in all that nature comprehends, according to her manner of combining. (p. 12)

Burke circumvents this problem by suggesting that there exists a universal experience where ideas about nature accord with nature itself. So far this appears to be uncontroversial, at least in debates about nature in the eighteenth century. However, the picture is complicated by Burke's account of Taste.

In his examination of Taste he states that there exists a pre-lapsarian moment when 'the pleasure of all the senses, of the sight, and even of the Taste, that most ambiguous of the senses, is the same in all, high and low, learned and unlearned' (p. 16). This can be altered by custom and national characteristics, so that 'opium is pleasing to Turks, on account of the agreeable delirium it produces. Tobacco is the delight of Dutchmen, as it diffuses a torpor and pleasing stupefaction' (p. 15). However, this claim for a universal experience poses a problem; Burke emphasises that Taste is universal 'in all, high and low, learned and unlearned', implying that Taste is unlearned and exists prior to knowledge. This claim is, however, undermined by Burke's further claim that 'the critical Taste does not depend upon a superior principle in men, but upon superior knowledge' (p. 19).

Burke, in attempting to separate 'critical Taste' from Taste (as some form of sense perception), makes a false opposition between the two and the reason for this is that Taste is itself externally ratified. This is apparent, for example, in his discussion of the national characteristics which inform Taste in which Taste is contingently defined (is nationally mediated). Burke deploys the term 'critical Taste' in order to try to account for variations in Taste-preference which are, paradoxically, inherent to pure Taste in the first place (informed, as they are, by national variations). Burke locates this idea of variance within the mind's operations: 'There is nothing which I can distinguish in my mind with more clearness than the three states, of indifference, of pleasure, and of pain' (p. 33). Although these are the necessary states of mind for Burke, it still leads him into a state of mourning for the now lost pre-lapsarian sense of the self. He writes that

> In the morning of our days, when the senses are unworn and tender, when the whole man is awake in every part, and the gloss of novelty fresh upon all the objects that surround us, how lively at that time are our sensations, but how false and inaccurate the judgements we form of things? (p. 25)

This pre-lapsarian state was something which Burke had previously seen as lying behind Taste, because Taste transcended knowledge. Burke's elevation of critical Taste above Taste leads him into a discussion of society and the influence which knowledge (education) has on informing critical Taste.

It is worth emphasising this Burkean argument about Taste because it has an important echo in Gothic discourse. It can be seen in the account of Taste that it is the status of knowledge which is the problem. The sense of nostalgia for an unmediated experience is clear. The fall away from this is a fall into representation; this in turn leads to a concern over the very status of the subject, of what it means to be 'human' (of what we are, of how we function). It is precisely these types of problems which Mary Shelley addresses in *Frankenstein*. The creature's authenticity is always in question: he is both an innocent who acquires knowledge of the world, and a perceived threat to a quasi-Burkean philosophy of nature which has, via a discourse of terror and monstrosity, formed him in the first place. Victor Frankenstein's scientific procedure bears analogy with the philosopher of the sublime who attempts to get beneath the appearance of reality in order to discover universal truths. The creature is produced out of this knowledge of nature but is paradoxically an affront to nature. The idea that he is simultaneously natural and unnatural rests on the same dilemma which Burke has concerning the status of knowledge in relation to Taste. The natural state of Taste becomes compromised because of the existence of contingent, mediating elements, so that what is 'natural' is itself compromised. It is this very undermining of the status of the 'natural' which is a product of an incoherence in Burke's *Enquiry*, an incoherence which the Gothic so readily exploits and provides solutions to. Shelley in part achieves this through an exploration of social injustice (giving back a political frame to an idealist philosophy). Also, revealingly, Burke proceeds to discuss society after his inconsistent account of Taste, a move which Shelley will similarly make, but in a more overtly critical way.

Burke attacks solitude because the subject realises his/her potential in the social sphere: 'we may discern, that an entire life of solitude contradicts the purposes of our being, since death itself is scarcely an idea of more terror' (p. 43). Burke redefines his theory of the universal subject in relation to the sociable subject, 'the purposes of our being' implying that the subject is naturally socially ordained, with solitude almost becoming a fate worse than death. However, there is the danger in this that the social world takes on a monochrome look, and so Burke introduces Ambition into his argument in order to account for social (class) variance. Some are more equal than others.

It is in Section Two of the *Enquiry* that Burke defines the sublime. In the sublime moment the mind is overcome by an object (or a feeling provoked by it) which destroys the mind's claim to reason: 'the mind is so entirely filled with its object, that it cannot entertain any other, nor by consequence reason on that object which employs it' (p. 57). Burke then itemises various sources of the sublime, such as Power and Obscurity but underlying this is the principal source of the sublime, terror: 'I know of nothing sublime which is not some modification of power. And this rises ... from terror, the common stock of every thing that is sublime' (p. 64). Terror is the result of the subject's confrontation with an awe-inspiring and overwhelming sense of the pantheistic; in this confrontation the individual is rendered insignificant:

> whilst we contemplate so vast an object, under the arm, as it were, of almighty power, and invested upon every side with omnipresence, we shrink into the minuteness of our own nature, and are, in a manner, annihilated before him. (p. 68)

We will briefly look towards the end of this chapter at *Frankenstein's* reading of the Burkean sublime, but at this stage it is worth exploring Burke's ideas concerning representation, ideas which have ramifications for our consideration of the Gothic.

In the *Enquiry* Burke outlines a taxonomy of responses that the subject makes when confronted by the sublime, beauty and Taste. Effectively, he produces a dictionary of what will cause which effect in each category. However, underlying these categories there exists a theory of resemblances which destabilises his closing section on language. It is in this theory of resemblances that Burke posits the existence of a full sign, whereby things mean what they say. On painting, for example, he writes that it can represent the sublime because: 'a judicious obscurity in some things contributes to the effect of the picture; because the images in painting are exactly similar to those in nature' (p. 62). Although here Burke is discussing the possibility of an accurate representation, he then proceeds to extend this into an account of how an outer form implies its inner 'reality'. In the section on physiognomy, for example, he argues that it is possible to 'read' somebody's face and so gauge their moral worth. It is this idea of the existence of a possibly full sign which leads Burke into an account of language. Language, as I mentioned earlier, is an important area of debate within accounts of the sublime and within that mode of the Gothic which samples such accounts. It is in Burke's analysis of language that problems about representation begin to emerge, problems which undermine his earlier view that the sublime can be portrayed.

For Burke, language is an essentially empty medium: 'Nothing is an imitation further than as it resembles some other thing; and words undoubtedly have no sort of resemblance to the ideas for which they stand' (p. 173). This means that Burke restates the same kind of problematic about language which can be found in Longinus; because language does not accurately represent the world, it may deceive us. Also, language cannot effectively represent the sublime (despite the allowance which Longinus believed should be made for figurative licence in the special case of sublimity). Burke juxtaposes language with painting:

> In reality poetry and rhetoric do not succeed in exact description so well as painting does; their business is to affect rather by sympathy than imitation; to display rather the effect of things on the mind of the speaker, or of others, than to present a clear idea of the things themselves. (p. 172)

Such a view does not cohere with his earlier view that painting can represent the sublime because it can capture obscurity. In his account of painting he had written that 'A clear idea is ... another name for a little idea' (p. 63). Here he reverses the tendency by suggesting that painting is able 'to present a clear idea of the things themselves'. It is this reversal which confuses the status which is ascribed to painting, and it is a confusion which, significantly, leads Burke into elevating rhetoric over painting:

> To represent an angel in a picture, you can only draw a beautiful young man winged; but what painting can furnish out any thing so grand as the addition of one word, 'The angel of the *Lord*?' It is true, I have here no clear idea, but these words affect the mind more than the sensible image did ... (p. 174)

Language, because it can represent obscurity, can thus represent the sublime. Words can show the unimaginable and are thus more effective in representing the sublime than painting: 'these words affect the mind more than the sensible image did'. Language, which was previously empty, has now been given a fuller, wider, meaning. This paradox of language, that it can represent the unrepresentable, is reasserted in Burke's analysis of lines 618–22, Book II, of *Paradise Lost*. He writes:

This idea or this affection caused by a word, which nothing but a word could annex to the others, raises a very great degree of the sublime; and this sublime is raised higher by what follows a *'Universe of Death'*. (p. 175)

So, for Burke, language now seems to possess a certain kind of representational efficacy; however, Burke then proceeds to remove its representative power through a conceptualisation of excess. Burke writes of his project on language that

Words were only so far to be considered, as to shew (*sic*) upon what principle they were capable of being the representatives of these natural things, and by what powers they were able to affect us as strongly as the things they represent, and sometimes much more strongly. (pp. 176–7)

It is this 'sometimes more strongly' which liberates words from describing 'the things they represent', meaning that the representational power of language is taken away.

Burke's model of language reveals a series of problematics which are familiar from Longinus. If language does not represent then there exists the possibility that language deceives. The similarity between Longinus and Burke lies in the suggestion that language can affect the subject as strongly as the thing which it is trying to represent. The major difference between the two is that Burke's sublime stands in opposition to social experience, whereas for Longinus the social and the sublime become linked due to the persuasiveness of public oratory.

It is worth summarising Burke's view of the separation between the sublime and the social because it is this kind of separation which the Gothic also makes. Burke believes that one shared trait between the sublime and the social is that of universalism. The status of the universal is compromised when the issue of education is introduced (as it is in the account of Taste). However, in his discussion of society Burke establishes a new kind of universalism which suggests that the subject is inherently social (and ambitiously so). Social isolation is unnatural – it is a death-like state – and this is because the proper understanding of death is in the sublime and not within the social. Burke, for example, discusses the power of the phrase *'Universe of Death'* (p. 175) in *Paradise Lost* as provoking a sense of the sublime. The social is characterised by development, ambition, procreation and presence, whereas the sublime is defined by death and absence. It is in the sublime that the subject loses a sense of social bonding; or as Weiskel puts it, 'As the Romantic ego approaches godhead, the minute particulars which are the world fade out' (p. 62). So, there exists a clear demarcation between the sublime and the social for Burke, but it is the presence of a universal tendency which underlies both. Such an attempt to claim a universal tendency for both the sublime and the social is problematic because they rest on different, and mutually exclusive, knowledge claims. The conclusion is that in Burke's *Enquiry* there are two different ideas about what a universal experience means.

We can see from this that what characterises Burke's text is an ambivalence concerning 'human' experience of the world. This is perhaps not surprising; after all, the social implies the subject's integration into the world whereas the sublime implies transcendence of it. The Gothic also focuses on this type of uncertainty (about issues of certainty). Jackson writes of the 'fantastic' text that: 'Uncertainty and impossibility are inscribed on a structural level through hesitation and equivocation, and on a thematic level through images of formlessness, emptiness and invisibility' (p. 49). The Gothic echoes the incoherence to be found in accounts of the sublime while at the same time traversing a similar terrain of formlessness. This kind of equivocation in the Gothic does not merely restate a problem found within accounts of the sublime, but rather leads to a dramatic reconstruction of sublime excess in order to expose the premises upon which sublime experience is allegedly founded. It is for this reason that the Gothic focuses on ideas about reason, language, and what it means to be 'human', all of which coalesce in any account of the sublime. Kant's version of the sublime is also, for example, critically 'read' by the Gothic.

Kant

Kant's 'Analytic of the Sublime' can only be properly understood through an analysis of the contrasts which he makes between the sublime and the beautiful.[6] Additionally, Kant breaks down the sublime into mathematical and dynamical modes; these are important sub-divisions, but first we will consider his general theory of the sublime.

For Kant the mind resonates with the structure of the sublime. To explore the sublime is to explore the structure of the mind. The beautiful is to be found in an object (of nature) whereas the source of the sublime is to be found in the mind. Kant comes to this conclusion by separating understanding from reason (by ascribing them to different faculties of the mind). Kant writes that:

> The beautiful in nature is a question of the form of the object, and this consists in limitation, whereas the sublime is to be found in an object even devoid of form, so as it immediately involves, or else by its presence provokes, a representation of *limitlessness*, yet with a super-added thought of its totality. Accordingly the beautiful seems to be regarded as a presentation of an indeterminate concept of understanding, the sublime as a presentation of an indeterminate concept of reason. (pp. 90–1)

It is this 'indeterminate concept of reason' which conditions Kant's view of the sublime. At this point Kant outlines what kind of pleasure is involved in sublime experience. In this experience, 'the mind is not simply attracted by the object, but is also alternatively repelled thereby, the delight in the sublime does not so much involve positive pleasure as admiration or respect, i.e. merits the name of a negative pleasure' (p. 91). As we shall see, it is this ecstatic revulsion which is more systematically developed in the Gothic. For Kant, the negative element involved in the sublime is caused by the mind's inability to properly comprehend the object which has stimulated it. This, however, is compensated because reason (or 'ideas of reason') creates a paradoxical (because incomplete) level of self-awareness. Kant writes:

> the sublime, in the strict sense of the word, cannot be contained in any sensuous form, but rather concerns ideas of reason, which, although no adequate presentation of them is possible, may be excited and called into mind by that very inadequacy itself which does not admit of sensuous presentation. (p. 92)

The very inadequacy of the imagination makes this possible. Ideas of reason, although imperfectly revealed (un-presentable) imply that the mind possesses an inner (higher) faculty which is obscurely at work within it. Kant proceeds to separate the sublime into mathematical and dynamical forms.

In the mathematical sublime, vastness becomes sublime when there is a failure of standards (the inability to quantify). This is again located in the mind of the subject: 'It is a greatness comparable to itself alone. Hence it comes that the sublime is not looked for in the things of nature, but in our own ideas' (p. 97). This internalisation of the sublime is linked to reason. It is this realm of reason, or of the super-sensible, which is gestured towards when imagination fails to grasp the sublime. Reason takes over

> because there is a striving in our imagination towards a progress *ad infinitum* while reason demands absolute totality, as a real idea, that same inability on the part of our faculty for the estimation of the magnitude of things of the world of sense to attain to this idea, is the awakening of a feeling of a supersensible faculty within us. (p. 97)

Kant's formulation of the mathematical sublime is summed up thus: 'An object is *monstrous* where by its size it defeats the end that forms its concept' (p. 100). Kant goes on to add that as the object in the sublime cannot be grasped numerically, it must be interpreted aesthetically because: 'it must be the *aesthetic* estimation of magnitude in which we get at once a feeling of the effort towards a comprehension that exceeds the faculty of imagination' (p. 103).

There is a problem here with Kant's construction of '*aesthetic* estimation'. The problem arises because Kant has linked aesthetic apprehension to judgement about the beautiful; as such it 'refers the imagination in its free play to the *understanding*' (p. 104). The effect of this is 'to induce a temper of mind conformable to that which the influence of definite (practical) ideas would produce upon feeling, and in common accord with it' (p. 104). This means that the experience is ratified by how the subject feels rather than by what the object is, and it is because of this that it is not linked at all to the aesthetic apprehension of beauty. There thus exists a division in the idea of aesthetic judgement. In one case aesthetic judgement is solely linked to an appreciation of the beautiful, but in the second case aesthetic judgement shares the universalising tendencies to be found in the sublime.

There is a difference between aesthetic judgement of the beautiful and aesthetic judgement of the sublime because: 'The mind feels itself *set in motion* in the representation of the sublime in nature; whereas in the aesthetic judgement upon what is beautiful therein it is in *restful* contemplation' (p. 107). Kant secularises the sublime in his account of the dynamical sublime. There, nature is referred to as a possible source which provokes sublime sensation. Kant writes that 'If we are to estimate nature as dynamically sublime, it must be represented as a source of fear' (p. 109). This is not to say that every state of fear is a sublime moment but that he shares with Burke the belief that terror is an integral part of the sublime and it is this which provides, for Kant, a useful means of gauging moral worth. It is this vision of heroism which informs the Gothic taste of the eighteenth century, and is one which Kant poses in universal terms:

> For what is it that, even to the savage, is the object of the greatest admiration? It is a man who is undaunted, who knows no fear, and who, therefore, does not give way to danger, but sets manfully to work with full deliberation. (p. 112)

There is a paradox here, because if the subject 'knows no fear' then it is difficult to ascribe moral worth to their actions (there needs to be some sense of overcoming fear). Kant proceeds to explore the relationship between religious contemplation and the sublime. He writes:

> The man that is actually in a state of fear, finding in himself good reason to be so, because he is conscious of offending with his evil disposition against a might directed by a will at once irresistible and just, is far from being in the frame of mind for admiring divine greatness, for which a temper of calm reflection and a quite free judgement are required. (p. 113)

Divine 'greatness' is not denied here, but it is separated from the sublime. It is in fact accorded the same status as aesthetic judgement in relation to the beautiful. This move towards a secular sublime is something which is also plotted in *Frankenstein*, when the cultural status of the creature compromises a notion of the divine. Victor Frankenstein's status as a divine creator is lampooned in this because his pantheistic understanding of the sublime is compromised by the material nature of the creature. Also, Victor perceives the creature's ugliness as a conundrum: his parts are beautiful but the organic whole is 'corrupt'. This means that the idea of aesthetics comes into play, and this lies uneasily with a conception of the sublime. This problem of aesthetic apprehension is also to be found in Kant's idea of the mathematical sublime.

Kant had said that in the mathematical sublime the object is perceived aesthetically. Kant, if he is to be consistent, needs to separate aesthetic apprehension from aesthetic judgement (the two might appear to be the same but one is linked to perception, the other to interpretation). Kant partially achieves this by placing aesthetic apprehension outside the realm of the imagination, which allies it with reason; whereas aesthetic judgement is related to the mind's understanding. It is in the sublime that innate moral behaviour can be discerned, meaning that aesthetic apprehension acquires a kind of moral distinction. Kant writes about moral ideas (here referring to the dynamical sublime) that: 'without the development of moral ideas, that which thanks to preparatory culture, we call sublime, merely strikes the untutored man as terrifying' (p. 115). Kant is careful to suggest that these ideas about morality are innate to the subject rather than culturally constructed. Instead, morality can be discerned within culture because it has been put there by human agency. He writes of morality:

> it is in human nature that its foundations are laid, and, in fact, in that which, at once with common understanding, we may expect every one to possess and may require of him, namely, a native capacity for the feeling for (practical) ideas, i.e. for moral feeling. (p. 116)

So, then, the sublime refers the subject to the existence of a higher realm of reasoning which is gestured towards rather than clearly discerned or grasped. Also, in the dynamical sublime, a universal moral tendency can be found, a tendency which suggests the subject's innate sense of courage.

After this definition of the sublime, Kant spends the rest of the analytic focusing upon the issue of representation. Unlike Burke, who believes that art can represent nature, Kant distinguishes between the two; 'fine art must be clothed *with the aspect* of nature, although we recognize it to be art' (p. 167). However, like Burke, he acknowledges that art needs to be governed by a set of external rules (by a theory of art) because 'fine art cannot of itself excogitate the rule according to which it is to effectuate its product' (p. 168). Also, like Burke, he regards representation as being governed by a series of resemblances. The artist can bring the object to life by the use of a set of 'appropriate' images:

> the soul of the artist furnishes a bodily expression for the substance and character of his thoughts, and makes the thing itself speak, as it were, in *mimic language* – a very common play of our fancy, that attributes to lifeless things a soul *suitable to their form*, and that uses them as its mouthpiece. (p. 188, my italics)

Such a view accords well with Victor Frankenstein's project, which is similarly concerned with finding a fitness for purpose in the construction of the creature. Victor is also attempting to find a suitable soul for 'lifeless things'. The novel ultimately works against this idea of aesthetics because the creature does not possess the moral mutilation which is suggested by his appearance. What Mary Shelley's novel does is highlight a problematic in such an aesthetic credo, and this occurs because Kant inherits a problem about representation which can be found in Longinus' account of figurative language (which takes us back to this central issue of language in treatises on the sublime). Kant, for example, attempts to separate poetic language from oratory by suggesting that the latter appropriates its manipulative tropes from the former. He writes that

> Rhetoric, so far as this is taken to mean the art of persuasion, i.e. the art of *deluding by means of a fair semblance* [my italics] (as *ars oratoria*) and not merely excellence of speech (eloquence and style), is a dialectic, which borrows from poetry only so much as is necessary to win over men's minds to the side of the speaker before they have weighed the matter, and to rob the verdict of its freedom. (p. 192)

It is this account of the delusive aspects of oratory which destabilises his theory of resemblances which, he had previously argued, reflected 'the soul of the artist'. Poetry can provide oratory with deceptive (seductive) rhythms; resemblance is thus based on a false use of rhetorical tropes and linguistic flourishes.

Almost as if this issue of being misled has become unconscious, Kant finishes his analytic with an account of jokes. For Kant, it is the deceptive element in jokes which creates their effect: 'It is observable that in all such cases the joke must have something in it capable of momentarily deceiving us' (p. 201). For Kant, this is due to the surprise element to be found in jokes which disrupt what otherwise resembles a realist narrative. The joke is thus an extension of his account of oratory because it deludes us by deflecting attention away from its structure. For Kant jokes offer 'a topsy-turvy view of things' (p. 203). This subversive element of the joke bears a similarity to the destabilising qualities of the Gothic text; the Gothic text (like the sublime itself) also offers 'a topsy-turvy view of things'. This apparently whimsical concluding note to Kant's analytic can thus be seen as a product of, rather than a refutation of, his concern with representation, a concern which the Gothic will also give prominence to in its exploration of the limits of the sublime and the limits of its representation.

At this juncture it is worth exploring an influential theoretical reading of the sublime. In its failures we can see a complex reworking of the sublime and its relationship to psychoanalysis, one which has important ramifications for an understanding of the Gothic. By looking at such meta-readings of the sublime we can observe how, and why, the sublime can infiltrate their analysis (something which we will also see in Freud's account of the uncanny).

Weiskel

Thomas Weiskel's seminal psychoanalytical study *The Romantic Sublime* was the first sustained attempt to explore the alleged psychodynamics which underpin the sublime. Although earlier I quoted some general observations from Weiskel, there are some issues in his work which need to be challenged. Weiskel's project is to examine the sublime as a codified Oedipal drama. His reading is therefore an overtly Freudian one, and is one which forms some intriguing, and as we will see, revealing, problems. The failure in Weiskel's argument, one which he acknowledges, is related to methodology; he just cannot fit the sublime into an Oedipal paradigm and the reasons for this return us to the sublime. It requires us to follow how Weiskel plots his arguments, as this reveals where and why these arguments start to disintegrate.

Weiskel begins his argument by suggesting that the Romantic sublime 'provided a language for urgent and apparently novel experiences of anxiety and excitement which were in need of legitimation' (p. 4). This urgency is caused by a Romantic perception that there was an emptiness in the soul, and it is this idea of absence which is, for Weiskel, a defining characteristic of the sublime. Weiskel writes, 'The soul is a vacancy, whose extent is discovered as it is filled. Inner space, the infinitude of the Romantic mind, is born as a massive and more or less unconscious emptiness, an absence' (p. 15). It is in these opening remarks that Weiskel discusses the possible conflation of the rhetorical sublime with the natural sublime. Weiskel argues that this is possible because both are associated with absence. With the rhetorical sublime, words themselves are empty, so that in Romanticism there is 'an unexamined convention that the meaning of words lies solely in the way they are used, for in principle an appeal beyond language to nature has no logical ground' (p. 15). There is, however, a problem here because Weiskel side-steps the central issue of language in philosophies of the sublime. In Longinus, Burke and Kant there is an attempt (no matter how problematic) to link language to nature. Language is granted some form of representational efficacy in relation to nature at some point. Weiskel's reasoning behind his conflation of the rhetorical with the natural is that 'A general semiotic of the sublime would find, I think, the same discontinuity between sensation and idea as between idea and word – this is, at any rate, the substance of my hypothesis in fusing the natural and rhetorical sublimes' (p. 17). Weiskel is only able to do this because he discerns a basic pattern behind the sublime which links the two. However, the rhetorical and the natural do not lie easily together in accounts of the sublime, and this basic pattern does not really exist in any manifest way. This criticism of Weiskel can be clarified if we briefly return to the issue of rhetoric in Longinus, Burke and Kant. In their writings there is no 'semiotic of the sublime' because there is no structure in place which can be examined in a semiotic fashion.

Longinus' account of the sublime, for example, lacks a sustained formulation of the natural sublime; rather we get a highly problematic account of the effects of rhetoric. Language (or precisely, figurative language) is the problem here because although it produces meaning, it is also capable of producing deception. This problem is never fully resolved by Longinus because he does not take up any consistent position on language, and consequently it is difficult to argue that his account is open to a semiotic investigation. Burke inherits this problem from Longinus and adds problems of his own. In the final section of his *Enquiry* there is an inconsistent account of the representational efficacy of language; sometimes language represents and at other times it does not. The sublime plays a part in this confusion, but this confusion is not available for structural analysis because of Burke's equivocation. In Kant there is no appeal to an 'objective' nature. The sublime is linked to a philosophy of the mind. Language is also defined by its deceptive possibilities, which serves to undermine Kant's previous privileging of poetic language as offering a 'full' representation.

Weiskel, paradoxically, proceeds not to imply that there is a coherent relationship between the rhetorical and natural sublimes, but that the sublime has been occasioned by the collapse of the former. He writes:

The sublime dramatized the rhythm of transcendence in its extreme and purest form, for the sublime began where the conventional systems, readings of landscape or text, broke down and, it found in that very collapse the foundation for another order of meaning. (p. 22)

This collapse however, can only be a partial one because rhetoric is still examined in relation to resemblance in the philosophy of the sublime. This means that the issue of rhetoric has not (as Weiskel here suggests) been banished from the debate but rather problematically informs it. Weiskel, nevertheless, proceeds to examine the natural sublime as an independent entity.

Weiskel discusses Kant's theory of the sublime in relation to alienation. Weiskel writes that 'The affective ambivalence of the sublime, which opposes the imagination's feeling of defeat to the reason's awe of itself, points to a cognitive alienation within the mind as a whole and invites a dialectical interpretation' (p. 41). This is then discussed in relation to repression, 'The imagination's feeling of sacrifice or deprivation, the relation of concealment between it and reason – these suggest the role of repression in the sublime' (p. 41). For Weiskel, this is implicit in Kant's separation of the beautiful from the sublime: 'In the sublime moment, dualism is legitimated and intensified. The beautiful intimates reconciliation, however precariously and ambiguously; the sublime splits consciousness into alienated halves' (p. 48). The sublime is then discussed in terms of how Kant relates it to negative pleasure, which Weiskel links to 'superego anxiety':

> The negative sublime apparently exhibits some features of a response to superego anxiety, for in the suddenness of the sublime moment the conscious ego rejects its attachment to sensible objects and turns rather fearfully toward an ideal of totality and power which it participates or internalizes. (p. 83)

Weiskel has now got to the point where he can advocate a psychoanalytical investigation of Kant. The reason for this is that for Weiskel there is an Oedipal anxiety which can be discerned behind Kant's failure of the imagination in the sublime. This anxiety concerning the failure of the imagination is compensated by the elevation of the ego (of reason). This leads Weiskel to the conclusion that, 'The sublime moment recapitulates and thereby re-establishes the oedipus complex, whose positive resolution is the basis of culture itself' (p. 94). Weiskel, however, acknowledges that this conclusion is rendered problematic by the negative sublime (in contrast to Wordsworth's egotistical sublime). In this instance, the Oedipal drama is reduced to a level of structural play, 'Since the defense is directed primarily against the dangerous passivity, the other component of the oedipus complex – the aggressive wish against the father – is only structurally motivated and fails to impress us as authentic' (p. 105). We now need to elaborate some criticism which can be made about a psychoanalytical approach to the sublime.

First, Weiskel tends to regard theoreticians on the sublime as forming an homogenous group. While there do exist some family resemblances, this is too simplistic a summary. Weiskel, for example, makes general statements about the Kantian sublime which imply that this reading will hold true for all accounts of the sublime. Also, at some point (early on) Weiskel has dropped the problem of representation. This is a significant omission because these tracts on the sublime are primarily influenced by a concern with the status, and uses, of representation. He has left this behind in his discussion of the breakdown in traditional ways of reading nature, landscape and so on, and thus fails to acknowledge the debate concerning the relationship between Art and nature. Additionally, he fails to address the status of Ambition and Taste in Burke, and Kant's idea of the 'moral' subject. Such areas are associated with the sublime and provide an important insight into their respective versions of it. Weiskel's psychoanalytical approach would appear, however, to have little to say about these related issues. Also, Weiskel observes a similarity between the sublime experience and superego anxiety, but whereas the latter is seen as a necessary stage in the Oedipus complex, the sublime is characterised by its arbitrary nature: 'What happens to you standing at the edge of the infinite spaces can be made, theoretically, to "mean" just about anything' (p. 28). The problem Weiskel has with psychoanalytically investigating the negative sublime is because it only structurally mimics Oedipal anxiety. It is 'empty', as the sublime itself is characterised by Weiskel as empty: 'the infinitude of the Romantic mind is born as a massive and more or less unconscious emptiness, an absence' (p. 15).

In this brief examination of Weiskel I have provided a synopsis of the problems, rather than dwelled on his more general comments, but the purpose of this is to highlight what happens to psychoanalysis when it attempts an analysis of sublimity. Ultimately psychoanalysis cannot account for the sublime because psychoanalysis is unable (like the subject in the sublime moment) to fully grasp the import of sublime experience. The reason for this is that psychoanalysis' object of investigation, the unconscious, is an internalised version of the sublime. This means that Weiskel is attempting to analyse the prototype of the very theoretical basis which underpins psychoanalysis in the first place. We will return to this point because it is *the* site of incoherence for psychoanalytical investigations of the sublime, an incoherence which later nineteenth-century Gothic texts, such as *The Strange Case of Dr Jekyll and Mr Hyde*, will indirectly acknowledge.

Fantasy: macabre versions of the sublime

So far my focus has been on the sublime but I now want to look more closely at the Gothic through Rosemary Jackson's account of fantasy. Jackson's arguments in *Fantasy: the Literature of Subversion* are largely confined to an analysis of post-Romantic fantasy, but her reading of the Gothic does have implications for an analysis of the sublime. Jackson's mode of analysis is principally a psychoanalytical one, and although I take issue with such an approach throughout this book, I feel that her work helpfully illustrates how the a certain type of criticism of the Gothic can (coincidentally) open up the Gothic for a reconsideration of the sublime. Jackson writes of the fantastic text that 'The fantastic opens on to a region which has no name and no rational explanation for its existence. It suggests events beyond interpretation' (p. 25). This bears some similarity to Kant's notion of the supersensible. However, in Kant's sublime there do not exist 'events beyond interpretation', but rather an intimation of the existence of reason and a revelation of moral worth. Despite this fundamental difference, there is a similarity in the concern over interpretation, and it is this issue of interpretation which Jackson regards as being integral to the fantastic text in which 'The narrator is no clearer than the protagonist about what is going on, nor about interpretation; the status of what is being seen and recorded as "real" is constantly in question' (p. 34). Jackson links this problem with interpretation to the anxiety which it pro vokes; whereas in the sublime there is no such anxiety, but rather a sense of frustration about the status of representation. She does, however, construct a theory of the fantastic which resembles a prototypical account of the sublime:

> It could be suggested that the movement of fantastic narrative is one of *metonymical* rather than of *metaphorical* process: one object does not *stand for* another, but literally becomes that other, slides into it, metamorphosing from one shape to another in a permanent flux and instability. (pp. 41–2)

This is similar to the position of the subject in the sublime moment; subject and object distinctions become erased in ways which undermine the subject's identity. In the sublime there is of course the pay-off that a realm of reason is gestured towards in this moment, a gesture which more than compensates for the apparent obliteration of selfhood. As we considered earlier, Kant's theory of the sublime accounts for the apparently indeterminate by resolving uncertainty through the revelation of the existence of some higher 'truth'. It is this moment of revelation which contrasts with Jackson's idea that the Gothic subject encounters incoherence because of an overwhelming objectivity: 'Other persons and objects are no longer distinctly other: the limit between subject and object is effaced, things slide into one another, in a metonymical action of replacement' (p. 50).

How incoherence can be resolved is, for Jackson, the central feature of the fantastic text. One possible resolution is associated with the status of the Other, which provides a political solution to a problem which was beginning to look like a purely psychological issue. Jackson writes of the Other that 'Any social structure tends to exclude as "evil" anything radically different from itself or which threatens it with destruction, and this conceptualisation, this naming of difference as evil, is a significant ideological gesture' (p. 52).

Nevertheless, Jackson's account of fantasy bears some structural similarity to how the subject is positioned in the sublime moment. There are some telling differences, but Jackson's account implicitly indicates how the sublime is reshaped through fantastic texts. Although Jackson is primarily interested in post-Romantic fantasy, she does at one point discuss Romantic fantasy. She writes that 'During the Romantic period, the sense of the "demonic" was slowly modified from a supernatural meaning into something more disturbing, something less definable' (p. 56). She regards this move as producing an inverted model of the sublime, in which 'the demonic pact comes to be synonymous with an impossible desire to break human limits, it becomes a *negative version* of desire for the infinite' (p. 57). We can take it here that the sublime is associated with a positive version of the same desire.

Jackson sees Romantic fantasy as being informed by a range of religious concerns which contrasts it with the more secular post-Romantic fantasy. However, even in these later secularised texts there is an identifiable reworking of the sublime taking place: 'Through secularization, a religious sense of the numinous is transformed and reappears as a sense of the uncanny, but the psychological origins of both are identical' (p. 66). This is an idea taken issue with elsewhere in this book, but at this point it is worth following how Jackson's argument concerning this reworking develops. Jackson writes that

'The formal and thematic features of fantastic literature are similarly determined by this (impossible) attempt to find a language for desire' (p. 62). This means that secular fantasy is defined by an inherent existential anxiety:

> whereas a religious subject has faith that a sense of unbeing, a disso-
> lution of the ego, will lead to ultimate unity with a divine beloved, a
> sceptical, atheistic subject has no such faith. In the place of tran-
> scendent ideals, there is discovered a zero point, a space of non-
> being, an absence. (p. 78)

Jackson thus argues that there is a development from religious to secular fantasy (from Romantic to post-Romantic). In this development a religious sense of the sublime becomes replaced by a threatening ontological absence. This absence is threatening for a culture dominated by a science which suggests the knowability of all things.

One question which can be raised at this point concerns the notion of evil because it is the labelling of evil which, in its secular manifestation, revises the form of transcendental idealism. 'Evil' has to come from somewhere outside religious conceptions of it and Jackson suggests this in the idea that political considerations (rather than theological ones) come into play. She argues that the norm (a bourgeois norm) defends itself against the Other, whereby that Other has to be expelled or destroyed since this Other is capable of: 'un-doing those unifying structures and significations upon which social order depends, fantasy functions to subvert and undermine cultural stability' (p. 69). This secularised notion of the fantastic contrasts with Kant's version of the sublime. For Kant, the subject's innate morality is expressed through cultural behaviour. Although this morality is in some sense uncon-scious (*a priori*) It does not undermine the social order, or cultural sta-bility, but rather ratifies both. Thus for Kant the 'law' (of culture, of reason) is upheld and expressed through its unknowability. This means that the unknowable is expelled in the secular fantastic, but not before such fantastic narratives have entertained the possibility of a worrying (but subversively exciting) unknowability; in the sublime and in Jackson's account of secularised fantasy there is thus a reliance upon comparable metaphysical systems.

Earlier we saw that what Jackson regards as characterising the Romantic fantastic is the demonic pact. In this pact there is a move towards 'something less definable' (p. 56), this 'desire for the infinite' (p. 57), which is a negative version of a pantheistic sublime, with a demonic authority being provisionally validated in its place. Although in this Romantic context 'evil' is something defined religiously, it nevertheless, for Jackson, has a lingering presence within secular fantasy. The secular fantasy inherits the sublime as a 'worrying absence', but even within this, 'without God, transgression is empty, a kind of profanation without an object' (p. 79). This is, however, exactly the same position occupied by the sublime. Without an externally ratifying discourse (such as Pantheism) its significance is unclear and it becomes associated with absence and emptiness. The result is that this vacuous sublime poses a problem for a culture which secures its authority on new (predominantly 'scientific') ways of seeing.

The precise point at which these moves and conflicts take place is unclear, but one novel which helps illuminate these concerns is *Frankenstein*. One notable feature of *Frankenstein* is the similarity between Victor's project and that of the philosopher of the sublime. Victor paraphrases Burke on the necessity for the philosopher (scientist) to go beyond the world of appearance in order to discover the 'rules' which govern the natural world. Victor's ideal critical tools come from natural science (which echoes Burke's own stress on the need to follow the 'correct' procedure when analysing the sublime). Natural science enables Victor to discover the fundamental laws of metaphysics, in which the meaning of life is associated with the ability to reproduce it. His procedure thus follows that of the sublime philosopher, but his endeavours are given a material slant through the creation of the creature. The creature, created through a parody of Burkean sublime inquiry, becomes both an object and a subject of the sublime. He is an object because (in the novel) he conforms to Burke's idea of the massive and the monstrous, and he is a subject because he is associated with Burke's idea of original innocence in which the subject is awed by nature. However, the creature receives no consolation in sublime reverie, he finds no God in nature because he is himself perceived as a profanation against nature. It is for this reason that he goes in search of his personal God (his own creator), a God who can grant him the kind of mental stability which the non-monstrous subject receives through divine rapport in the sublime moment.

The creature, like the Burkean subject, loses his pre-lapsarian status through 'education' and through the way that he is treated by others. The central issue of language is developed in the novel because it is through language that the creature's true nature is revealed; the monster should be understood as he speaks not as he looks. The novel therefore provides a critique of society for its way of seeing. It is for this reason that the labelling of 'evil' in the novel becomes highly problematic.

In *Frankenstein* the sublime is an empty experience because it disrupts the possibility of making a true assessment of the creature's worth. The novel provides a parody of sublime endeavour and also plots the sublime within a secular, pseudo-scientific, context. *Frankenstein* combines Romantic with post-Romantic thought in order to formulate the sublime as an absence which is, paradoxically, defined through the (parodic) use of religious iconography. A close investigation of *Frankenstein* will provide us with an example of how the Gothic critically reads the sublime.

2
Frankenstein: Sublimity Reconsidered, Foucault and Kristeva

Frankenstein provides us with some unique insights into the sublime, insights which also have ramifications for an understanding of contemporary critical theory. Shelley's complex critique of sublimity bears a direct correlation with Foucault's work on the arrival of modernity and its struggle to throw off the Classical episteme. Foucault's *The Order of Things* is especially useful in this context as, although he does not explicitly refer to the sublime, he does identify an emerging mode of experience which helps us to account for Shelley's representation of subjectivity. Additionally, the novel parallels Kristeva's construction of the subject as constituted through a series of drives. Kristeva may seem to be an odd choice of theorist given the premise of my book, but what I want to explore is how the novel prefigures her version of the subject. Ultimately *Frankenstein* replaces the sublime with a nascent form of the unconscious, one which looks forward to psychoanalysis but which is used by Shelley in order to provide an antidote to sublime excess. To get to this unconscious we need to start by looking at how the sublime is played out as a complex series of exchanges between a variety of characters in the novel, exchanges which imply the existence of a variety of perceptions on the sublime, and which in turn invite an investigation into its social provenance.

Victor Frankenstein has a series of strained relationships with his family, his fiancée Elizabeth, and the creature. The only character that he feels comfortable with, because less intimate with, is his friend Henry Clerval. What conditions this friendship is the attempt to resolve a clash between science and sentimentality. It is Henry, the sentimentalist, who tries to reintroduce Victor to sublime pleasures which are precisely the kind of pleasures lost in Victor's scientific deliberations; although there is an irony here in that it is this science which creates a, paradoxically, unnatural form of the sublime (a Burkean monster). Victor acknowledges that it is his scientific endeavours which estrange him from both nature and his family; he says of his scientific project:

> I knew well ... what would be my father's feelings, but I could not tear my thoughts from my employment, loathsome in itself, but which had taken an irresistible hold of my imagination. I wished, as it were, to procrastinate all that related to my feelings of affection until the great object, which swallowed up every habit of my nature, should be completed.[1]

Here Victor's project has the same irresistible qualities associated with the all-consuming Burkean sublime; like the sublime his project 'swallowed up every bit of my nature' and he 'could not tear my thoughts from my employment'. For Burke, the sublime is related to terror, but here it is related to repulsion; Victor's employment is 'loathsome in itself', yet it 'has taken an irresistible hold of my imagination'. Also, like the sublime, it leads to social isolation which is expressed as a guilty lack of filial duty, 'I knew well ... what would be my father's feelings.' The sublime is not transcendent here, at least not properly so; rather it is replaced by the synthetic functions of scientific experimentation. However, it is close enough to the sublime to supplant the Burkean natural sublime, meaning that Victor becomes immunised to this seemingly older version of sublimity.

As I mentioned, Clerval's task is to attempt to re-educate Victor about the pleasures to be found in the sublime. Victor says that 'Clerval called forth the better feelings of my heart; he again taught me to love the aspect of nature and the cheerful faces of children' (p. 117). However, the fact that this is learned means that it compromises the supposedly natural status of the sublime; although, provisionally, it enables Victor to reclaim his past, a past which is associated with the sublime:

> I became the same happy creature who, a few years ago, loved and beloved by all, had no sorrow or care. When happy, inanimate nature had the power of bestowing on me the most delightful sensations. A serene sky and verdant fields filled me with ecstasy. (p. 117)

Later, Victor links this contemplation of nature to Pantheism:

> the dashing of the waterfalls around, spoke of a power mighty as
> Omnipotence – and I ceased to fear or to bend before any being less
> almighty than that which had created and ruled the elements, here
> displayed in their most terrific guise. (p. 140)

Victor would appear to have reclaimed his prelapsarian self. Science now
becomes represented as a false model of the sublime when compared
with nature. There is, however, a contradiction here: the sublime is not
truly natural but, rather, cultural because it requires Clerval's pedagogic
intervention ('he taught me again'). Victor is left to perceive in Clerval
something about his own past, 'in Clerval I saw the image of my former
self; he was inquisitive and anxious to gain experience and instruction'
(p. 203). Earlier he had said of Clerval that 'He was a being formed in the
"very poetry of nature". His wild and enthusiastic imagination was
chastened by the sensibility of his heart' (p. 201). It is Victor, to hold the
analogy, who is ruled by his head. However, all of this reveals that Victor
is an outsider, an observer who cannot quite regain his earlier self and is
left merely to observe its preservation within Clerval.

Clerval is only able to give Victor a precarious re-education in the
sublime because the sublime is repeatedly transgressed through the
appearance of the creature. The failure of the natural sublime is linked
to the appearance of the creature within the natural settings which
Victor so problematically contemplates. Victor, for example, seeks consolation in nature after the death of his brother, William, and the exe-
cution of Justine; just prior to the arrival of the creature he says of the
landscape, 'These sublime and magnificent scenes afforded me the
greatest consolation that I was capable of receiving. They elevated me
from all littleness of feeling, and although they did not remove my
grief, they subdued and tranquillized it' (p. 142). On first seeing the
creature, 'I was troubled; a mist came over my eyes, and I felt a faint-
ness seize me; but I was quickly restored by the cold gaie of the moun-
tains' (p. 144). In contrast to the mountain scenery, Victor sees that
the creature's 'unearthly ugliness rendered it almost too horrible for
human eyes' (pp. 144–5), and so destroys the serene mood.

The creature does not solely disrupt the sublime, he also represents
death, and in this sense he becomes a form of the sublime made flesh.
The sublime, instead of provoking feelings of transcendence, now
results in a confrontation with death. The creature represents, physically, the awesome power associated with the sublime, a power which

kills off the natural sublime in a move which is echoed in his killing of Clerval. After the death of Clerval, Victor acknowledges that the sublime is irrevocably lost:

> The cup of life was poisoned forever, and although the sun shone upon me, as upon the happy and gay of heart, I saw around me nothing but a dense and frightful darkness, penetrated by no light but the glimmer of two eyes that glared upon me. (p. 226)

Victor the observer now becomes the observed. These penetrating glaring eyes become confusingly linked to both Clerval and the creature. Victor says of the eyes, 'Sometimes they were the expressive eyes of Henry' but sometimes they were 'the watery, clouded eyes of the monster' (p. 226). Here the live eyes of the creature become conflated with the dead eyes of Clerval; after this, oppositions in the novel are progressively conflated and Victor gives up on any attempt to reclaim the natural sublime.

All of these moments in the novel testify to the failure of the sublime to adequately supply an interpretative model of nature. The novel constructs a parallel version of the sublime through the creation of the creature. Victor's absorption by his scientific investigations echoes the natural sublime's own arresting presence. However, it is the existence of the creature which implies that the sublime is to be engaged physically rather than mentally; in this way the novel satirises the idealism of the sublime by the introduction of a material element which personifies it. Ultimately the natural sublime is exposed as a cultural fiction.

Culture and experience, sublime (re)considerations

Throughout *Frankenstein* there is a series of misrecognitions and mis-understandings. Often these are related to how the sublime supplies a false perception of the world. However, the idea of misinterpretation and misunderstanding is introduced early on in the novel in the relationship between Victor and Robert Walton. If it had been Clerval's task to try and re-educate Victor about the sublime, it becomes Victor's to try and disabuse Walton of his own apparent overreaching. There are some significant similarities between Walton and Victor's quests. Victor tries to create life out of death and Walton is in search of a tropical paradise at the North Pole.[2] Also, Walton's endeavours have something of the sublime tremor about them; he writes to his sister,

'It is impossible to communicate to you a conception of the trembling sensation, half pleasurable and half fearful, with which I am preparing to depart. I am going to unexplored regions, to "the Land of mist and snow", but I shall kill no albatross' (p. 69). The reference to 'The Rime of the Ancient Mariner' is telling, as it is Victor who passes on his own precautionary tale to Walton: 'Unhappy man! Do you share my madness? Have you drunk also of the intoxicating draught? Hear me; let me reveal my tale, and you will dash the cup from your lips!' (p. 77). In Walton, Victor sees an image of his earlier self, one poised between his early ambitions and the adult Clerval. The encounter becomes another opportunity to satirise Romantic abstractions.

The novel achieves its critique through the introduction of cultural elements which undermine the supposedly authentic and innate experience of the sublime. This is the painful knowledge which Victor gains and which he attempts to pass on to Walton.

The explicit denunciation of the sublime as a cultural experience takes place in the scenes where the creature encounters the De Laceys. The monstrosity of the creature becomes an issue in this encounter, and it is one in which the creature comes to conform not only to Burke's idea of the monstrous, but also to the category of 'natural' objects in part Five of Burke's *Enquiry*, where 'natural objects affect us, by the laws of that connexion, which Providence has established between certain motions and configurations of bodies, and certain consequent feelings in our minds' (p. 163). This idea of an innate recognition is also played upon when the creature sees himself reflected in a pool of water. He tells Victor:

> how was I terrified when I viewed myself in a transparent pool! At first I started back, unable to believe that it was indeed I who was reflected in the mirror; and when I became fully convinced that I was in reality the monster that I am, I was filled with the bitterest sensations of despondence and mortification. (p. 159)

This is not as clear as it might first appear; this recognition coincides with the creature's introduction to language which suggests that this is a cultural recognition. It is these ideas concerning culture and society which are played out in the creature's rejection by the De Laceys. The rejection of the creature becomes the rejection of a certain type of culture. It is the creature's acquisition of language, his status as a speaking subject, which means that he is a cultural artefact and not a natural object.

Chris Baldick, in *Frankenstein's Shadow: Myth, Monstrosity and Nineteenth-Century Writing*, briefly outlines the history of the representation of monstrosity, concluding that 'monsters were understood primarily as exhibitions of moral vices: they were to be seen and not heard'.[3] The creature in *Frankenstein* does not in any coherent way represent a series of moral vices, and although he becomes a 'murderer' (problematically, as in a legal sense he is outside of the law because he is not recognised as a 'real' man), this is due to circumstance and not because of a natural disposition. As he puts it, 'I am malicious because I am miserable' (p. 190). Victor empathises with the creature's words but cannot but perceive him in terms of moral turpitude:

> His words had a strange effect upon me. I compassionated him and sometimes felt a wish to console him, but when I looked upon him, when I saw the filthy mass that moved and talked, my heart sickened and my feelings were altered to those of horror and hatred. (p. 192)

The monster confuses Victor because he is not as he sounds, so he compromises Victor's claims to certainty and in doing so the creature highlights the problems which are associated with the sublime.

These problems are not unique to Burke's version of the sublime. That there is a problem with the Kantian sublime is something which Stephen Knapp addresses in his *Personification and the Sublime*. Knapp's argument is that in Kant the sublime ceases to be discovered in an external object and instead becomes associated with an internal set of feelings. The danger in this is that the sublime lacks any external ratification and becomes a purely subjective experience. It is this problem which conditions Victor's anxiety when confronted by the creature. The creature should be anchored to a discourse of monstrosity, one marked out by Baldick, which is mediated through a Burkean sense of monstrosity as a source of sublime terror. However, the creature cannot be externally ratified in this way, because it is his speech which defines him as a cultural subject. This means that Victor is faced with the terrifying possibility that the sublime may be pure subjectivity because the sublime does not now seem to relate to the world in any meaningful way. Knapp writes of this moment of slippage in the sublime in ways which are relevant to Victor's plight:

> the sublime itself now depends on an act of reference: the terrible object must be taken to signify a power in the self. The sublime

experience, no longer an instinctive reflex, turns out to be doubly inauthentic: first, because the power thus internalised is no real property of the self: second, because even this illusory aggrandizement is in the service not of the self but of Providence, which conforms even the vice of pride to social ends.[4]

The creature therefore evades Victor in two ways; firstly because he does not exist as a simple natural object, and secondly because his speech, although seductive, does not equate to any form of 'authentic' sublimity. The sublime cannot be apprehended, which echoes with the way that the creature, spatially, evades Victor in his pursuit of him towards the end of the novel. The sublime fails even to make sense as a set of feelings, the authenticity of which is taken away because they are plotted through a wider, obscure, providential design (a sense that this is all fated). This all means that the subject loses control, specifically over the possibility that the sublime possesses meaning.

David E. Musselwhite, commenting on the creature's teasing evasion of Victor, writes, 'The monster is always ahead or behind, always elsewhere, ever in a condition of migratory adjacency.'[5] This is because the creature eludes forms of classification, ones which would relate him either to the sublime and/or monstrosity. This failure to classify is significant because it relates the novel to a wider set of anxieties associated with modernity. The creature echoes Foucault's notion that modernity is characterised by the creation of 'man' as an object of knowledge. As Musselwhite puts it, 'what has been Mary Shelley's most remarkable achievement, even though it is thrust before us on almost every page of the novel ... is the invention of "man"' (p. 71). The fact that the creature poses a problem for classification means that for Musselwhite, 'Anomalous and exorbitant with respect to all that would define it the Monster is the very figure of the unknown that haunts modern thought' (p. 73). To understand how this works we need to look at how Foucault plots the arrival of modernity, an account which has implications for an understanding of why the sublime becomes so problematic a category in the late eighteenth and early nineteenth centuries.

Foucault's man

In *The Order of Things* Foucault writes that modernity emerges against the backdrop of the decline of Classicism.[6] This emergence was in part registered through a problematisation in the representational efficacy of language, which takes us back to the issue of language to be found in accounts of the sublime. Foucault explains, 'The threshold between Classicism and modernity ... had been definitively crossed when words ceased to intersect with representations and to provide a spontaneous grid for the knowledge of things' (p. 304). Because words cease to co-incide with what they should represent, it means, according to Foucault, that the possibility of self-reflexive thought is undermined. In this process the subject becomes constituted as a new object of knowledge, moving away from a faith in subjectivity to an emphasis on how the subject can be classified (can be more 'scientifically' understood) as an object of knowledge. As Foucault puts it, 'It seems obvious enough that, from the moment when man (*sic*) first constituted himself as a positive figure in the field of knowledge, the old privilege of reflexive knowledge, of thought thinking itself, could not but disappear' (p. 326).

This movement, which constitutes the subject as an object of knowledge, is not solely linked to a new need for external ratification; it is also associated with the belief that language is not only non-representational but lacking an origin. In this way language is doubly problematised because it fails to represent and its origins have become occluded. Foucault writes of the subject that 'all he ever finds is the previously unfolded possibility of language, and not the stumbling sound, the first word upon the basis of which all languages and even language itself became possible' (p. 330). This means that the subject has no origin. He writes, 'things began long before him, and that for this very reason, and since his experience is wholly constituted and limited by things, no one can ever assign him an origin' (p. 331). Here, where Foucault is referring to 'things' he is also in part referring to language. The subject is formed through a language which is linguistically and historically displaced, and the subject follows this displacement; consequently, like the creature in *Frankenstein*, the subject escapes a particular type of (Classical) knowledge which regarded subjectivity as a guarantor of truth.

For Foucault then, the advent of modernity is associated with the breakdown of meaning in language (a moment which Foucault locates at the beginning of the nineteenth century).[7] The subject follows this displacement and becomes reconstituted as a problematic object of knowledge. To understand how this directly relates to Shelley's novel we need to explore how the creature is inserted into the symbolic and so how his language acquisition reflects on the status of the sublime and on Foucault's modern man.

The creature overhears the speech of the De Laceys and attempts to construct a rudimentary grammar. He says of the De Laceys, 'Their pronunciation was quick, and the words uttered, not having any apparent connection with visible objects, I was unable to discover any clue by which I could unravel the mystery of their reference' (p. 158). The creature is, as Musselwhite points out, baffled by words which designate subject positions: 'The youth and his companion had each of them several names, but the old man had only one, which was "father." The girl was called "sister" or "Agatha," and the youth "Felix," "brother," or "son"' (p. 158).[8]

The creature's introduction to language illustrates what Foucault sees as characterising the emergence of 'man'. Words are no longer (as they were in Classicism) perceived as simply representative; subject positions are potentially confusing, suggesting that linguistic meaning is dependent upon the position of the speaking (designating) subject within a social context (here, the family). By extension, it is because the creature has no family that he remains unnamed and unnameable in what is, at some level, a novel about families, whether it is the De Laceys, or the Frankensteins, or even Walton with his letters to his sister.

It is the creature's education which is contrasted with Victor's, although the novel also establishes an initial contrast between Victor's and Elizabeth's education. Victor tells Walton about his childhood and dwells on the fact that he developed an early interest in searching for profound truths, whereas Elizabeth enjoyed the surface of things: 'While my companion contemplated with a serious and satisfied spirit the magnificent appearances of things, I delighted in investigating their causes' (p. 85). This search for origins becomes transformed into an adult search for the origins of life. Victor's education is above all bookish and consequently largely theoretical. The creature acquires language (and knowledge of Plutarch, Goethe and Milton) through hearing, whereas Victor acquires knowledge through reading. This constitutes the basis for the hearing/seeing paradox which will later condition Victor's encounter with the creature; an encounter in which language becomes problematised because the creature does not objectively represent the monstrosity that Victor sees.

For the creature, language is problematically representative, whereas for Victor language is seemingly transparent. It therefore becomes appropriate and revealing that Victor's early reading is confined to the Classics. Ultimately the novel poses the question which Foucault saw as characterising the emergence of the modern episteme: 'The whole curiosity of our thought now resides in the question: What is language, how can we find a way round it in order to make it appear in itself, in all its plenitude?' (p. 306). It is this question which returns us to the sublime and to the role of language.

We saw that in Burke's *Enquiry*, language is constituted as a problematic; sometimes it is representational, at others times it appears to either overwrite or underwrite its object. In Kant's treatise, there is a confused account of poetic language. Longinus' exploration of rhetoric leads him to the conclusion that language can mislead us. Thus at the heart of these debates about the sublime there is an argument about language taking place which informs the status of the sublime itself. What is also to be found in such accounts is a problematic search for plenitude, one which is suggested in Victor's quest and in Foucault's question. Foucault argues that this search for a full representation was linked to a conception of human nature which helped to ratify such a search. Foucault writes that:

> the great, endless, continuous surface is printed with distinct characters, in more or less general features, in marks of identification – and, consequently, in words. The chain of being becomes discourse, thereby linking itself to human nature and to the sequence of representation. (p. 310)

It is this which characterises the Classical episteme, but it is also connected to the sublime which contains within it the traces of just such a plenitude, as well as an anxious registering of that plenitude's potential disappearance. In *Frankenstein* these 'marks of identification' are apparently observed by a sublime gaze which attempts to decode the creature via a discourse of monstrosity. This gaze is also tied to ideas about 'human nature' because it is associated with a concept of universality, one which the creature ultimately destabilises. The creature resists these attempts to categorise him because of what Foucault sees as a change in the conception of representation itself: 'It is no longer their identity that beings manifest in representation, but the external relation they establish with the human being' (p. 313). This faith in representation is revealed in the creature's belief that language can accurately reveal his 'humanity'. The creature is contrasted with Victor in a variety of ostensible ways. The creature craves community, which contrasts with Victor's desire for seclusion. Both the creature and Victor live in solitude, one enforced, the other desired. Victor does, however, hold on to an older form of 'humanity' which demonises the creature. This clash between the creature and Victor captures Foucault's idea about the arrival of an 'analytic of finitude', one which challenges the claims of Classical thought. The arrival of this analytic underlines the struggle between the Classical and the modern. Foucault writes:

> Where there had formerly been a correlation between a *metaphysics* of representation and of the infinite and an *analysis* of living beings, of man's desires, and of the words of his language, we find being constituted an *analytic* of finitude and human existence, and in opposition to it … a perpetual tendency to constitute a *metaphysics* of life, labour, and language. (p. 317)

It is Victor who comes to personify the position of 'a *metaphysics* of representation and of the infinite', something which relates Victor to the sublime. This opposes an '*analytic* of finitude' which Foucault associates with death. It is this latter position which the creature fills, being literally made out of dead parts, as well as being a creature which kills (this also explains why the creature seems to fulfil Burke's notion of death as a source of the sublime). Victor can also be linked to this idea concerning 'a *metaphysics* of life, labour, and language' because his position in the novel suggests that the creation of life, the labour required to attain it, and language itself, should be tied to a metaphysics. It is the creature's language which problematises all of this for Victor, and it is this idea of appearance and representation which becomes, according to Foucault, the object of analysis in the modern episteme:

> analysis seeks to articulate the possible objectivity of a knowledge of nature upon the original experience of which the body provides an outline; and to articulate the possible history of a culture upon the semantic density which is both hidden and revealed in actual experience. (p. 321)

In *Frankenstein* it is the case that the body and semantics are conflated. The body is read in a certain way, only for that reading to generate false meanings. In the novel what is revealed in the 'experience … of the body', is that it is tied to a 'history of a culture' which 'sees' in a certain way.

Mary Shelley's novel can thus be read through Foucault's account of the emergence of 'man' as an object of knowledge in modern thought. Foucault also, implicitly, provides us with an historicisation of the sublime and its decline as a metaphysic, a decline in part inaugurated by the failure of language which we have seen as characterising these problematic accounts of the sublime. Additionally, in the clash between Victor and the creature, there is a representative clash between Classicism and modernity. The creature personifies this newly created 'man' who cannot be understood by an older Classical discourse. The sublime becomes internalised because it is no longer properly held in place by a coherent discourse about human nature. The sublime's new internal status heralds the arrival of the unconscious and Foucault writes about this in ways which are applicable to the problematisation of the status and function of the subject in the old sublime moment: 'How can man think what he does not think, inhabit as though by a mute occupation something that eludes him, animate with a kind of frozen movement that figure of himself that takes the form of a stubborn exteriority?' (p. 323). For Foucault, the way in which this dilemma is resolved is through the creation of an Other who stands in opposition to the subject:

> the *cogito* will not therefore be the sudden and illuminating discovery that all thought is thought, but the constantly renewed interrogation as to how thought can reside elsewhere than here, and yet so very close to itself; how it can *be* in the forms of non-thinking. (p. 324)

Structurally this bears some similarity with the pantheistic sublime, but it also applies to the creature in *Frankenstein*. The creature is granted a provisional and precarious status as a sublime object which implies that he is non-thinking (a monster). In Baldick's terms he is supposed to exemplify moral mutilation. The fact that the creature speaks means that he undermines this attempt to categorise him as an objective exemplar of moral vice. The creature does, however, become Other to Victor; he becomes what Foucault regards as thought residing in the inanimate, 'of non-thinking'. This means that it becomes possible to see the relationship between Victor and the creature as defined by a dynamic between self and Other. Significantly, it is Foucault's notion of the emergence of the Other which has parallels with the creation of the creature. Foucault writes:

> the Other that is not only a brother but a twin, born, not of man, nor in man, but beside him and at the same time, in an identical newness, in an unavoidable duality. This obscure space so readily

interpreted as an abyssal region in man's nature, or as a uniquely impregnable fortress in his history, is linked to him and indispensable to him: in one sense, the shadow cast by man as he emerged in the field of knowledge; in another, the blind stain by which it is possible to know him. (p. 326)

The creature mirrors this 'birth', and he also parallels the way that, as a sublime object of terror, he is 'so readily interpreted as an abyssal region in man's nature'. The creature becomes both Other to Victor and his shadow. This paradox, of Otherness and nearness, would suggest that at some level there is a possible convergence between them. This is something which Mary Poovey has identified in the novel:

> In *Frankenstein*, the monster simply acts out the implicit content of Frankenstein's desire: just as Frankenstein figuratively murdered his family, so the monster literally murders Frankenstein's domestic relationships, blighting both the memory and the hope of domestic harmony with the 'black mark' of its deadly hand.[9]

We observed earlier that there seems to be an inverse relationship between the two because the creature desires the kind of domesticity which Victor rejects. However, the creature becomes both Other and the same to Victor, for in killing his family, for example, the creature, at some level, becomes the same as Victor.

These similarities between the creature and Victor take place at a necessarily covert level. Victor has no overt hatred of Elizabeth or his family, but what this suggests is that the novel constructs an unconscious level at which these transferences take place. It is this idea of the unconscious which also distances the novel from an endorsement of the sublime. It also accords with Foucault's idea of the 'unthought' (the unconscious), whereby 'it is always concerned with showing how the Other, the Distant, is also the Near and the Same' (p. 339). This gives us another, complementary, explanation as to why Victor can only with difficulty perceive in the creature the desired objective presence of an alien monstrosity. The sublime becomes internalised in *Frankenstein*, as exterior moments of discovery are retranslated into interior moments of anxious identification, all of which implies the emergence of the unconscious. It is this emergence which brings back into focus the status of representation in accounts of the sublime. The creature is used to demonstrate that Burkean sublime monstrosity can only be ascribed to him if he is seen from a certain cultural position. The creature appears to capture this Burkean moment, but in fact he undermines it. This can also be linked to Foucault's account of the relationship between representation and perception:

> the analysis of man's mode of being as it has developed since the nineteenth century does not reside within a theory of representation; its task, on the contrary, is to show how things in general can be given to representation, in what conditions, upon what ground, within what limits they can appear in a positivity more profound than the various modes of perception. (p. 337)

Sublime speculations are thus replaced by questions about representation. This in turn becomes problematised by the emergence of the unconscious, a particular version of the unconscious which can be profitably approached through a Kristevian reading of *Frankenstein*. The following reading is not, as it might appear, a straightforward endorsement of a psychoanalytical approach; rather, what I want us to consider is the way that Kristeva's sense of the subject is structurally echoed in Victor's own creation of his subject: the creature. This is a good example of how the Gothic formulates an antidote to the sublime, its tentative development of an unconscious dimension which will in turn ghost psychoanalysis. Psychoanalysis thus owes a largely unacknowledged debt to the Gothic, one which it is my aim to unravel.

Kristeva: semiotic sublimity

In *Revolution in Poetic Language* Kristeva outlines the different functions of the semiotic and the symbolic. The symbolic is associated with language and the semiotic to an ordering principle which is behind language, but which is non-linguistic and unconscious; both are present at the same time in the subject, and cannot be separated. She writes, 'the subject is always *both* semiotic *and* symbolic, no signifying system he (*sic*) produces can be either "exclusively" semiotic or "exclusively" symbolic, and is instead necessarily marked by an indebtedness to both'.[10] Kristeva also formulates a theory of drives, drives which control both the semiotic and the symbolic; in her account of this 'chora' it is possible to see a relation between the chora and the creation of the creature in *Frankenstein*. Kristeva writes that

> Discrete quantities of energy move through the body of the subject who is not yet constituted as such and, in the course of his develop-ment, they are arranged according to the various constraints imposed on this body – always already involved in a semiotic process – by family and social structures. In this way the drives, which are 'energy' charges as well as 'psychical' marks, articulate what we call a *chora*: a non-expressive totality formed by the drives and their stases in a motility that is as full of movement as it is regulated. (p. 25)

The subject is thus both essential (motivated by innate drives) and nur-tured (formed by 'social structures'). To locate this chora poses a problem because it is non-figurative and it is manifested only through 'vocal or kinetic rhythm' (p. 26), and so appears to have rather more to do with form than with content: 'the semiotic *chora* is no more than the place where the subject is both generated and negated, the place where his unity succumbs before the process of charges and stases that produce him' (p. 28). The chora, like the Freudian uncanny, is that which is hidden.

So, for Kristeva, the subject is produced through a range of social structures which serve to highlight the subject's initiation and inser-tion into the symbolic realm; the acquisition of language being the key here. Underlying this language there exists an unconscious, unspoken semiotic which is in turn controlled by energy charges in the drive of the chora. What we find here is the suggestion that there is an inevitable lack of unity. The subject is constituted through a series of drives and encounters with the world over which he/she has no conscious control.

This lack of unity in the Kristevian subject has echoes with the crea-ture's lack of corporal unity. Victor perceives this lack when he writes of his attempt to cover the body with skin: 'His yellow skin scarcely covered the work of muscles and arteries beneath' (p. 105). Beneath the surface (the level of appearance) there is an excess which undermines Victor's sense of aesthetics, but which also represents a series of drives which, in some sense, energise the creature. As stated earlier, Kristeva has written that 'Discrete quantities of energy move through the body of the subject who is not yet constituted as such' (p. 25). It is later, when the semiotic chora is arranged 'by family and social structures' (p. 25), that the subject enters the symbolic. The creature early in the novel has a similar status when he is pre-linguistic, and this sense of pre-insertion into the symbolic is referenced through the failure of the skin to properly contain his component parts; he is not yet properly constituted as a subject. The creature retains this status until the sublime is exposed as a cultural (symbolic) form of perception.

As we have seen, Victor's initial perception of the creature is one which connects the creature to the sublime. The creature is a sublime object of monstrosity: 'A flash of lightning illuminated the object and discovered its shape plainly to me; its gigantic stature, and the deformity of its aspect, more hideous than belongs to humanity' (p. 123). The creature seems to be naturalised in such moments which connect him to a set of emotional triggers; this is because the sublime is felt to be 'innate' rather than understood as a cultural taxonomy. Victor, for example, says of his early life that:

> During my youthful days discontent never visited my mind, and if I was ever overcome by *ennui*, the sight of what is beautiful in nature or the study of what is excellent and sublime in the productions of man could always interest my heart and communicate elasticity to my spirits. (p. 205)

This sub-linguistic encounter with the world controls Victor's response to the creature, one which the creature unsettles through his almost grandiloquent speech. In Kristevian terms it could be argued that the creature is both semiotic and symbolic. The semiotic is here associated with the sublime and the symbolic with speech; both are seemingly irreconcilably present. Victor comes to acknowledge this troubling moment of recognition in the apparent contradiction between the creature's appearance and his words, and ultimately this will lead Victor to the covert conclusion that the sublime is in reality a culturally organised form of perception. What happens then is that the sublime, like the creature, becomes constituted as both semiotic and symbolic. This is a process worth our reconsideration.

The creature is initially identified with the sublime, and thus he equates to the semiotic. When the sublime is revealed to be a culturally organised form of perception, then that form of perception is exposed as symbolic (cultural) rather than semiotic (sublime). However, the creature does partially retain a semiotic status (gestured to in his unnaming) which confounds attempts to classify him; he remains an 'impossible' body. The creature is thus simultaneously symbolic and semiotic. We can see this, for example, in Victor's reaction to the creature's taunt that he would be with him on his wedding night: 'still the words of the fiend rang in my ears like a death-knell; they appeared like a dream, yet distinct and oppressive as a reality' (p. 214). The creature's words are both real and unreal, they are dream-like and yet as 'oppressive as a reality'. The semiotic and the symbolic merge here and this is something which is also evident in Victor's confusion on his destruction of the creature's mate: 'The remains of the half-finished creature, whom I had destroyed, lay scattered on the floor, and I almost felt as if I had mangled the living flesh of a human being' (p. 215). It is, of course, the dead flesh of several human beings.

We saw earlier that Foucault identifies the modern in terms of how the emergence of 'man' becomes constituted as a subject and object of knowledge. In this constitution the unconscious is granted a particular privilege as in it the truth of the subject is to be found; this coheres with how *Frankenstein* constructs a version of the unconscious which explains Victor's own confused motives. Additionally, Kristeva's notion of the 'thetic' is linked to these arguments, a notion which we need to consider before returning to the sublime.

Death, creation, and the thetic

David Ketterer argues that in *Frankenstein* there are parallels made between artistic practice and scientific endeavour.[11] Victor's craving for isolation echoes that of the artist's, or as Ketterer puts it, 'The writer, like the scientist, works best in isolation' (p. 12). Indeed, according to Ketterer, the two practices are almost identical, 'In many respects ... scientific and artistic creation are understood as indistinguishable' (p. 12). For Ketterer this is exemplified by Victor's, rather than Walton's, control over the narrative; he points out that Walton writes to his sister, 'Frankenstein discovered that I made notes concerning his history; he asked to see them and then himself corrected and augmented them in many places' (p. 253). For Ketterer, Victor creates the creature and the narrative and they bear similarity to each other because both are potentially open to mutilation. Victor says to Walton, 'Since you have preserved my narration ... I would not that a mutilated one should go down to posterity' (p. 253). Ketterer links this idea of Victor as creator to an anxiety about masturbation; he writes that 'To the extent that creativity calls for isolation and self-absorption, it might be regarded as a perversion of sexuality, specifically a form of masturbation or incest' (p. 47).[12]

This idea of self-love is one played on in a variety of ways throughout the novel. The creature, for example, as we have seen, catches sight of himself in a pool in a clear, although usurped, reference to the myth

of Narcissus. Victor explains that he is motivated by a need for adoration, and he says of his scientific project that he hoped that 'A new
species would bless me as its creator and source; many happy and
excellent natures would owe their being to me. No father could
claim the gratitude of his child so completely as I should deserve
theirs' (pp. 101–2). The creature becomes, however, instead of a doting
child, 'an abortion to be spurned at, and kicked, and trampled on'
(p. 263). Walton also shares Victor's desire for adoration and self-
aggrandizement, as he writes to his sister:

> you cannot contest the inestimable benefit which I shall confer on
> all mankind to the last generation, by discovering a passage near the
> pole to those countries, to reach which at present so many months
> are requisite; or by ascertaining the secret of the magnet, which, if
> at all possible, can only be effected by an undertaking such as mine.
> (p. 64)

Walton apes Victor here in his desire to become a blessed parent who
provides a 'benefit ... on all mankind to the last generation'.

In *Frankenstein*, then, these moments of self-love function to obscure
the need for self-aggrandisement. Kristeva writes of narcissism in *Freud
and Love: Treatment and its Discontents* that 'Narcissism and its lining,
emptiness, are ... our most intimate, brittle and archaic elaborations of
death drive. The most advanced, courageous and threatened sentries of
primal repression.'[13] According to Kristeva, narcissism is regulated by
the death drive because it expresses a desire for isolation (and so has
echoes with Burke's account of the sublime). It is this social 'death'
which is overcome by eros because love leads the subject into an
identification with, and a separation from, another subject. Kristeva
writes that, 'In being able to receive the other's words, to assimilate,
repeat and reproduce them, I become like him: One. A subject of
enunciation. Through psychic osmosis/identification. Through love'
(p. 244). Kristeva, like Musselwhite and Ketterer, links narcissism to
creativity although, paradoxically, it is a form of creativity conditioned
by the operations of the death drive. In *Revolution in Poetic Language*
this notion of creativity is associated with a rupture in the thetic;
her definition of the thetic and its functions is given as: 'thetic
signification is a stage attained under certain precise conditions during
the signifying process ... it constitutes the subject without being
reduced to his process precisely because it is the threshold of language'
(pp. 99–100). She proceeds to explain why the thetic becomes

ruptured, 'Though absolutely necessary, the thetic is not exclusive: the semiotic, which also precedes it, constantly tears it open, and this transgression brings about all the various transformations of the signifying practice that are called "creation"' (p. 113).

With Kristeva it is the case that the subject learns identification and separation through language acquisition which again puts the focus on an issue which is central to accounts of the sublime: the function and status of language. According to Kristeva the thetic is the 'threshold of language'; it is the primary stage which enables language acquisition to occur. It is also the stage which, potentially, can lead the subject away from this dangerous narcissism. The acquisition of language can, however, be problematised because language can be ruptured by a fragmented Otherness which leads to an irruption of the semiotic, whereby 'the Other has become heterogeneous and will not remain fixed in place: it negativizes all terms, all posited elements and thus syntax, threatening them with possible dissolution' (p. 108). For Kristeva, when language breaks down like this, it destabilises what we understand to be true or false propositions. She writes that 'all transgressions of the thetic are a crossing of the boundary between true and false – maintained, inevitably, whenever signification is maintained, and shaken, irredeemably, by the flow of the semiotic into the symbolic' (p. 110). As we saw earlier, the creature in *Frankenstein* personifies this process in his wavering between the semiotic and the symbolic, and then semiotic-symbolic. It is when the creature speaks that, for Victor, the boundaries 'between true and false' are 'shaken, irredeemably'.

Kristeva's account of symbolic disruption is not a negative one, as we saw earlier it is associated with creativity. She links this creativity to the functions of the death drive when she writes: 'In all known archaic societies, this founding break of the symbolic order is represented by murder – the killing of a man, a slave, a prisoner, an animal' (p. 119).

The creature inaugurates 'this founding break of the symbolic order' through murder; the symbolic order in *Frankenstein* being defined in terms of family, lovers, friends and servants. It is also the creature who is observed in 'archaic' ways. We can see this by a reconsideration of Foucault's argument that the arrival of modernity is shadowed by the presence of an older, Classical, knowledge. Victor has studied the now arcane works of Albertus Magnus, Paracelus and Cornelius Agrippa. Victor effectively brings back to life a dead knowledge through the creation of a creature from 'dead' body parts. All of this makes a clear connection between death and creativity, and in Kristevian terms it becomes possible to see the creature as personifying this death drive. What this means is that the creature represents (figuratively) an emerging modernity which usurps the claims to truth to be found in Classicism (even though he is a product of a kind of classical knowledge). The creature challenges now outmoded ways of seeing, and this usurpation is represented through the creature's literal killing of the symbolic order of the old regime.

What we have seen is that *Frankenstein* challenges theories of the sublime. This challenge conforms to Foucault's idea that the emergence of 'man' characterises the arrival of modernity and the break-up of the Classical episteme. Victor is conditioned by this older Classical knowledge, whereas the creature is associated with a new understanding of the world based on the exposure of the cultural partisanship to be found in the sublime gaze. All of this suggests that Shelley's novel runs together a complex series of historical and cultural references in order to construct a new way of looking at sublime experience, one which is also influenced by the arrival of the unconscious.

We have also seen that the dynamics of the sublime in the novel can be read through Kristeva's account of the semiotic and the symbolic. The sublime bears an analogous relationship to the semiotic, whereas the creature's speech implies his entry into the symbolic. Victor is thus forced to recognise, in Kristevian terms, that the creature is both semiotic and symbolic. The sublime's cultural determination is highlighted in the novel partly because of the latent presence of the semiotic, and in part because Shelley is also making wider, overtly politicised, comments about exclusion and social injustice. In using Kristeva in this way it might appear that one essentialist philosophy (the sublime) is being replaced by another. However, as we shall see, the status of the precursor is problematic because one of the peculiar features of the sublime is that it ghosts, at some level informs, psychoanalytical accounts of the subject. I have looked at Kristeva in order to reveal the structural similarities between Shelley's critique of the sublime and Kristeva's formulation of the subject. An analysis of this Gothic sublime will also reveal its presence within Freudian thought and how it is that this Gothic presence compromises Freud's version of the unconscious. The history which I am mapping out is one that historicises the Gothic and historically accounts for the emergence of Freud. This history of the Gothic sublime thus embraces the Freudian moment as well as observing the Gothic deconstruction of that moment.

What we will find is that the Gothic emphasises a disunity of the self, a disunity to be found within psychoanalysis itself; what this means is that this Gothic sublime can be used to critically read psychoanalytic versions of the self *avant la lettre*. Ultimately, *Frankenstein* can be interpreted as accounting for the break between the Classical and the modern epistemes and it does so by establishing a clash between a potential plenitude and a threatened absence; as the creature puts it at the end of the novel, 'I cannot believe that I am the same creature whose thoughts were once filled with sublime and transcendent visions of the beauty and the majesty of goodness' (p. 263).

3
History and the Sublime

We have seen how in *Frankenstein* a dead language is brought back to life. This is a resurrection of the dead science of Albertus Magnus, Paracelsus and Cornelius Agrippa. This idea of using the past in order to define the present is something which Mary Shelley also explores in two of her tales, 'Valerius: the Reanimated Roman' and 'The Mortal Immortal: a Tale'. As in *Frankenstein*, it is the return of the past which unsettles the sublime in these tales, but before looking at them in detail it is helpful to explore Walter Jackson Bate's contention that the remnants of a Classical culture can be found within Romantic thought. Bate's argument provides us, indirectly, with an explanation as to why the Romantics' attachment to the past destabilises the Romantic sublime.

In *The Burden of the Past and the English Poet* Bate explores some of the more problematic moments within Romanticism.[1] Bate outlines the decline of Classicism and the emergence of Romanticism (in ways which, incidentally, structurally echo Foucault's reading of the emergence of modernity). Bate argues that the end of Classicism was brought about through its apparent perfection. The rules of composition for the Epic, for example, had become so codified that the only possible form of artistic practice was that of imitation: in effect meaningful creativity had disappeared. Romanticism's role was to develop new forms of writing in a process through which originality and experimentation replaced imitation. There was also a concurrent move towards nature as the possible source of inspiration, and as the site which could ground a philosophical system such as the sublime.

According to Bate, the emergence of Romanticism was characterised by this evolving concept of the sublime and by the appearance of a new aesthetics designed to represent this experience. For Bate,

Classicism is associated with Roman culture and its influence within Augustan thought. However, he also claims that Classicism retains a grip on Romanticism and it is this continuing presence which suggests a possible return to *Frankenstein*. Bate, for example, explore Hume's interest in the Roman historian Velleius Paterculus (at this point Bate is still exploring the place of imitation within poetic models). Bate writes that, 'In bringing up this directly human problem of emulation, Hume resurrects some remarks by Velleius Paterculus (I. xvii), written about the year A.D. 30' (p. 82). Bate states that Hume's argument can be found at the end of his essay 'Of the Rise and the Progress of the Arts and Sciences'. Bate proceeds to quote Paterculus:

> Genius is fostered by emulation .... As in the beginning we are fired with the ambition to overtake those whom we regard as leaders, so, when we have despaired of being able either to surpass or even equal them, our zeal wanes with our hope. It ceases to follow what it cannot overtake, and abandoning the old field as pre-empted, seeks a new one. (p. 83)

Hume, however, does not directly quote from Paterculus, rather he writes that:

> Had Waller been born in Rome, during the reign of Tiberius, his first productions had been despised, when compared to the finished odes of Horace. But in this island the superiority of the Roman poet diminished nothing from the fame of the English. We esteemed ourselves sufficiently happy that our climate and language could produce but a faint copy of so excellent an original.
> In short, the arts and sciences, like some plants, require a fresh soil; and however rich the land may be, and however you may recruit it by art or care, it will never, when once exhausted, produce anything that is perfect or refined in the kind.[2]

Bate assumes that Hume is paraphrasing Paterculus. There are, however, some telling differences here: notably the nationalism and the metaphor of Nature as Nurture. What remains however (if we can plausibly read this as an unacknowledged paraphrase of Paterculus) is the irony of Hume emulating Paterculus on emulation. It is this lack of direct acknowledgement by Hume which Bate associates with a variety of other philosophers, such as Kames, Gerard, and Priestley, who had also referred to Paterculus in a somewhat unfocused way: 'Their speculations tend to be limited and indirect, revealing a general, unlocalized suspicion that they seem unwilling to apply to literature in detail' (p. 83). In the case of Hume the paradox is that he is using the arguments of the ancients in order to banish Classical philosophy from modern thought. Bate's wider claim is that these moments of discrete appropriation suggest the continuation of Classicism within the philosophical systems which influenced Romantic thought.

In *Frankenstein* it is Classical knowledge which produces the creature. The knowledge of the ancients is resurrected in the creation of the creature. This idea of a resurrection is punned on (unconsciously) by Bate: 'Hume resurrects some remarks by Velleius Paterculus' (p. 82). Also, in the Introduction to Paterculus' *The History of Rome*, Frederich W. Shipley writes of this brief history that:

> Abridgements are usually little more than skeletons; but Velleius has succeeded, in spite of the brief compass of his work, in clothing the bones with real flesh, and in endowing his compendium with a mere shadow of vitality ....[3]

These historical accounts are thus ghosted by metaphors of resurrection. However, as we saw with *Frankenstein*, it is resurrection which disrupts a culture's sense of its natural order. It is the creature's mere existence which compromises the claims made for the natural sublime, and what we tend to lose sight of is the role that Classicism (Magnus, Paracelsus, Agrippa) has played in his construction. Importantly this Classical past has no model of the sublime within it, meaning that the creature is the product of a discourse which exists outside of Romantic philosophies. It is this idea, of the resurrected past undermining the present, which we can also see at work in two of Mary Shelley's tales.

Roman(tic) displacements

'Valerius: the Reanimated Roman' is the strange tale of Valerius, an ancient Roman citizen who is reintroduced to modern-day Rome.[4] The tale emphasises the contrast between modern and ancient perceptions of Rome; it is a contrast in which the sublime plays an important role. In order to grasp the central dynamics of the tale I will quote from it at length because, revealingly, it is constructed from two eye-witness accounts which bestow importance on the function of subjectivity in the interpretive process.

The initially striking feature of the tale is its convoluted structure; the story represents a clash between the past and the present in terms of narrative control. The two narratives of the tale, Valerius' account to an unnamed Englishman, and the account of Valerius by Isabell, his guide around modern-day Rome, grate against each other. The unidentified narrator who presents us with both accounts is outside of the action of the story but they present us with a revealing preliminary comment concerning Valerius; they write 'I can compare him to nothing that now exists – his appearance resembled that of the statue of Marcus Aurelius in the Square of the Capitol at Rome' (p. 332). It is this comparison between Valerius and Marcus Aurelius which bears significance to a claim that Marcus Aurelius makes in his *Meditations*. He writes:

> Consider for example the times of Vespasian, and you will see all these things: people marrying, rearing children, falling ill, dying, making war, holding festivals, trading, farming, flattering, asserting themselves, suspecting, plotting, praying for other people's death, muttering about present conditions, making love, hoarding money, wanting the consulship, wanting the throne. Now that life of theirs exists no more anywhere. Pass on, again, to the times of Trojan. Again, all the same. That life is dead too.[5]

Shelley's tale, in a broad sense, provides a reply to Marcus Aurelius in its exploration of social change. Isabell tries to place Valerius in a continuum which links him to the past through a nebulous concept of humanity, one which Aurelius endorsed, but one which Valerius challenges. Isabell takes Valerius to the Coliseum, built in the time of Vespasian. Valerius' response to the now crumbling Coliseum takes on a sublime quality, 'The moon shone through the broken arches and shed a glory around the fallen walls, crowned as they are by weeds and brambles. I looked around, and a holy awe seized me' (p. 335). Valerius will ultimately be unable, for telling reasons, to generate a sustained state of sublimity. However, Valerius elects to live in the Coliseum because, 'If Rome be dead, I fly from her remains, loathsome as those of human life. It is in the Coliseum alone that I recognise the grandeur of my country – that is the only worthy asylum for an antient Roman' (p. 336).

Valerius comes to recognise his historical and cultural displacement, and it is a recognition which culminates in feelings of alienation: 'Yet suddenly, the feeling so dreadful to the human mind, the feeling of utter solitude, operated a new change on my heart. I remembered as it were but of yesterday all the shews which antient Rome had presented' (p. 336). The collapse of Rome is associated with the collapse of Classicism, and also with a moral decline. Valerius says:

> When I died, I was possessed by the strong impression that, since philosophy and letters were now joined to a virtue unparalleled upon earth, Rome was approaching that perfection from which there was no fall; and that, although men still feared, it was a wholesome fear which awoke them to action and the better secured the triumph of Good. (p. 336)

Valerius perceives the decline of Rome as indicating a moral decline, one which, paradoxically, is revealed by the presence of Christianity. He says 'Modern Rome is the Capital of Christianity, and that title is that which is crown and top of my despair' (p. 337). However, what we see is that Valerius becomes, in a Christian sense, redeemed through an apprehension of a higher, divine authority. He says of his early feelings of desperation that 'It was then that a kind deity interfered and, sending my good genius to watch over me, extricated me from any difficulties' (p. 338). Valerius also projects this sense of salvation on to Isabell:

> She is so frank-hearted, and yet so tender, that she wins my soul and binds it up in hers in a manner that I never experienced in my former life. She is Country, Friends – all, all, that I had lost is she to me. (p. 339)

Isabell becomes caught between two worlds: a modern one, she lifting his soul 'in a manner that I never experienced in my former life' and an ancient one, 'She is ... all, all, that I had lost'.

Valerius' historical displacement is echoed in Isabell's repositioning as both ancient and modern. There are two crucial movements in the tale; one is in Valerius' attempt to re-evoke the past and the other is, as we will see, Isabell's problematic attempt to reinscribe the modern back into the past. It is because of these overdetermined historical clashes that the sublime becomes undermined. It is also at this point in the narrative, after Valerius' salvation, that Isabell takes control. The anonymous narrator informs us that, 'The story ends at this point, but another and fragmentary version, told from Isabell Harley's point of view, follows in the manuscript' (p. 339). The narrative as a whole therefore has the status of an historical artefact and this is in keeping with the conflation of textual and historical claims. It is also this idea of displacement which Isabell first addresses in her fragmentary narrative; she writes of Valerius that 'He appeared to regard every thing around him as a spectacle in which he had no concern. He was indeed a being cut off from our world' (pp. 339–40). Isabell takes Valerius to a tower which provides a grand view of Rome. It is a scene in which the veracity of the sublime is brought into question. Isabell tells Valerius:

> This is of all others the place I delight most in Rome to visit: it joins the beauty and fragrance of Nature to the sublimest idea of human power; and when so united, they have an interest and feeling that sinks deep into my heart. (p. 341)

For Valerius, however:

> 'You bring me here,' he said, 'to view the works of the Romans, and behold nothing but destruction. What crowds of beautiful temples are fallen to the dust. My eyes wander over the seven hills, and all their glories are faded.' (p. 341).

The sublime's metaphysical status is exposed by this historical repositioning.

Valerius' status in the narrative suggests that the present is inhabited by the past in a fashion which creates a precarious evocation of a prelapsarian state: 'the modern city is filled with the ruins of the antient. But to me it all appears void' (p. 341). This has echoes with Weiskel's claim, discussed earlier, that, 'standing at the edge of the infinite spaces can be made, theoretically, to "mean" just about anything' (p. 28). Isabell attempts to forge a continuity with the past by trying to reinsert Valerius into the modern world. The object which she selects as an example of this continuity is the Pantheon which she regards as evocative of a modern-day pantheism:

> It is at such a time when one feels the existence of that Pantheic Love with which Nature is penetrated – and when a strong sympathy with beauty, if such an expression may be allowed, is the only feeling which animates the soul. (p. 342)

Valerius is only able to partially identify with this. For him this modern-day pantheism is different to the power of the ancient god(s) he is used to. It is the issue of historical displacement which ultimately defies Isabell's attempts to form a coherent continuity with the past, and again it is Christianity which highlights this. In a temple they see a crucifix. While for Isabell:

> The cross did not alter my feelings ... those of my companion were embittered. The apple so fair to look at had turned to brackish dust. The cross told to him of change so great, so intolerable, that that one circumstance destroyed all that had arisen of love and pleasure in his heart. (p. 343)

After this, Valerius' Otherness is increasingly emphasised.

Shelley's tale critiques the claims made for a pantheistic sublime. Isabell is imbued with this sublimity and she tries to underline the sublime's trans-historical status by attempting an awakening of its pleasures in Valerius. Isabell's position on the sublime appears to survive Valerius' alternative version of events because he becomes defined as irretrievably alien. Isabell writes:

> With my other feelings towards him, I had joined to them an inexplicable one that my companion was not a being of the earth. I often paused anxiously to know whether he respired the air, as I did, or if his form cast a shadow at his feet. His semblance was that of life, yet he belonged to the dead. I did not feel fear or terror: I loved and revered him. (p. 343)

This kind of ambivalence can be read as a gloss on Victor's own ambiguous relationship to the creature in *Frankenstein*. This ambivalence also, however, suggests an ambivalence about the past. Valerius possesses a 'semblance ... of life', but 'he belonged to the dead'. He is both attractive and repulsive: 'there was mingled with these commoner sensations an awe – I cannot call it dread, yet it had something slightly allied to that repulsive feeling – a sentiment for which I can find no name' (pp. 343–4).

The repulsion is a result of a fear of the return of the 'physically' dead and Valerius is described in ways which reinforce his corpse-like status. His historical displacement is not, however, entirely forgotten. The tale suggests that there exists a possible romantic attachment between Isabell and Valerius, which then becomes used as, paradoxically, a further opportunity to reinforce Valerius' Otherness. For Isabell, 'If he put his hand upon mine, I did not shudder, but, as it were, my thoughts paused in their course and my heart heaved with something of an involuntary uneasiness until it was removed' (p. 344). The physical and the historical collapse into each other. Valerius is ancient and yet exists, for Isabell, in the present as an ambivalent object of desire and repulsion. This strangely implies that the past is attractive precisely because it is dead. The ruins of Rome, for example, are a sublime, pantheistic object; they are regarded as representing a triumph of modern religion over the now-decayed Roman myths. Valerius is revered by Isabell as an object of the past, one which she is ambivalently attached to, ambivalently because the physical revulsion implies necrophilia.

This tale can be read as an analogue of the attempt made by the Romantics to banish Classical thought (or to lay it to rest). It also possesses the same kind of paradox identified by Bate, in that it becomes necessary to revive the past in order to conduct a superior dialogue with it. Although Valerius is the modern's Other, he is not fully marginalised by modern thought. What we find is that he 'owns' part of the narrative, and although his voice is superseded by Isabell's (the triumph of the modern), his arguments are never fully refuted; instead Valerius and Isabell talk past each other and any attempt to unite the ancient with the modern becomes impossible because the past is couched in a metaphor of tabooed necrophilia. This breakdown in the dialogue with the past does not banish its influence; rather what we find is that the past unsettles claims made in support of sublimity. This means that the Classical legacy which operates within Romantic thought brings with it destabilising tendencies. The Romantic sublime, at its very inception, begins to look like a troubled experience; even Burke's *Enquiry* is dominated by the kind of systematising which Bate associates with Classicism.

As we saw in the previous chapter, the internalisation of the sublime is predicated on a rupture with the pantheistic sublime. It is this internalisation which, in Foucault's terms, coincides with the emergence of 'man' as an object of knowledge. However, as we can see, it is not just the progressive internalisation of the sublime which frees it from a pantheistic presence, it is also challenged by the continued existence of Classical ideas within Romanticism. This use of the past introduces an historical relativism which undermines the transhistorical claims made for the sublime in general and the pantheistic sublime in particular. The problematic status of the pantheistic sublime in Shelley's tale exemplifies how the debate with Classicism has been lost, and that in that defeat the sublime becomes ghosted by an ambivalent attachment to the past (expressed in the tale through attraction/repulsion).

Fuseli and the problem with art

Another example of this ambivalent attitude towards Classicism can be found in Henry Fuseli's sketch, 'The Artist in Despair over the Magnitude of Antique Fragments'. According to Bate, this sketch captures the position of the artist burdened with the past, and struggling with the 'new'. Bate writes:

> What is shown of the 'grandeur' of the past is only the gigantic foot of some classical colossus and, above it, a great hand pointing upward. The modern artist cannot touch the hand. He is seated at the pedestal, half-bowed, with his left hand to his forehead, as if in despair. (p. 90)

Bate implies that this break with Classicism is, paradoxically, confused with a nostalgia for its very 'grandeur'. The sketch can be understood as representing an anxious search for new artistic direction. The sketch relies on organicist imagery; it is not a fully integrated body which we see (echoing with the creature's in *Frankenstein*) but only a severed foot and hand. To put it simply, the hand gestures towards a higher authority, an older inspiration, whereas the artist reclines across the foot which represents more earthly, secular considerations. Within this tableau there is a juxtaposition of bodies in which the broken body of the Colossus is contrasted with the human (complete) body of the artist. There is also a juxtaposition between the living and the dead and the real and the imaginary. Foucault revealingly writes in *The Order of Things* that, 'No doubt, on the level of appearances, modernity begins when the human being begins to exist within his organism, inside the shell of his head, inside the armature of his limbs, and in the whole structure of his physiology' (p. 318). This is represented in Fuseli's sketch in the contrast between the figure of the artist and the Classical, excessive, human figure which now lies in ruins. The artist has to construct new rules for art because Classical art has been destroyed. The artist, however, is in mourning for Classicism, meaning that the past haunts the present in ways which indicate, as Shelley does in 'Valerius', that the present might be an empty experience. As Valerius says about the modern world 'to me it all appears void' (p. 341).

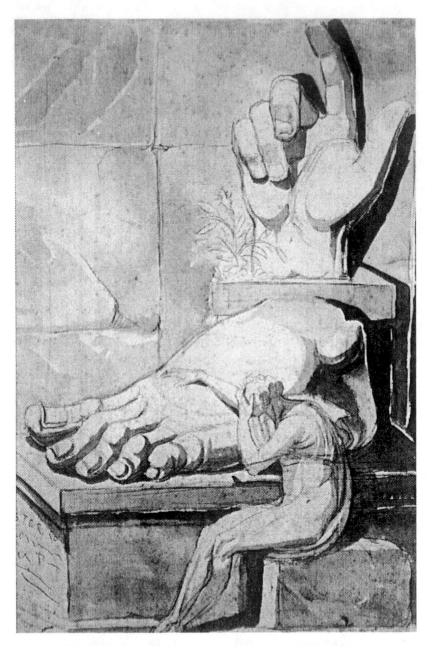

Henry Fuseli, 'The Artist in Despair over the Magnitude of Antique Fragments (Right Hand and Left Foot of the Colossus of Constantine)', 1778–80.

Again the past is evoked in order to grieve over it, rather than to celebrate a decisive rupture from it.

We can also see that the sketch contains images which Isabell perceives as a source of the sublime. Isabell too observes the ruins of Rome, but here it is the idea of grief which resituates this experience and suggests that instead of a pantheistic plenitude there is only absence and loss. In this way the giant hand pointing towards heaven mocks the notion of its possible interpretation as a source of splendour. It is this idea of a return of the past which we can see being played out in a rather different way in another Shelley tale, 'The Mortal Immortal: a Tale'.

The persistence of the past

In *Frankenstein* Shelley makes reference to Victor's indebtedness to Cornelius Agrippa, who reappears in 'The Mortal Immortal'. The narrator, Winzy, is a pupil of Agrippa's and the relationship between the two is described as a demonic pact. Winzy tells us that 'when Cornelius came and offered me a purse of gold if I would remain under his roof, I felt as if Satan himself tempted me.'[6] Winzy drinks Agrippa's formula for the elixir of life believing it to be a potion which would cure him of his apparently unrequited love for Bertha. After taking this elixir Winzy is transported in a way which suggests sublime transcendence:

> Words would be faint and shallow types of my enjoyment, or of the gladness that possessed my bosom when I woke. I trod air – my thoughts were in heaven. Earth appeared heaven, and my inheritance upon it was to be one trance of delight. (p. 223)

This state of sublime rapture is only slightly diminished as the years pass and Winzy ceases to age:

> I often called to mind that period of trance-like inebriation with wonder. The drink of Cornelius had not fulfilled the task for which he affirmed that it had been prepared, but its effects were more potent and blissful than words can express. (p. 224)

Winzy comes to personify the sublime, as he is quite literally a transhistorical subject who is imbued with the spirit of the sublime. Whereas in 'Valerius' it was a case of the dead being brought back to life, here we have a life which cannot die. In 'Valerius' the potential romance between Valerius and Isabell is tabooed as necrophilia, whereas here it takes on the form of a suggested incest taboo between mother and son. Winzy says of Bertha after several years of marriage that, 'We sat by our lone fireside – the old-hearted youth and his antiquated wife' (p. 227).

Winzy begins to find immortality burdensome, and this is exposed through a telling irony. Winzy's sense of the sublime is a pantheistic one ('Earth appeared heaven'); however, it is his very immortality which means that he cannot join with God through death. Rather he is overwhelmed by a sense of loss for those whom he has loved. At the end of the tale he talks of returning his body to nature by leaving it open 'to the destructive elements of air and water' (p. 230). If this fails then:

> I shall adopt more resolute means, and, by scattering and annihi-
> lating the atoms that compose my frame, set at liberty the life
> imprisoned within, and so cruelly prevented from soaring from
> this dim earth to a sphere more congenial to its immortal essence.
> (p. 230)

Here, unlike in 'Valerius', there is no collapsing of the physical into the historical. Rather Winzy's transcendence of the historical means that the physical stays the same; for this reason his soul is imprisoned 'for ever within its carnal habitation' (p. 226). Winzy's reference to 'annihi-lating the atoms that compose my frame' echo with the creature's final words in *Frankenstein* where the creature tells Walton, 'I shall ascend my funeral pile triumphantly and exult in the agony of the torturing flames. The light of that conflagration will fade away; my ashes will be swept into the sea by the winds' (p. 265). All of this works against Burke's notion of a fear of death as a source of sublime terror, as in these instances it is a desire for death which motivates.

We can see that in 'The Mortal Immortal' the present is endlessly repeated and thus takes on a transcendental quality, whereas in 'Valerius' it was the case that the past returns and undermines the present. In 'The Mortal Immortal' the sublime is lost because death, and so the 'real' ascendency to heaven, becomes impossible. It is the idea of a problematic return of the past which can be helpfully recon-sidered by exploring how Freud's notion of the uncanny reveals a similar range of disabling aporias.

The return of the past: Freud and Mary Shelley

In his essay on the uncanny, Freud writes that 'the uncanny is that class of the frightening which leads back to what is known of old and long familiar' (p. 340). Life itself is uncanny in 'The Mortal Immortal', becoming subject to an endless repetition. For Winzy it is the present which, paradoxically, is 'known of old and long familiar'. In 'Valerius' it is the persistence of the past which ultimately becomes frightening for Isabell.

Freud, in his account of the etymology of the uncanny, acknowledges that 'many languages are without a word for this particular shade of what is frightening' (p. 341). It is this very wordlessness which aligns the uncanny with the sublime, and the link with fear also echoes Burke's notion that terror is a source of sublimity. Additionally, in 'Valerius' the sublime is defined as a sub-linguistic pleasure for Isabell:

> Why cannot human language express human thoughts? And how is it that there is a feeling inspired by the excess of beauty, which laps the heart in a gentle but eager flame, which may inspire virtue and love, but the feeling is far too intense for expression? (p. 342)

Freud defines the uncanny through its relation to the *unheimlich* or the unhomely. His reference is to Schelling, 'Everything is *unheimlich* that ought to have remained secret and hidden but has come to light' (p. 345). This is played out in 'Valerius' in the very homelessness of the past, in Valerius' search for both literal and metaphysical accommodation. Famously, Freud's registers, *heimlich* and *unheimlich*, slip into each other in ways which destabilise their respective meanings. Freud quotes from a dictionary, '*Heimlich* ... as withdrawn from knowledge, unconscious ... *Heimlich* also has the meaning of that which is obscure, inaccessible to knowledge' (p. 346). In this alienation Freud suggests that at least the subject gains some awareness that there exists an Other from which they are estranged. It is this Other which dramatises an aspect of the self which is hidden or made 'inaccessible'. What this means is that the return of the past is in fact a return of the same; it represents a return of an Other from which the subject is apparently alienated. This all becomes related to Freud's wider purpose, which is to explain the feelings generated by an encounter with the double. Freud writes:

the fact ... that man is capable of self-observation – renders it possible to invest the old idea of a 'double' with a new meaning and to
ascribe a number of things to it – above all, those things which seem
to self-criticism to belong to the old surmounted narcissism of earliest times. (p. 357)

Although Freud is writing about Hoffmann's 'The Sandman', this also
applies to 'Valerius'. Valerius threatens the present through his very
existence, as he is the past repeated. Also, the casual acceptance of
Valerius' existence by the other characters implies that there is nothing
particularly strange about his presence. There is an air of inevitability
about Valerius' return which is echoed in Freud's notion of repetition;
Freud writes that, 'this factor of involuntary repetition which surrounds what would otherwise be innocent enough with an uncanny
atmosphere ... forces upon us the idea of something fateful and
inescapable' (pp. 359–60).

Freud is careful to separate clinical practice from literary configurations of the uncanny, although he does so in a way which renders literature doubly uncanny. I will discuss this later, in Chapter 7, but for the
purpose of the current argument we will look at what Freud writes
about the uncanny's relationship to literature. Freud writes that literature 'is a much more fertile province than the uncanny in real life, for
it contains the whole of the latter and something more besides, something that cannot be found in real life' (p. 372). This 'something more
besides' is the fantastic (certainly so in relation to Hoffmann). Freud,
because he sidesteps a discussion of creativity, leaves the fantastic
unexplored. What Freud does is use a literary text as an example of the
uncanny, only to then create a separation between the 'real' and the
literary, one which ultimately destabilises his account of the real. For
Freud, literature is itself a source of the uncanny because within it he
sees a problematic representation of the real. Freud tries to play down
the literary status of 'The Sandman' in order to appropriate its content;
however, what this signals is the fact that it is within literature that a
model of the self can be discerned. Freud often uses fiction to support
his scientific findings and this strange status accorded to the literary
implies that it contains a version of the self, one which predates psychoanalytical investigations of it.

This is a crucial point because it now becomes possible to observe
how it is that the literary contains the very basis of psychoanalysis
itself. It is not the case that Freud can illuminate literature, rather it is a
re-investigation of the literature which illuminates Freud. It is literature

which represents the emergence of 'man' as a category of knowledge (as a subject who can be placed within a psychoanalytical taxonomy). The figurative status of the unconscious is thus clear, but in order to identify its emergence we need to look at how the fantastic prefigures the Freudian unconscious, how it already produces an image of the subject which, in Foucauldian terms, indicates the arrival of this problematically categorised 'man'. Foucault, for example, writes about this emergence in a way which enables us to return to 'Valerius' and reconsider Valerius' own arrival into the modern world. There is an inevitability about Valerius' presence which corresponds to what Foucault writes about this new 'man':

> He is a quite recent creature, which demiurge of knowledge fabricated with its own hands less than two hundred years ago: but he has grown old so quickly that it has been only too easy to imagine that he had been waiting for thousands of years in the darkness for that moment of illumination in which he would finally be known. (p. 308)

Valerius represents this move from Classicism to modernity in which 'in the profound upheaval of such an archaeological mutation, man appears in his ambiguous position as an object of knowledge and as a subject that knows' (p. 312). The problem is that this familiarity with the past represents what Bate terms 'the burden of the past' in Romanticism. The past becomes merely the return of the same (which gestures towards Freud's uncanny), a return which unsettles the sublime.

In 'The Mortal Immortal' we can see that the tale provides us with a problematic reworking of what Foucault sees as the 'Analytic of finitude' which we explored earlier in relation to *Frankenstein*. It is this analytic which is externally determined by 'labour, life, and language' (p. 313). Central to this idea is the notion of repetition and of a culture reproducing itself and it is one which anticipates Freud but which also captures Winzy's own condemnation to a life of endless repetition. In Shelley's tale it is this repetition which leads to alienation, as the uncanny does for Freud. Winzy is alienated from the 'real' source of pantheism by being condemned to repeat the weaker version of the natural sublime, while the Freudian subject possesses an essential estrangement from the primary cause of the reason to repeat.

In 'Valerius' the past is evoked in order to pose troubling questions about the present. In the tale there is a clash taking place which conforms to Foucault's idea that the emergence of modernity is characterised by conflict. He writes:

> there is a *nature* of human knowledge that determines its forms and that can at the same time be made manifest to it in its own empirical contents. There were also analyses that – by studying humanity's more or less ancient, more or less easily vanquished illusions – functioned as a sort of transcendental dialectic. (p. 319)

It is this '*nature* of human knowledge' which in the Romantic texts discussed here is associated with the sublime. It is the sublime which is 'made manifest' through a prescribed way of seeing found in Burke's precise itemisation of cause and effect.

What we find in the two Mary Shelley tales is that there persists in Romantic thought an interest in 'studying humanity's more or less easily vanquished illusions'. It is in this fascination with the past that the sublime becomes undermined. The sublime is challenged, not by an external threat but by Romanticism's failure to properly distance itself from Classicism.

The progressive internalisation of the sublime in the work of Kant (and indeed in Schiller)[7] appears to pose the major threat to the pantheistic sublime. However, as we have seen, there is an alternative threat which comes from the refusal to break with the past. The irruption of the past into the present provides an equally disabling critique of the pantheistic sublime. Indeed, when we consider the correspondence between Shelley's tales, Freud, and the observations of Foucault, it becomes possible to see that this refusal to break with the past makes possible the internalisation of the sublime: an internalisation which leads to Freud. In this way the pantheistic sublime incorporates its own critique within it when it resurrects the past. This means that the pantheistic sublime is subverted from within rather than marginalised by an external, radical critique. This return of the past can now be seen as clearing the way for Kant's version of the sublime.[8] This idea of a new self-consciousness is captured in Winzy's comment from 'The Mortal Immortal' that:

> All the world has heard of Cornelius Agrippa. His memory is as immortal as his arts have made me. All the world has also learned of his scholar, who, unawares, raised the foul fiend during his master's absence, and was destroyed by him. (p. 219)

The scholar is here emblematic of the self-subverting Romantic subject. The question is, where does the sublime go from here? The sublime's post-Shelleyan transformations are a complex matter and they are not solely associated with its internalisation. As we will see in the next chapter there is an important stage of development that it goes through first, one which wrings a confession from the subject.

4
Sublime Utterance: Gothic Voyages, Going Public with the Private

So far we have considered how the Gothic reshapes the sublime for certain ends. If one threat posed to the sublime is its reliance on Classicism, another threat is associated with changes in attitude towards solitude. This is particularly relevant for the Romantic era, in which the roots of this change can be observed. In Romanticism there emerges a fascination with public discourse which is ultimately matched by a Gothic rewriting of the sublime; one that adapts it to provide an account of communal, rather than solitary, experience. This modification of the sublime eventually shifts the emphasis from the natural to the urban. This history is, as we shall see, played out through a range of disparate writings which includes Romantic poetry and encompasses Freud's failure to make the joke conform to the isolating, apparently rebellious, features of the unconscious. First we need to reconsider *Frankenstein* and see how it develops these ideas, ideas which are subsequently developed by Poe.

Telling monstrosity

In *Frankenstein* Victor explains to Walton why he feels morally compelled to tell his story. He says to Walton:

> Learn from me, if not by my precepts, at least by my example, how dangerous is the acquirement of knowledge and how much happier that man is who believes his native town to be the world, than he who aspires to become greater than his nature will allow. (p. 101)

76

Victor's tale critiques Walton's own search for scientific knowledge. Walton's quest is to 'discover the wondrous power which attracts the needle and may regulate a thousand celestial observations that require only this voyage to render their seeming eccentricities consistent forever' (pp. 63–4). Victor's challenge to this search for 'pure' knowledge comes out of the novel's staging of a debate about the relationship of ethics to scientific practice. What characterises the status of this debate is the need for its public dissemination. In this process of public disclosure we witness the transformation in the period from a stress placed on private experience to a new, emerging emphasis placed on public discourse.[1]

We can see this move from the private to the public in the developments within the Gothic sublime. While the sublime becomes progressively internalised, there is a contrary movement which demands that this private experience needs to be refashioned for public consumption. In *Frankenstein*, for example, there is a movement from Victor's solitary studies to a new need for a public commentary on where those private studies have taken him.

As we saw earlier, there is an ostensible oppositional relationship between Victor and the creature. The former shuns society whilst the latter is shunned by society. Victor not only works in solitude, but his early acquisition of knowledge is gleaned in isolation; he tells Walton that, 'I was, to a great degree, self-taught with regard to my favourite studies' (p. 88). Victor works in secret in order to create another secret (the creature) whose existence needs to be explained, first to the Judge shortly after Clerval's murder, and latterly to Walton when the story is retranslated into a moral discourse. As we have seen, the novel links Victor's desire for isolation to the actions of the creature. The creature, in killing members of Victor's family, enacts out Victor's craving for isolation. Victor recognises this after the death of William, where the creature is described as 'my own vampire'. Victor tells Walton of 'the deed which he had now done, nearly in the light of my own vampire, my own spirit let loose from the grave and forced to destroy all that was dear to me' (p. 124).

Victor, rather belatedly, comes to recognise the importance of the community which he is vicariously destroying. This loss of community is linked to a loss of self; as he had said to Walton, 'happier that man is who believes his native town to be the world' (p. 101). It is this loss of community which is acknowledged by Victor after his destruction of the creature's 'mate': 'I walked about the isle like a restless spectre, separated from all it loved and miserable in the separation' (p. 214). In this loss of community Victor becomes ghost-like, 'a restless spectre', an unreal, because not socially integrated, subject. This is an issue which Victor's narrative readdresses when it effects an entrance into the public domain. However, these debates over the role of the community are not solely associated with Victor: they are also prompted by the creature's sense of exclusion.

The creature says to Victor during their first meeting, 'Everywhere I see bliss, from which I alone am irrevocably excluded' (p. 146). The creature later gives Victor an account of his relationship with the De Laceys. The significant scene here is Safie's French lesson. Peter Brooks writes of this scene that:

> with the arrival of Safie, we have a lesson in French being offered to a Turkish Arab, in a German-speaking region, the whole rendered for the reader in English. This well-ordered Babel calls attention to the fact and problem of transmission and communication, the motive for language, and reminds us that the framing structure of the novel – Walton's letters to his sister ... evokes the same concerns.[2]

It is this notion of a 'well-ordered Babel' which provides a prototype of a truly metropolitan community. Raymond Williams writes of the modernist metropolis in ways which (coincidently) open up the Safie–De Lacey scene for us:

> language was perceived quite differently. It was no longer, in the old sense, customary and naturalised, but in many ways arbitrary and conventional. To the immigrants especially, with their new second common language, language was more evident as a medium – a medium that could be shaped and reshaped – than as a social custom.[3]

In the scenes involving Safie and the De Laceys it is possible to see a similar sense of an emergent community being represented, a community which the creature wishes to join. The creature also comes to understand that language is a cultural artefact, which in turn leads him to meditate on the supposed opposition between nature and culture. We explored this in depth earlier in an analysis of how the sublime is exposed as a cultural way of seeing. It is also the case that although language places the creature on the side of culture this becomes linked to the (ultimately unrealisable) aspirations he has for insertion into the cultural order of a community. The cottagers perceive the creature as a natural threat rather than a cultural product and they reject him. The creature rejects what they stand for by burning down their empty cottage which symbolically represents his rejection of a society which refuses (quite literally) to accommodate him. The creature tells Victor of the burning-down of the cottage that:

> As the night advanced, a fierce wind rose from the woods and quickly dispersed the clouds that had loitered in the heavens; the blast tore along like a mighty avalanche and produced a kind of insanity that burst all bounds of reason and reflection. (p. 183)

The creature here aligns himself with nature, behaving in ways opposed to the 'bounds of reason and reflection'. This is, however, only temporary because with his request for a mate he seeks to re-enter the cultural by gaining access to some kind of companionship. He tells Victor:

> My vices are the children of a forced solitude that I abhor, and my virtues will necessarily arise when I live in communion with an equal. I shall feel the affections of a sensitive being and become linked to the chain of existence and events from which I am now excluded. (pp. 192–3)

It is Victor's destruction of this mate which leads the creature to destroy Victor's community when he becomes his 'vampire'. The opening and final scenes of the novel, set at the North Pole, bear testimony to how far the creature has pulled Victor away from civilisation. These scenes also develop the notion of solitude, an idea which takes over the lives of both the creature and Victor. The creature leaves Victor a note:

> Follow me; I seek the everlasting ices of the north, where you will feel misery of cold and frost, to which I am impassive. You will find near this place, if you follow not too tardily, a dead hare; eat and be refreshed. Come on, my enemy; we have yet to wrestle for our lives, but many hard and miserable hours must endure until that period shall arrive. (p. 248)

The North Pole as a symbol of solitude is thus associated with struggle and death.

In *Frankenstein* then, there is a clash between the desire for solitude and the desire for community. It is the creature who mirrors Victor's desire for solitude through the killing of William, Clerval, and

Elizabeth. Victor, as we have seen, proceeds to repeat this story as a morally instructive tale for Walton's benefit. It is in this process of telling that we see how the movement from the private to the public takes place.

It is this notion of going public with the private which also governs 'The Rime of the Ancient Mariner', a poem which Shelley's novel makes direct reference to in Walton's claim to his sister that 'I am going to unexplored regions, to "the land of mist and snow", but I shall kill no albatross' (p. 69) – that is, if he pays proper attention to what Victor has to say to him. Coleridge's poem bears many similarities to *Frankenstein*, an exploration of which will help to open up this theme of community.

The loquacious mariner

> The answer to parched isolation is community.
>
> (Woodring, 1972)[4]

An interesting way to explore 'The Rime of the Ancient Mariner', one which looks towards the issue of community and bears testimony to the complexity of the poem, is to look at a range of criticism of it. This might seem to be a somewhat oblique approach, but the reason why it is so productive is because the critical responses bear an analogy to the relation which the poem has to its gloss (I refer throughout to the 1817 version) and the relationship which the mariner has to the world. The poem covertly acknowledges that the mariner's isolated experiences require interpretation but that any act of interpretation will actually mediate experience and so endanger the authentic expression of the mariner's 'feelings'. This position is echoed in the various difficulties expressed in a range of critical readings, an echo which generates its own kind of critical community.

As to the poem itself, what we find is that it takes us from scenes of isolation to a community through the direct physical relocation of the mariner, but we also see that telling itself is motivated by a form of moral compulsion. As the mariner tells the wedding guest:

> Since then, at an uncertain hour,
>   That agony returns:
> And till my ghastly tale is told,
>   This heart within me burns.
>
> (576–9)[5]

The precise nature of the mariner's experience has always been in doubt. The problem of explication is compounded by the way that the gloss seems to impose a limit on interpretation. In some sense it seems to control any dangerous excess generated by sublime terror. It is this idea of a secret, barely contained, sublime presence which Lockhart referred to in 1819. He observed that: 'the very music of its words is like the melancholy mysterious breath of something sung to the sleeping ear – its images have the beauty – the grandeur – the incoherences of some mighty vision'.[6] Richard Haven suggests that the poem tries to externalise this presence through the use of an objective correlative: 'the poem is the final and successful culmination of a series of efforts to create in a poetic object an "objective correlative" for "inner" phenomena which the philosophy tries to account for in abstract theoretical terms'.[7] In this sense we can see that the poem dramatises a move towards the communal through its very philosophy, a philosophy which Lockhart had associated with the sublime. This means that the objective correlative enables the private to be expressed in the public realm; or as Haven puts it, 'the Mariner stands as a bridge between the familiar and the unfamiliar, between the commonplace reality of the outer, public world and the extraordinary reality of the inner world of consciousness' (p. 20).

It is the gloss which seems to problematise this. For Jean-Pierre Mileur the gloss's relation to the poem exemplifies the failure of Rationalism, so that:

> The inadequacy of the gloss's attempts at allegorization to enclose the action of the poem or to disclose the order conditioning the apparent contingency governing the world in which the mariner finds himself reveals that coincidence is not a sufficient ground of meaning.[8]

The suggestion is that the gloss cannot properly hold in check the disruptive force of the sublime. For Katherine Wheeler the gloss should be seen as a version of a threshold philosophy (the kind of philosophy which refers to the sublime); thus, 'The gloss ... would be a caricature of the irony of conventional perception, where the threshold experiences are constantly resolved into certainties.'[9] It is a caricature because the apparent certainties in the gloss are challenged.

It is this problem of the gloss and how it problematises certainty which Jerome McGann links to the critical history of the poem itself. This is also implicit within the poem because of the way that the gloss provides a form of interpretation which itself invites further interpretation.[10] The suggestion is that what we have is a community of critics who paradoxically enact out the mariner's compulsion to tell, meaning that other readings should be seen as a meta-gloss on the poem. This is typified in Edward Bostetter's account of Robert Warren's article 'A Poem of Pure Imagination: an Experiment in Reading'. Bostetter writes that, 'It superimposes upon the poem a rigid and consistent pattern of meaning which can only be maintained by forcing certain key episodes into conformity with the pattern and ignoring others.'[11] The 'pattern' is Warren's referencing between a 'sacramental' vision and 'the One Life'. What we can see is that the critical responses to the poem emphasise a problematic which other critics have identified as central to the poem: 'this vision of obedient community [the mariner at the Kirk] is, literally, no resting place for the Mariner'.[12] So that for Wheeler,

> Since the verse text as a whole is explicitly about both the tale and the telling, it becomes itself tainted by the never-ending repetition: the telling is never finished, and, as a result, neither is the verse text. The end of the verse is practically the beginning of the search for a new listener. The gloss writer may act as an example of such a continuation. (p. 45)

The poem thus generates critical responses which enact out the poem's own problematic sense of the possibility of interpretation. The poem also suggests that the movement to community is the moment in which interpretation becomes crucial because it is the moment when the mariner has to provide his own incomplete explanation. What happens in the poem is that the mariner's experience gleaned in isolation is relocated in the community, so that what appears to be sub-linguistic (the sublime) can be communicated. It is this emphasis on interpretation and communication which so peculiarly anticipates critical readings of the poem. It also anticipates *Frankenstein*'s own emphasis on the act of telling rather than on the 'felt' isolated experience of the subject. This act of telling is also couched in terms of a moralistic pedagogy so that Coleridge can say of the wedding guest:

> A sadder and a wiser man,
> He rose the morrow morn.

(614–15)

So then, the poem internally dramatises what would be subsequently echoed in critical commentaries upon it. The poem dramatises a move from the specific to the paradigmatic (its critical history) and a dramatisation of the local to the communal.

Coleridge's poem, like *Frankenstein*, stresses the importance of dialogue. Isolated experiences need to be publicly transmitted in a moralistic discourse which makes sense of such experience. It is therefore significant that Victor's experiences are ultimately expressed in the form of a letter sent to Walton's sister. Mary Shelley also focused on these themes of community, language and culture in a revealing letter which provides us with a useful insight into this process of public transmission; one which problematises the idea of community by introducing the issue of nationality.

Community as ambiguity

On 22 January 1819 in Naples, Mary Shelley wrote a letter to Maria Gisborne which includes the passage:

> The Italians are so very disagreeable, and you live in the same kind of solitude that we do – There is no life here – They seem to act as if they had all died fifty years ago, and now went about their work like the ghostly sailors of Coleridge's enchanted ship – except indeed when they cheat. Yet no doubt, there would be many things to teize one in England, and I remember when I set my foot on the shore in Calais, I seemed to break the thread of my annoyances. But I find care to be the thing that Horace describes it to be – and yet mine came from outward circumstances in a great part, and not from my self. The reports, you mention, have nothing to do with these – I seldom suffer them to torment me. When we see you again, we can talk them over, if you have any curiosity on the subject – but it was a kind of treat when we came to Italy to be acquainted with friends who knew nothing of us, as it were, in a public light – and that kept me silent.[13]

Shelley's reference to 'The Rime of the Ancient Mariner' is one which is linked to the idea of solitude. It is her xenophobia, 'The Italians are so very disagreeable', which defines an apparently alien cultural community, one which compounds these feelings of alienation and isolation; feelings which she perceives as being echoed in the experiences of the reader (Gisborne), 'you live in the same kind of solitude that we do'. The community is jokingly referred to as a dead one, although one which is spectrally animated. Shelley is quick to counter the view that this could be extended to all countries, but she does emphasise the bridging of geographical rather than cultural boundaries, as in 'when I set my foot on the shore of Calais'. Shelley proceeds to construct internal boundaries, writing of anxiety ('care') that 'mine came from outward circumstances in a great part, and not from my self'. The cumulative effect is that Shelley defines community as an external force which stands in opposition to the individual; anxiety is generated by the value systems of this community rather than through the psychological disposition of the individual. Solitude is therefore due to cultural difference, or else it is enforced due to 'mass' opinion, 'it was a kind of treat when we came to Italy to be acquainted with friends who knew nothing of us, as it were, in a public light'. This letter is formed out of a set of competing anxieties concerning the function of the community. The community may stand in opposition to the individual, but the individual can resist the pressure of community values by finding strength from within, seen in the claim that 'The reports you mention, have nothing to do with these [external pressures] – I seldom suffer them to torment me.' Also, paradoxically, Shelley finds friendship outside this mass opinion, although it is public opinion which has led to her isolation. In Italy, Shelley finds both isolation and community because neither has been unambiguously defined. Her final comments add to the confusion when she writes of having found a new community of friends who were unacquainted with public opinion 'and that kept me silent'.

What we can see in this letter is a similar range of concerns expressed in both *Frankenstein* and 'The Rime of the Ancient Mariner'. Like them this letter reveals that what constitutes a community can only be problematically understood. Community is nationally defined in a way that leaves Shelley feeling alienated. Additionally there exists a community of friends, but they can only remain friends if they stay unaware of any 'scandal' associated with the Shelleys. What we also witness is the isolated subject expressing the need to publicly express those feelings of isolation. Shelley is also writing to what she sees as a sympathetic reader who occupies a position similar to her own. This echoes the respective positions of Victor and Walton. Victor relays his secret knowledge to Walton in a process of enlightenment based on the similarities between their personalities and quests. Also, the epistolary nature of these kinds of narrative underlines the importance of making the private public; self-isolation becomes the subject matter for communication.

There are obvious differences between this letter and *Frankenstein* and Coleridge's poem; it certainly lacks the moralising overtones of the fictional works. Rather it is largely made up of a series of confused observations. All three, however, are addressed to an implied reader and, as we will see, the status of the implied reader becomes central to Freud's treatise on jokes. Before discussing Freud we need to consider Karl Kroeber's *Romantic Fantasy and Science Fiction* because he examines two issues, scepticism and reiteration, which Freud also explores. Kroeber, importantly, throws light on how these issues are related to Romanticism and (implicitly) to the idea of going public with private experience.

The sceptic and the scientist

Karl Kroeber writes that 'the Romantic fantastic is a mode of turning critical skepticism against itself. Romantic fantasy in so doing seeks not to destroy skepticism but to define its limits.'[14] In *Frankenstein* we can see that there is a pervasive scepticism concerning communal values. Victor works in isolation in order to free himself from communal, and therefore cultural, constraints. The creature embodies this sense of being outside cultural norms and he goes on to affect a direct challenge to cultural values as they are represented by Victor's family and friends, the very people whom Victor has rejected in the first place. What appears to be Victor's biggest crime is conducting his scientific experiments in a moral, and so cultural, vacuum. It is therefore not so much Victor's endeavours which are criticised as his scientific practice. This is something which Victor also acknowledges towards the end of the novel when he tells Walton:

> Seek happiness in tranquillity and avoid ambition, even if it be only the apparently innocent one of distinguishing yourself in science and discoveries. Yet why do I say this? I have myself been blasted in these hopes, yet another may succeed. (p. 260)

This success depends upon Walton learning from Victor that the acquirement of knowledge has cultural and moral ramifications. In this way the novel critiques the idea that there exists an obtainable, purely abstract and absolute knowledge. It also indicates to us that there is an essential lack, a dissatisfaction, to be found within culture itself. Kroeber writes:

> Romantic fantasy does not defamiliarize the commonplace so that we may perceive the usual with its veil of familiarity torn off. It attempts, rather, the highly peculiar task of creating awareness that what we have come to accept as the only possible reality may not be as absolute, complete, or comprehensive as we think, and of urging us to imagine what in a progressive and enlightened and incredulous world must seem inconceivable. (p. 71)

In this instance scepticism does not destroy cultural practice but rather leads to a renegotiation of what is meant by culture, something which is acknowledged in Victor's speech to Walton concerning the possibility of success.

Kroeber associates this idea of scepticism with Romantic fantasy. He then proceeds to explore how reiterability is linked to science fiction. Kroeber makes this link because he perceives a similarity between scientific experimentation and the discourse of science fiction. Kroeber, for example, writes that H. G. Wells' *The Time Machine* formulates a version of experimental replicability which is central to scientific practice itself. He writes about the time-shifts in the novel that:

> Without a potential of reiterability the experience of a distant place or time could not to a scientific mind seem entirely authentic. Extrapolation of scientific attitudes implies emphasis on replicability, and the work of art of an age of mechanical reproduction appropriately diminishes the importance of uniqueness. (p. 25)

The ability to repeat an experience gives it scientific credence. In an extended sense this idea of reiterability informs 'The Rime of the Ancient Mariner' with the mariner's condemnation to a life of an endless repetition of his moral instruction. This does not quite conform to Kroeber's notion of experimental replicability, and he observes that the poem expresses an essential incoherence, the kind of incoherence which we saw governing Mary Shelley's letter to Maria Gisborne. Kroeber writes that in 'The Rime of the Ancient Mariner' there is 'The refusal of fantasy to cohere with ordinary systems of order, so that in the very mode of its telling it casts doubt on the meaning of what it tells' (p. 35). This also characterises some of the more problematic attempts to interpret the poem. Kroeber links this lack of coherence to a model of communication disorder: 'Most simply, the story is of a conversation, the intersecting of two utterances, which means that for either speaker the speech of the other is unpredictable' (p. 75). Additionally, it is possible to link, where Kroeber does not, this problem with dialogue to scepticism. It is the public discourse which is developed out of a scepticism concerning the value of purely private experience. We will see later how Freud's account of what he terms sceptical jokes provides an 'acceptable' public expression of anti-social (or potentially private) experiences. It is speech itself which seems to provide some form of moderation; Kroeber unconsciously acknowledges this when he writes, 'The Mariner undergoes radical shifts in his physical circumstances, travelling through tumultuous arctic seas to oppressive tropic calm back to his pleasantly temperate home port' (p. 75). The mariner's experience is sub-linguistic, but it is in the middle, between the 'tumultuous arctic' and the 'oppressive tropic calm' that speech becomes possible, when the mariner is returned to 'his pleasantly temperate *home* port' (my italics), to a community which enables communication.

Scepticism and replicability thus influence Romantic fantasy. Kroeber relates scepticism to a linguistic, conversational, sphere. What, however, is also required is an implied reader/listener, a position which may be occupied within the narrative itself, as in, for example, Walton's letter to his sister. Also, the role of this hypothetical reader is tied to the idea that language, as a cultural product, is closely related to an implied culture of readers waiting to consume such products. At this point we need to turn to Freud. His account of jokes echoes these issues of transmission, and, yet again, enables us to see how his writings are ghosted by concepts to be found within both Romanticism in general, and the Gothic in particular, although I do acknowledge that the similarities are largely structural. This might appear to be a peculiar Freudian text to explore in this instance, but Freud's treatise on jokes (and its failures) throws a revealing light on the continuing presence of a Romantic culture in the late nineteenth century.

Have you heard the one about ... ?

To discuss jokes at this juncture might seem to inaugurate a genre shift. However I want to pull Freud into these arguments and to do so via his treatise on jokes because of its conclusion that jokes need to be socially understood. Freud reaches this conclusion when he gives up on the attempt to make the joke conform to the rebellious impulses of the unconscious. Freud's *Jokes and their Relation to the Unconscious* is therefore (structurally speaking) a reworking of this Romantic movement from solitary to collective experience, one which, along the way, tells us something about culture.[15] First it is worth considering Freud's categorisation of a variety of forms of joke.

One type of joke which Freud explores is what he terms the sceptical joke. This kind of joke problematises the claims made about knowledge (as scepticism does for Kroeber in the Romantic fantastic). Freud investigates this troubling aspect of the joke through a series of questions:

> Is it the truth if we describe things as they are without troubling to consider how our hearer will understand what we say? Or is this only jesuitical truth, and does not genuine truth consist in taking the hearer into account and giving him a faithful picture of our knowledge? (p. 161)

Freud highlights the social nature of jokes because they are constructed for public transmission. This is also echoed in Freud's series of questions which are not purely rhetorical but rather are addressed to an implied reader (or hearer). For Freud, jokes exist independently of the teller; they only make sense when interpreted by another and understood by that Other on their own terms. In this way a contract is covertly made between the teller and the addressee. Freud essentially regards jokes as expressions of altruism, and it is altruism which he believes helps to bind a community together. The importance of community for Freud appears in an aside in his main treatise; he writes that:

> One must bind one's own life to that of others so closely and be able to identify oneself with others so intimately that the brevity of one's own life can be overcome; and one must not fulfil the demands of one's own needs illegitimately, but must leave them unfulfilled, because only the continuance of so many unfulfilled demands can develop the power to change the order of society (p. 155).

For Freud it is the possibilities provided by scepticism which makes this feasible because scepticism implies the possibility of social change. In this process the joke provides an attack on claims made about the world, subjecting such claims to critical scrutiny, so that: 'What they [sceptical jokes] are attacking is not a person or an institution but the certainty of our knowledge itself, one of our speculative possessions' (p. 161). So, the critique of knowledge benefits the community and this social altruism is represented through an internal–external relationship. Freud writes that, 'The external obstacle which is to be overcome in the hearer corresponds to an internal inhibition in the maker of the joke' (p. 184). Freud thus accounts for jokes through a metaphor of balance and loss; this notion of the economics of the joke is also to be found in his account of the tendentious joke where he writes, '*this yield of pleasure corresponds to the psychical expenditure that is saved*' (p. 167). Freud restates this metaphor of balance and loss when he writes that, 'Relief from psychical expenditure that is already there and economizing in psychical expenditure that is only to be called for – from these two principles all the techniques of jokes, and accordingly all pleasure from these techniques, are derived' (p. 177). The subject is thus psychically integrated into the experience of the joke-work, which is placed within a social, communal context that implicitly exerts a pressure for change.

Freud tries to integrate this communal dimension of the joke with his theory of the unconscious. His idea is that the joke gives an acceptable expression to that which has been tabooed; in this way it retains a rebellious aspect which challenges social norms (rather like the unconscious itself). Freud, however, is forced to recognise that the relationship between the joke and the unconscious is a problematic one. This is because of the inherently social nature of jokes as distinct from the private world of the unconscious. Freud writes of the difference between jokes and dreams that:

> The most important difference lies in their social behaviour. A dream is a completely asocial mental product; it has nothing to communicate to anyone else; it arises within the subject as a compromise between the mental forces struggling in him (*sic*), it remains unintelligible to the subject himself and is for that reason totally uninteresting to other people. (pp. 237–8)

Dreams are thus defined by their asocial nature whereas the joke is outward- rather than inward-looking. The joke can only work through a social contract in which the teller and addressee agree to how the joke is received, so that Freud asks the questions: 'Why is it ... that I do not laugh at a joke of my own? And what part is played in this by the other person?' (p. 195). For Freud this governs the structure of all forms of joke-telling, including the 'innocent' joke (one which does not mischievously refer to taboos), 'Innocent jokes, too, jokes that serve to reinforce a thought, require another person to test whether they have attained their aim' (p. 196). Freud extends this social aspect of the joke by arguing that it can help bind a community together. Early on in his treatise he writes that:

> We may ... bear in mind the peculiar and even fascinating charm exercised by jokes in our society. A new joke acts like an event of universal interest; it is passed from one person to another like the news of the latest victory. (p. 46)

This also links with the idea that in 'The Rime of the Ancient Mariner' the mariner passes on his information, his particular brand of scepticism, for the benefit of the community, and it also relates to Kroeber's notion of reiterability within Romantic fantasy. We saw earlier that for Kroeber, scientific method is characterised by the possibility of repetition, meaning that scientific verification is established through experimental replicability. Similarly, both Victor and the mariner tell their tales, reconstructing the events by repeating them as moral parables. Their narratives demonstrate a scepticism about experience 'learned' in isolation and repeat that experience (as telling) for the benefit of the community. Likewise for Freud sceptical jokes benefit society because they critique (lampoon) various kinds of social (and sexual) knowledge. The idea of repetition, so important to *Frankenstein* and 'The Rime of the Ancient Mariner', is an issue which Freud also addresses. He writes that:

> When a joke is repeated, the attention is led back to the first occasion of hearing it as the memory of it arises. And from this we are carried on to an understanding of the urge to tell a joke one has heard to other people who have not yet heard it. (p. 207)

Behind the apparent banality of this claim there is the suggestion that the subject becomes both psychically and socially united through this act of remembrance, and the subsequent desire to tell. If one controlling metaphor in Freud's treatise is that of balance and loss, here it is one of contagion. A joke only works if it is told 'to other people who have not yet heard it', who would, to follow Freud's reasoning, have a similar 'urge' to repeat the joke in the same way. Freud also argues that this urge to repeat is an integral part of the joke-work because, 'It is ... generally acknowledged that rhymes, alliterations, refrains, and other forms of repeating similar verbal sounds which occur in verse, make use of the same source of pleasure – the rediscovery of something familiar' (p. 170). The 'rediscovery of something familiar' here relates to memory. This is similar to the stress placed on memory in *Frankenstein* and 'The Rime of the Ancient Mariner', where the past is constantly kept alive through a process of retelling.

What we find in Shelley's novel and Coleridge's poem is that there is a mapping out of an area which would later be indirectly discussed by Freud. Shelley and Coleridge anticipate Freud's ideas through their representations of the communal as that which replaces individual experience. In Freud's writings this is echoed by the status of the public joke in relation to the private, personal status of the unconscious. Also, the issue of repetition is directly linked to the transmission of the joke. We have looked at Freud here because what is so significant about his account is the way that it reveals how the theme of the communal has entered a discourse – psychoanalysis – which is largely designed to explore private, asocial, experience.

So far we have looked at how this theme of an emergent community is played out through a range of different texts, and observed how this theme is prefigured within Romantic fantasy. One issue which we have yet to address is that of the voyage-narrative. Both *Frankenstein* and 'The Rime of the Ancient Mariner' are accounts of sea voyages, and an exploration of another such narrative, Poe's *Narrative of A. Gordon Pym*, will provide us with an interesting example of how the form (and the issues associated with it) developed during the early part of the nineteenth century.[16] In Poe's novel we find that the sublime is reintroduced as a source of secularised mystery, from which the detective elements of the story are generated. However, before discussing this new emphasis on the detective we need to look at how the novel constructs notions of community and how they accord with the earlier narratives.

Mysterious communities and hybrid beings

In *Frankenstein*, as we saw earlier, Walton believes that he will discover a tropical paradise at the North Pole. Walton's misguided optimism is exposed in the novel, but Poe begins, rather than ends, on a note of pessimism. Pym's initial visions of the voyage are ones of

> shipwreck and famine; of death or captivity among barbarian
> hordes; of a lifetime dragged out in sorrow and tears, upon some

gray and desolate rock, in an ocean unapproachable and unknown. Such visions or desires – are common, I have since been assured, to the whole race of the melancholy among men ... (p. 757)

The novel's story is indeed a bleak one: Pym is a stowaway on a ship, the *Grampus*, where there is a mutiny and, after some adventures, the sailors find themselves on an island called Tsalal. There they are attacked by the inhabitants and only Pym and one of the mutineers survives; Pym makes good his escape but the novel concludes on a note of mystery which throws this escape into some doubt.

Pym is discovered during the earlier mutiny, and in the consequent chaos the survivors quickly run out of provisions, a plight which echoes that of the mariner's in Coleridge's poem. A ship seems to offer salvation but as it draws near:

Of a sudden, and all at once, there came wafted over the ocean from the strange vessel (which was now close upon us) a smell, a stench, such as the whole world has no name for – no conception of – hellish – utterly suffocating – insufferable, inconceivable. (p. 809)

This resembles the mariner's, although rather less olfactory, response when spotting the ship of death:

> *Her* lips were red, *her* looks were free,
>   Her locks were yellow as gold:
> Her skin was as white as leprosy,
> The Night-mare LIFE-IN-DEATH was she,
> Who thicks man's blood with cold.

(190–4)

Death is described here in vampiric terms, and in *Pym* the narrator is confronted with the death of a community:

Twenty-five or thirty human bodies, among whom were several females, lay scattered about between the counter and the galley in the last and most loathsome state of putrefaction. We plainly saw that not a soul lived in that fated vessel! (p. 809)

The survivors are eventually picked up and when Pym reaches Kerguelen Land images of a harmonious community are evoked. Significantly, given that the novel is in a tradition of seafaring voyage-narratives, it is the albatross which is discussed. This construction is couched in a pseudo-natural, scientific discourse, which I need to quote from at length:

> The albatross is one of the largest and fiercest of the South Sea birds. It is of the gull species, and takes its prey on the wing, never coming on land except for the purpose of breeding. Between this bird and the penguin the most singular friendship exists. Their nests are constructed with great uniformity upon a plan concerted between the two species – that of the albatross being placed in the centre of a little square formed by the nest of four penguins. Navigators have agreed in calling an assemblage of such encampments *a rookery*. These rookeries have been often described, but as my readers may not all have seen these descriptions, and as I shall have occasion hereafter to speak of the penguin and the albatross, it will not be amiss to say something here of their mode of building and living. (p. 834)

The idea of communal life is naturalised in such descriptions. The narrator proceeds to describe how this bipartite community operates through a policy of reciprocal altruism. The metaphor which predominates here is one of an idealised version of the metropolis. Pym recounts that:

> Having defined the limits of the rookery, the colony now begin to clear it of every species of rubbish, picking up stone by stone, and carrying them outside of the lines, and close by them, so as to form a wall on three inland sides. Just within this wall a perfectly level and smooth walk is formed, from six to eight feet wide, and extending around the encampment – thus serving the purpose of a general promenade. (p. 835)

Here is an image of community as harmonious town planning. The rookery is also described as a fully integrated community, one in which no clear hierarchy exists. Pym, for example, writes of the paths which run through the rookery that:

> At each intersection of these paths the nest of an albatross is constructed, and a penguin's nest in the centre of each square – thus every penguin is surrounded by four albatrosses, and each albatross by a like number of penguins. (p. 835)

This idealistic utopian community is also an open one. Pym again; 'Although there are some rookeries in which the penguin and albatross are the sole population, yet in most of them a variety of oceanic birds are to be met with, enjoying all the privileges of citizenship ...' (p. 835). I have quoted at length here as it is important that we consider this model of community because it is one which is constantly threatened throughout the novel.

Pym's descriptions of a naturalised integrated community life is juxtaposed with the island community of Tsalal which is hierarchically organised and defined as essentially barbaric. The island community is described as an unnatural one in which its 'savage' inhabitants only serve to underline the fact that benign nature has been excluded from it. The Islanders are a community, but they do not form a civilisation; the novel suggests (as it does in the accounts of the rookery) a link between geography and community. Pym writes of the island that:

At every step we took inland the conviction forced itself upon us that we were in a country differing essentially from any hitherto visited by civilised men. We saw nothing with which we had been formerly conversant. The trees resembled no growth of either the torrid, the temperate, or the northern frigid zones, and were altogether unlike those of the lower southern latitudes we had already traversed. The very rocks were novel in their mass, their color, and their stratification; and the streams themselves, utterly incredible as it may appear, had so little in common with those of other climates, that we were scrupulous of tasting them, and, indeed, had difficultly in bringing ourselves to believe that their qualities were purely those of nature. (pp. 851–2)

The sailors are thus confronted by this mysterious alien community, one which contravenes all their notions of what constitutes nature. That the islanders are placed in opposition to the well-regulated natural communism to be found in the rookery is also revealed in a village that the sailors are taken to, where some shelters are tent-like, while:

Others were formed by means of rough limbs of trees, with the withered foliage upon them, made to recline, at an angle of forty-five degrees, against a bank of clay, heaped up, without regular form, to the height of five or six feet. Others, again, were mere holes dug in the earth perpendicularly, and covered over with similar branches, these being removed when the tenant was about to enter, and pulled on again when he had entered. (p. 853)

The haphazard structure of the village is a reference to its inhabitants; the novel implies that they are untrustworthy because they are themselves ill-formed.

The villagers kill the crew of the ship (with the exception of Pym and an original sailor from the *Grampus*, Peters), leaving these two survivors to hide on the island. At this point in the novel the peculiar, mysterious nature of the island is emphasised. The novel suggests that these mysteries of nature are open to interpretation. Pym and Peters, for example, discover a chasm of black granite; again this is defined by its 'unnatural' qualities: 'It was, indeed, one of the most singular-looking places imaginable, and we could scarcely bring ourselves to believe it altogether the work of nature' (p. 870). They find some marks on the walls, which according to Pym 'bore also some little resemblance to alphabetical characters' (p. 873). It is this idea of the possibility of decoding the mysterious nature of the island which turns Pym into a prototypical detective. The narrative effectively swaps genres as Pym addresses the possibility of decoding this 'natural' writing. This 'writing' is caused by marks which, 'had evidently been broken off by some convulsion from the surface where the indentures were found, and which had projecting points exactly fitting the indentures; thus proving them to have been the work of nature' (p. 873).

The novel constructs a separation between art and nature, a separation referred to in the difference between the rookery and the villages of the islanders. Pym increasingly finds it difficult to separate the two, the problem being that he finds it problematic to read this mysterious nature of the island, although he does acknowledge its natural status, as in the discovery that 'the surface of the ground in every other direction was strewn with huge tumuli, apparently the wreck of some gigantic structures of art; although, in detail, no semblance of art could be detected' (p. 876). It is this notion of mystery which also governs the closing lines, at the end of the quest: 'there arose in our pathway a shrouded human figure, very far larger in its proportions than any dweller among men. And the hue of the skin of the figure was of the perfect whiteness of the snow' (p. 882).

It is this idea of the mystery which we need to pay closer attention to, but it is worth at this point underlining some of the principal differences between Poe's novel and the other voyage-narratives which we have so far considered. Poe's novel sets up a difference between ideal and human communities. Poe uses a motif of 'The Rime of the Ancient Mariner', the albatross, in order to represent this ideal community. However, the novel develops into a mystery story towards the end. Pym becomes an unreliable detective because he cannot read the clues (the strange writing to be found in nature) and the story closes on the appearance of the mysterious figure which defies interpretation. These features distance the novel from Coleridge's poem and *Frankenstein* because Poe's narrative does not turn into a moral parable but, rather, undermines the notion of certainty by developing into a mystery story. However, Pym's narrative is not the final one in the text: there is also an anonymous final explanatory note which attempts an interpretation. It is also this final commentary which extends the idea of the detective narrative which had been gestured towards in Pym's own attempts at effecting a reading of the landscape.

The closing narrative explores the prevalence of references to black and white in Pym's narrative. The 'Note' explains that some sketches which Pym had recorded of a chasm refer to 'an Ethiopian verbal root' which is 'To be shady' (p. 883). The marks which Pym had noted on the wall of the chasm are also interpreted and translated as 'the Arabic verbal root ... 'To be white' (p. 883). The author of the Note also explains the meaning behind one of the native refrains 'Tekeli-li':

> Tekeli-li! was the cry of the affrighted natives of Tsalal upon discovering the carcass of the *white* animal picked up at sea. This also was the shuddering exclamation of the captive Tsalalian upon encountering the *white* materials in possession of Mr Pym. This also was the shriek of the swift-flying, *white*, and gigantic birds which issued from the vapory *white* curtain of the South. Nothing *white* was to be found at Tsalal, and nothing otherwise in the subsequent voyage to the region beyond. (p. 883)

Pym is unable to effect this kind of interpretation because he is caught up within the ongoing action and so the mystery itself.

This issue of black and white refers to representations of race. What we have so far seen is how the novel contrasts the natural community of the rookery with the 'barbaric' unnatural community of the Islanders. In the rookery community is an open one where all can enjoy 'the privileges of citizenship' (p. 835), whereas the Island community is a closed one, hierarchically organised and constructed around notions of racial purity. It is this idea of purity which the novel develops early on through Pym's description of the mutineer, and his subsequent companion, Dirk Peters:

> This man was the son of an Indian woman of the tribe of Upsarokas, who live among the fastnesses of the Black Hills, near the Missouri. His father was a fur-trader, I believe, or at least connected in some manner with the Indian trading-posts on Lewis river. Peters himself was one of the most ferocious-looking men I ever beheld. (p. 776)

It is Peter's hybridity which initially makes him an object of terror. Pym's description goes on to mention that his

> ruling expression may be conceived when it is considered that the teeth were exceedingly long and protruding, and never even partially covered, in any instance, by the lips. To pass this man with a casual glance, one might imagine him to be convulsed with laughter; but a second look would induce a shuddering acknowledgement, that if such an expression were indicative of merriment, the merriment must be that of a demon. (p. 777)

The description also possesses a hybridity of its own, defining Peters as part animal, part demon, as warped by nature and as a supernatural subject. There is also anecdotal information about him, and 'These anecdotes went to prove his prodigious strength when under excitement, and some of them had given rise to a doubt of his sanity' (p. 777). Unnatural physicality and madness define him, the novel suggesting that the two terms are interchangeable.

These descriptions of Peters share an obvious similarity to the creature in *Frankenstein*, who is also a hybrid being: 'His yellow skin scarcely covered the work of muscles and arteries beneath' (p. 105). This in part indicates the failure of language to account for this new, composite being, which is echoed in Peters' own appearance and in the mythologising anecdotal accounts of him. Both novels will ultimately challenge this perception by breaking down the conventional (naturalised) connections between appearance and reality.

Peters' hybridity synecdochically represents the polyglot community of sailors. He also functions as a clue as to the nature of racial opposition in the novel. It is Peters' hybridity (both black and white) which conflicts with the model of racial purity to be found on Tsalal. The narrative has therefore prearranged this issue before its more systematic development in the scenes on the island. It is notions of racial purity which are the true sources of disorder, not Peters' own 'disordered' physicality. The Islanders' killing of the sailors is ostensibly for financial gain, but in reality there is a covert policy of eugenics in operation. What we see is a community purifying itself through the extermination of a threatening, white (or in Peters' case, mixed-race) other.

So, we have seen that the novel constructs a representation of an idealised, natural community which inheres to the images of the rookery. This contrasts with the hierarchical, mono-racial, community of the Islanders. The polyglot nature of the sailors is represented through the figure of Peters. This racial confusion also surfaces in the warning made to Pym by his friend Augustus about the impending mutiny on the *Grampus*. Pym only manages to catch part of the final sentence, '*blood – your life depends upon lying close*' (p. 770). He recounts, 'I was inspired by the fragmentary warning thus received. And "blood," too, that word of all words – so rife at all times with mystery, and suffering, and terror' (p. 770). In this description blood itself takes on a hybridity, here defined as mysterious, related to suffering and to terror. It is this idea of blood as mystery, and as a basis for racial purity, which becomes the source of terror in the demonisation of Peters because it is linked to his own hybridity (being of mixed blood).

What is at issue in the novel is the status and function of community life. The novel constructs conflict between a eugenically controlled mono-racial society and a multi-racial, multi-national community. In the latter, with its various cultural and linguistic practices, we can observe a version of urban metropolitan experience. This form of experience, as we will see, creates new types of mystery.

Language and community

So far we have explored a development which takes place in the nineteenth century in which isolated experience is reconstructed for public transmission. This is expressed in the narratives through their fascination with linguistic practices and cultural experiences. These issues are displaced along a culture/nature axis in *Frankenstein*. Victor recognises, perhaps grudgingly, that the creature is an object of culture, and that this linguistic subject means that he should, properly, be located within a cultural order (the community from which he is excluded). This challenge to ideas about nature, made from a cultural standpoint, theoretically means that isolation could be overcome because the creature does not conform to 'natural' paradigms of monstrosity. This theme of culture is echoed in the loquacity of the narrative (its status as reported speech sent in a letter). As we have seen, the novel has to overcome this disjunction between language and appearance, a disjunction made so clear in the early encounter between Victor and the creature, where, as we have seen, Victor notes that, 'His words had a strange effect upon me. I compassionated him' yet 'when I looked upon him ... my heart sickened and my feelings were altered to those of horror and hatred' (p. 192). It is the possibility that the creature may be cultural rather than natural which accounts for Victor's revulsion.

A similar loquacity is to be found in 'The Rime of the Ancient Mariner' in the mariner's compulsion to repeat his tale; a compulsion which leads to his concluding affirmation of community in his 'celebration' of the impending wedding, and the extended family which this implies. We find in Coleridge's poem, and in Shelley's novel, a shared connection made between telling and community. What we also find is the suggestion that telling requires a reconstruction of the events, meaning that experience is always indirectly expressed through a mediating (largely, in this instance, morally pedagogic) narrative.

These issues inform Freud's work on jokes, especially in how they discursively prefigure the importance which he accords to the respective positions of the teller and the listener. In Shelley's novel and Coleridge's poem there exists an opposition between nature and culture; in Freud's treatise there is an opposition between the private and the public, or between the dream and the joke.

One other factor touched on here was the emergence of the mystery tale, an emergence which has importance for a reconsideration of sublimity. Poe's novel turns into a mystery tale, one which suggests the possibility of interpretation: a possibility more fully developed in Poe's characterisation of his detective, C. Auguste Dupin. We will see that the sublime becomes relocated to an urban context where it becomes the source of this new sense of the mysterious. To understand this we need to return to the Kantian sublime.

The Kantian sublime

We saw that Kant in 'The Analytic of the Sublime' (following Burke) makes a distinction between beauty and sublimity. Beauty has a limitation imposed upon it and is defined by its objective value, whereas the sublime is not. This means that the sublime can only be apprehended through clues to its presence, in which a part implies 'a super-added thought of its totality' (p. 90). This is complicated because Kant removes the sublime from an understanding of the world of objects, so that: 'the sublime is not to be looked for in the things of nature, but only in our own ideas' (p. 97). The reason being that, 'the sublime [is] a presentation of an indeterminate concept of reason' (p. 91). The sublime, in its failed attempt to encompass the object, maps out the limits of reason. This failure is, of course, ambiguous because the potential *for* reason is intimated in the process. Kant thus suggests that a totalising knowledge is referred to within the realm of the supersensible. The importance of the supersensible is that it possesses this regulatory function which makes reason possible. Kant writes that: 'the *mere ability even to think* the given infinite without contradiction, is something that requires the presence in the human mind of a faculty that is itself supersensible' (p. 103). This totality may be gestured towards but it is not grasped, and as such it fails to provide an epistemological closure which can guarantee absolute truth.

An example of this can be found in Kant's idea of the mathematical sublime. In this instance there is a failure of standards to properly measure the experience of the sublime, so that the sublime can only be understood in aesthetic terms. Again this failure indicates to the subject that reason is only just beyond their grasp because: 'the Subject's very incapacity betrays the consciousness of an unlimited faculty of the same Subject, and the mind can only form an aesthetic estimate of the latter faculty by means of that incapacity' (p. 108). All of this would appear to construct a version of events which is very different from the totalities found in detective fictions. Nevertheless, as we shall see, Poe's detective tales do relate to Kant because they can be understood as fully developed versions of what an attainment of the supersensible would be. Poe's detective is positioned in a similar relationship to the mystery as Kant's subject is in the moment of sublime reverie. Poe's detective is all mind, and as Kant writes, 'instead of the object, it is rather the cast of the mind in appreciating it that we have to estimate as *sublime*' (p. 104). The function of the mind's capacity for reason becomes sublime indeed.

In Poe's tales we find that Dupin's pre-investigative state of inertia is overcome by an animating mystery, which bears similarity to how the subject is animated in the moment of sublime contemplation. As Kant writes, 'The mind feels itself *set in motion* in the representation of the sublime' (p. 107). Dupin also shares Kant's notion that morals unite a community, revealed in Dupin's attempt to reinstate social order after the community's 'rules' have been violated by the crime. In Kant's sense, morals refer to the wider philosophical aspect of being, one which accords with some aspects of ethics. In this sense it also conforms to some of the defining features of *Frankenstein* and 'The Rime of the Ancient Mariner', in which the community is associated with some inherent moral integrity. Kant writes that

> the fact that culture is requisite for the judgement upon the sublime in nature ... does not involve its being an original product of culture and something introduced in a more or less conventional way into society. Rather it is in human nature that its foundations are laid, and, in fact, in that which, at once with common understanding, we may expect every one to possess and may require of him, namely, a native capacity for the feeling for (practical) ideas, i.e. for moral feeling. (p. 116)

This idea of an innate sense concerning judgement on the sublime is something exposed in *Frankenstein*, but we can see that this description is echoed in Pym's account of an harmonious community in his description of the rookery. This Kantian internalisation of a moral law means that culture does not (as it does for Freud) place constraints upon the subject. What, however, we see in this is Kant's concern with the importance of communal life and communal values. All of these texts testify to the necessity of getting beyond the individual and their personal needs in order to focus on the role which the individual has in supporting a value system which makes community life possible.

Earlier we explored how Freud constructs an opposition between dream-work and joke-work which dramatises a clash between private and public realms. Kant, as a result of his discussion on culture, focuses on certain cultural artifacts, one of which is the joke. In Chapter 1 we observed how Kant perceives jokes as posing a threat to order because they can trick us: 'It is observable that in all such cases the joke must have something in it capable of momentarily deceiving us' (p. 201). The reason for this is because of the difference between enjoying the joke and trying to analyse it, or, as Freud puts it: 'If one laughs at a joke really heartily, one is not in precisely the best mood for investigating its technique' (p. 85), so that, 'it remains an uncontradicted fact if we undo the technique of a joke it disappears' (p. 113). For Kant, the joke offers 'a topsy-turvy view of things' (p. 203).

I earlier touched on how this idea of a 'topsy-turvy view of things' also occurs within fantasy fiction. It is also relevant to detective fiction, in that the disorder introduced by the mystery needs to be explained away. For Freud, jokes represent an acceptable expression of what is otherwise tabooed. In fantasy there is an 'ethical', covertly politicised, triumph over the anti-social (at least in the texts we have looked at so far) which is both gestured towards and marginalised. It is this notion of the anti-social which is also developed in detective fiction via a discourse of criminality. These fantastic narratives (and here I include Poe's detective tales for reasons which I hope will become clear) problematically question the limits of cultural knowledge. They possess the kind of scepticism which Kroeber links to Romantic fantasy, and which Freud links to certain types of joke. However, it is this kind of scepticism which ultimately exposes and indeed explains the presence of some of the more disabling elements of Freudian thought, no matter how politically 'conservative' these narratives might be.

In this chapter we have followed the movement from the private to the public, a movement which charts the development from isolation to community. This is echoed in the move from silence to speech (such as in the creature's language acquisition and all that it implies in *Frankenstein*). As we will see in relation to the detective tales, public loquacity takes over from private experience and in the process the Kantian sublime becomes reshaped as an integral feature of the urban landscape.

5

The Urban Sublime: Kant and Poe

The idea of going public with the private would appear to gesture towards psychoanalysis; however, the roots of this gesture are to be found in Poe's reworking of the Kantian sublime. This is, I would argue, an unconscious echo in Poe's writings. Poe inherits a philosophical language which reveals his indebtedness to Kant, and Poe unknowingly looks back to Kant and forward to Freud.[1] Many of Poe's tales appear, on the surface, to be explorations of complex psychological disturbances. However, there is more to them than this: there is also a problematic attempt to situate the individual within the collective through an exploration of urban experience. Such an attempt forces Poe's characters into public, urban domains; ones in which the encounter between the subject and society becomes the site of disorientation, but also, crucially, analytical thought. To illustrate this we will look at a range of Poe's detective tales. When discussing these tales my emphasis is on the accounts of reasoning which each tale constructs rather than on their respective plots. This is because it is in Dupin's theorising, rather than in his actions, that we can see neo-Kantian ideas at work. What we will see is that Poe reconfigures the sublime in order to create specifically urban mysteries: mysteries which will require an analytical explanation.[2]

First I want to consider the older, more properly Romantic, sense of the sublime and how it relates to the urban. The clearest example of this is to be found in Wordsworth's complex refutation of urban life in Book VII of *The Prelude*. In Wordsworth's arguments, hesitancies and anxieties we can see a subtle undermining of the sublime being staged; one which, ironically, points towards Poe.

Wordsworth and the problem of the city

In *The Prelude* Wordsworth contrasts his imaginings of London with his experience of it as a lived reality.[3] He writes that:

> My fancy had shap'd forth, of sights and shows,
> Processions, Equipages, Lords and Dukes,
> The King, and the King's Palace, and not last
> Or least, heaven bless him! the renown'd Lord Mayor.
>
> (109–12)

These preconceptions of social grandeur are in contrast to the babel-like mercantilism and crude representation of grandeur which confront the poet in the city:

> Here there and everywhere a weary throng
> The Comers and the Goers face to face,
> Face after face; the string of dazzling wares,
> Shop after shop, with Symbols, blazon'd Names,
> And all the Tradesman's honours overhead;
> Here, fronts of houses, like a title-page
> With letters huge inscribed from top to toe;
> Station'd above the door, like guardian Saints,
> There, allegoric shapes, female or male;
> Or physiognomies of real men,
> Lord-Warriors, Kings, or Admirals of the Sea,
> Boyle, Shakespear, Newton, or the attractive head
> Of some Scotch doctor, famous in his day.
>
> (171–83)

It is the 'symbols' and 'blazon'd Names' which Wordsworth perceives as falsehoods. The experience of the city is at one remove from his pre-conception of it. Instead of finding 'Lords and Dukes,/The King', there are 'allegoric shapes', 'physiognomies of real men'. He thus focuses upon forms of false representation, as in, for example, the shops which are represented as text, 'Here, fronts of houses, like a title-page/with letters huge inscribed from top to toe', in this sense the city is too open to reading. He develops this more fully when writing of the 'mechanic Artist' who represents:

By scale exact, in Model, wood or clay,
From shading colours also borrowing help.
Some miniature of famous spots and things
Domestic, or the boast of foreign Realms;

(266–9)

So then, the poet's journey into the city is prefigured by a preconception of the city as the site of social grandeur. The actual experience of that city is 'felt' as a play of representation, an idea of the city as aping that from which it is excluded: nature. At these moments Wordsworth introduces a nature/culture divide which separates the city from a natural, pantheistic conception of what constitutes the 'real':

At leisure let us view, from day to day,
As they present themselves, the Spectacles
Within doors, troops of wild Beasts, birds and beasts
Of every nature, from all climes convened;
And, next to these, those mimic sights that ape
The absolute presence of reality,
Expressing, as in mirror, sea and land,
And what earth is, and what she has to shew;

(244–51)

This 'absolute presence of reality' is in contrast to the mental experience of the city which is conditioned by the play of representation:

Though rear'd upon the base of outward things,
These, chiefly, are such structures as the mind
Builds for itself.

(624–26)

The urban experience is not suited to sublimity becuse it possesses a false logic of its own. As Max Byrd puts it: 'the construction remains incomplete, and Wordsworth fails to grasp some essential element of what he is describing, fails to compress his perceptions into a metaphor of sublimity: no face appears.'[4] It is, however, the absence of sublimity which, ironically, conjures up the 'true' version of the sublime. The city negatively refers the poet, in compensation, to the natural sublime. Wordsworth writes of the city that:

> If aught there were of real grandeur here
> 'Twas only then when gross realities,
> The incarnation of the Spirits that mov'd
> Amid the Poet's beauteous world, call'd forth,
> With that distinctness which a contrast gives
> Or opposition, made me recognise
> As by a glimpse, the things which I had shaped
> And yet not shaped, had seen, and scarcely seen,
> Had felt, and thought of in my solitude.
>
> (508–16)

The closing lines refer to the poet's authentic feel for the sublime, and the authentic representation of it. The urban is seen as conditioned by mimicry, whereas 'truth' is to be found in nature. This connection between artifice and nature is established earlier in Book VII, in the representation of mother and child. Here Wordsworth writes of:

> A rosy Babe, who, for a twelvemonth's space
> Perhaps, had been of age to deal about
> Articulate prattle, Child as beautiful
> As ever sate upon a Mother's knee;
> The other was the Parent of that Babe;
> But on the Mother's cheek the tints were false,
> A painted bloom.
>
> (368–74)

Here culture is post-lapsarian. Mary Jacobus writes of this scene that:

> I want to emphasize the displacement from mother to child, since it will help to refine one common reading of the episode: namely, that it allows Wordsworth to depict himself as ultimately uncontaminated by the fall into writing or representation which London symbolises in Book VII of *The Prelude*.[5]

The implication is that the sublime cannot be represented because it cannot be contained within the representative structures of Art or language.

The significance of all of this lies in the way that sublimity in *The Prelude* is used as a device to establish moral judgements. This is particularly apparent in the account of Bartholomew Fair, where Wordsworth writes of:

> All out-o'-the'-way, far-fetch'd, perverted things,
> All freaks of Nature, all Promethean thoughts
> Of man; his dulness, madness, and their feats,
> All jumbled up together to make up
> This Parliament of monsters.
>
> (688–92)

Earlier in the poem the mass is defined as an enemy to escape from:

> Meanwhile the roar continues, till at length,
> Escaped as from an enemy, we turn
> Abruptly into some sequester'd nook.
>
> (184–6)

This means that added to the nature/culture (or True/False) opposition is an Individual/Collective opposition. This is echoed in the passage I quoted earlier, when the poet writes of his isolated experiences of the sublime which he 'Had felt, and thought of in my solitude.'

What we can see is that the sublime organises perceptions of the urban in Book VII of *The Prelude*. The dilemma the poet finds himself in is similar to the one that Weiskel sees in Schiller, 'How is one to distinguish between what is intrinsically incomprehensible and what one merely fails to understand?' (p. 35).[6] In one way this is a question which Weiskel answers when he writes that, 'All versions of the sublime require a credible god-term, a meaningful jargon of ultimacy, if the discourse is not to collapse into "mere" rhetoric' (p. 36).

In Wordsworth's representation of the crowd as a polyglot entity there is a break-up of any unifying national principle. This is not to suggest that nationalism offers a 'credible god-term', but it does function as a belief system in this instance. The danger of a rhetorical displacement referred to by Weiskel is apparent in Wordsworth's association of the city with empty forms of representation. Also, Wordsworth overtly mentions the use of rhetoric in his account of the legislature. This echoes Longinus' account of 'delusive' rhetoric:

> Marvellous!
> The enchantment spreads and rises; all are rapt

> Astonish'd; like a Hero in Romance
> He winds away his never-ending horn,
> Words follow words, sense seems to follow sense;
> What memory and what logic! till the Strain
> Transcendent, superhuman as it is,
> Grows tedious even in a young man's ear.

(536–43)

Wordsworth couches this speech in the discourse of the Romantic hero and as such it represents a false rhetorical experience. This idea of the false experience of the Romance hero is something we will look at shortly in an alternative use of the Romance narrative in Sade's 'Florville and Courval'.[7] However, at this moment in *The Prelude* we can see that there are comparisons with Weiskel's version of the Romantic sublime.

The poet does not fully understand how the city can appear sublime; as from a distance it has a visual prospect of sublimity and yet fails to produce it. What the poet finds as representative of this apparent sublimity is merely a series of rhetorical strategies: signs, symbols, allegories and a legislative oratory linked to the oratory of the Romantic hero.

Weiskel's ultimate failure to psychoanalytically account for the sublime is in part illuminated by a reading of Wordsworth's own sense of aesthetic failure in the account of London. For Weiskel, Wordsworth's poetry is, following Keats, characterised by an egotistical sublime because experience is mediated through a controlling consciousness. There is an apparent rapport between nature and subject, or between object and the consciousness which apprehends it. However, in Book VII of *The Prelude*, there is a formulation of a potential sublime experience (the urban) which more properly falls within Weiskel's categorisation of the negative sublime. He writes that 'Our line of thought postulates a wish to be inundated and a simultaneous anxiety of annihilation: to survive, as it were, the ego must go on the offensive and cease to be passive' (p. 105). Wordsworth seems to pose a practical, passive, solution to this; as quoted earlier, he writes of seeking solitude from 'the roar' of the mass:

> Escaped as from an enemy, we turn
> Abruptly into some sequester'd nook.

(185–6)

Yet there is an emotional resistance to the mass at play; he writes of Bartholomew Fair that:

> Above the press and danger of the Crowd,
> Upon some showman's platform: what a hell
> For eyes and ears! what anarchy and din
> Barbarian and infernal! 'tis a dream,
> Monstrous in colour, motion, shape, sight, sound.
>
> (658–62)

This emotional response is a morally informed one, and this becomes associated with a superior perception which sees through the 'false' logic of urban existence:

> Nothing is listen'd to. But these, I fear,
> Are falsely catalogu'd, things that are, are not,
> Even as we give them welcome, or assist,
> Are prompt, or are remiss.
>
> (642–45)

These 'things that are, are not' highlights the apparently fabricated experience of urban life (whereby the activities of one class are used to suggest the ubiquity of all such activity). This idea of a fabricated experience is seen by Wordsworth to lie behind the split between nature and culture. The effect is that (and here Wordsworth is discussing love):

> Absorb'd and buried in the immensity
> Of the effect: a barrier seemed at once
> Thrown in, that from humanity divorced
> The human Form, splitting the race of Man
> In twain, yet leaving the same outward shape.
>
> (423–7)

The poet resists this possibility through a championing of a moral certainty gained in solitude, which is a response to the threat of becoming 'Absorb'd and buried' within a false experiential structure. Thus the poet's response to the city is similar to the Oedipal drama, one which I explored in Chapter 1, and which, as we saw, is mapped out by Weiskel in this way:

> The negative sublime apparently exhibits some features of a response to superego anxiety, for in the suddenness of the sublime moment the conscious ego rejects its attachment to sensible objects and turns rather fearfully toward an ideal of totality and power which it participates or internalizes. (p. 83)

Weiskel acknowledges that this does not convince, but rather appears to be a formal, structural version of an Oedipal drama; one which like Wordsworth's anxiety over representation, appears in a mimic form. Wordsworth rejects the city-scape in favour of a totalising, authentic, sublime moment which is suggested by its very absence; because the 'gross realities' of the city reveal 'The incarnation of the Spirits that mov'd/Amid the Poet's beauteous world, call'd forth,/With that distinctness which a contrast gives' (510–12). The sublime experience here is truly negatively defined because it is seen as an absent presence.

So, for Wordsworth, the city initially offers a prospect of sublimity. Once, however, it is seen as controlled by the 'false' logic of representation, rather than by the authentic vision of the sublime, then the city fails to participate in an overall picture of sublime grandeur. This is similar to Weiskel's failure to appropriate the negative sublime for the Oedipus complex. In this way, the negative sublime mimics a structural version of the Oedipal drama; it is associated with mimicry because filial anxiety is absent from the schema. Likewise in *The Prelude* the poet encounters a similarly 'structurally motivated' (p. 105) form of sublimity. However, it is mimicry because it 'plays' upon the sublime but lacks the necessary emotional basis for its production. There is also a sense of overcoming a 'dangerous passivity' when the poet resists the inauthentic urban sublime by a retreat into personal experience and by an artistic rebellion which defines the urban in terms of a 'fallen' aesthetic.

In this process experience is controlled by a moralising creative aesthetic, which stands in opposition to a homogenising false aesthetic in such a way that it means that form controls content. In *The Prelude* the sublime shapes what an authentic aesthetic experience is. In this the paradox is that that which is fundamentally fictive (the sublime) defines 'true' experience.

Living the text: the case of Sade

Earlier I touched on Wordsworth's link between legal oratory and Romance; where the barrister is 'Astonish'd; like a Hero in Romance/

He winds away his never-ending horn' (538–9). Experience is fiction-ally constructed and a false aesthetic controls the 'real'. This is also played out in the work of Radcliffe, especially with her 'villains' who have a false position upon nature which is contrasted with the hero/heroine's virtuous sensibility. In *The Italian*, for example, the villain, Schedoni, 'cared not for the truth, nor sought it by bold and broad argument, but loved to exert the wily cunning of his nature in hunting it through artificial perplexities'.[8] Such characters are neces-sarily estranged from nature and, consequently, any sustainable code of ethics. The excesses of the Romance are satirised in *Northanger Abbey*, but such a critique is also apparent at a more implicitly satiric level in Sade's 'Florville and Courval'. In this story, which is in part a parody of the Romance, we witness the unfolding of the history of Madame Courval, née Florville, who has, through no fault of her own, slept with her brother, killed their child, condemned her mother to death and then married her father. All of this works through a series of misrecognitions. Fate is portrayed as morally blind, and the dénouement reveals the true identities of the characters who have died in the course of the story. Madame Courval, however, was justified in her previous actions. She was unaware of the true identi-ties of any of the characters; her son had attempted to rape her and she had unwittingly testified against her mother who had murdered a love rival. It is, however, in the fictive sense of the Romance that experience becomes self-consciously defined. Towards the end of the story the 'heroine's' trials appear to be at an end. It is, however, a ref-erence to reading which prefigures the revelations and which disturbs the domestic tranquillity:

> One evening, this tender and loving wife was sitting next to her husband reading an unbelievably gloomy English novel which at the time was being much discussed.
> 'I must confess,' she said, dropping her book, 'here is a creature almost as miserable as I.' (p. 173)

Her husband thinks that it is a memory provoked by the novel which has caused this distress. However, the process of fictive interpellation is more complete than this; she tells him:

> 'Tis not memory that alarms me, but forebodings which terrify me ... I see myself happy with you, Monsieur ... yes, very happy ... and I was not born to be happy. 'Tis impossible that I remain so

very long, for it is ordained that the dawn of my happiness will never be aught but the lightning which precedes the thunderbolt. (p. 173)

This immediately precedes the arrival of Monsieur Courval's son, who exposes her past. A fictional experience, the 'gloomy English novel' comes, in a concrete way, to inform experience. The implication is that life runs true to fiction because there is no exterior totality, as in the sublime, which can effectively anchor moral conduct; instead there exists a fatalistic moral relativity. This, however, is only a position which the 'heroine' can arrive at through a reading of a particular type of Romantic text. What Wordsworth associates with false experience in *The Prelude* is used here to explain experience; the Romantic novel becomes a rhetorical paradigm for 'true' understanding.

One theme which unites Wordsworth and Sade, is that experience (whether it be urban or familial) is relationally defined. For Wordsworth sublimity controls experience and for Sade it is a notion of fictional efficacy. Consequently experience is always already defined and mediated, with Wordsworth and Sade employing a specifically aesthetic mediation, although both with varying intensities. Wordsworth's 'true' aesthetic is represented by the creative poet in opposition to the false aesthetic of the urban. It becomes a more 'natural' form of aesthetics because it is grounded in an idea of moral apprehension. Sade collapses moral distinctions and in privileging 'fate' makes them arbitrary; but both understand the world through fictive strategies. Therefore it means that some strategies are more 'honest' than others: 'As by a glimpse, the things which I had shaped/And yet not shaped' (514–15). The poet has given shape to 'nature' through an act of aesthetic construction.

Memory also plays a part in this act of aesthetic construction and this confirms that Book VII is partially defined by a process of aesthetic reconstruction. The poet writes early on in Book VII:

> A thing that ought to be. Shall I give way,
> Copying the impression of memory,
> Though things remembered idly do half seem
> The work of Fancy, shall I, as the mood
> Inclines me, here describe, for pastime's sake
> Some portion of that motley imagery,

(145–50)

London is made present then, not solely through an aesthetic reconstruction but through a temporal one as well: 'Copying the impression of memory', which highlights how experience is mediated through telling. The poet in this account of London is reader, interpreter of signs, symbols and false allegories, and writer/teller whereby the city is reconstructed through the act of telling. It disturbs Wordsworth's aesthetic sensibility because it lacks the moral certainty inherent in his own aesthetic of the sublime. What we see in this is an essential instability within the sublime. Wordsworth's fragile attempts to reassert its authority within the urban are challenged by an aesthetic process of reconstruction which undermines notions of authenticity. The irony is that the urban possesses a mysterious quality, one which accords with a more fully developed notion of the sublime than that nervously discovered by Wordsworth down some back street. To understand how the urban generates the sublime we need to turn to Poe. By looking at Poe's 'The Man of the Crowd' we will see how its handling of aesthetic, social and psychological demarcations is, perhaps paradoxically, illuminated by Wordsworth's reading of the urban.

Defying interpretation: Poe's 'The Man of the Crowd'

Poe's tale develops the observations of an anonymous narrator as he pursues an alleged criminal through the streets of London.[9] The narrator is baffled by what kind of criminal conduct is suggested by this man and by the fact that no one else in the crowds that they pass through sees anything peculiar in that man's behaviour. What we witness is the narrator's attempt at constructing an objective explanation for the man's actions.

Initially the narrator uses a programmatic conception of crime in order to account for the apparent villainy of this man, whom he subsequently pursues around the city. He notes that

> There are some secrets which do not permit themselves to be told. Men die nightly in their beds, wringing the hands of ghostly confessors, and looking them piteously in the eyes – die with despair of heart and convulsion of throat, on account of the hideousness of mysteries which will not *suffer themselves* to be revealed. Now and then, alas, the conscience of man takes up a burden so heavy in horror that it can be thrown down only into the grave. And thus the essence of all crime is undivulged. (p. 475)

Here secrecy is equated with mystery, which is then defined in terms of criminal behaviour. What is mysterious has thus already been defined as criminal. The last sentence suggests that it is not crime which remains hidden, but rather it is the 'essence' of crime which remains secret.

Poe's tale is relevant to Jackson's formulation of fantasy because it deals with a similar concern, the questioning of cultural and epistemological boundaries. She writes that, 'Presenting that which cannot be, but *is*, fantasy exposes a culture's definitions of that which can be: it traces the limits of its epistemological and ontological frame' (p. 23). Jackson defines the fantastic as a form which is opposed to the apparently unifying strategies of realism, and this idea is also thematically and categorically present in Poe's tale. It is possible to see the narrator as representing a realist position, as his concern with social hierarchy suggests that he is on the side of order (of a kind of social realism). Opposed to this is the mysterious 'villain', who appears within the crowd but is not of its order (and therefore on the side of 'fantasy').

The man of the crowd poses a problem for interpretation because the narrator cannot inscribe him within his exacting class observations. The narrator passes comment on the crowd as it passes his window and identifies a range of social classes from which the crowd is composed. The man of the crowd does not appear to belong to any class and this failure to socially place the man is augmented by a failed attempt to psychologically assess his character. The narrator attempts to gain knowledge of character by analysing the man's facial expressions, only to find that he resists interpretation:

> As I endeavoured, during the brief minute of my original survey, to form some analysis of the meaning conveyed, there arose confusedly and paradoxically within my mind, the ideas of vast mental power, of caution, of penuriousness, of avarice, of coolness, of malice, of blood-thirstiness, of triumph, of merriment, of excessive terror, of intense-supreme despair. (p. 478)

This apparent incoherence places the man of the crowd outside a rationalistic order. This character also echoes a more coherent picture of suggested evil that can be found in earlier Gothic texts. In *The Italian*, for example, the 'evil' monk Schedoni is seen by the virtuous Vivaldi:

> Vivaldi thought he beheld a man, who passions might impel him to the penetration of almost any crime, how hideous soever. He

recoiled from him, as if he had suddenly seen a serpent in his path, and stood gazing on his face, with an attention so wholly occupied as to be unconscious that he did so. (p. 51)

Schedoni is thus defined as constitutionally criminal. In Poe's tale an idea of criminality also defines the man of the crowd, but there is a strange doubling between that man and the narrator.

In tracking the man of the crowd the narrator echoes the man he is pursuing, so that who the man of the crowd is (the narrator or the alleged criminal) is unclear. He cannot understand the man because there is no linear development in the man of the crowd's reversals and repetitions, they do not tell a story: 'I was surprised, however, to find, upon his having made the circuit of the square, that he turned and retraced his steps. Still more was I astonished to see him repeat the same walk several times' (p. 479). The man, rather like the tale itself, goes nowhere. The tale folds back on itself and implicitly acknowledges that this notion of hesitancy is perhaps its real subject matter.

The link between *The Prelude* and 'The Man of the Crowd'

A fascination with social and metaphysical systems links Wordsworth's account of the city with Poe's tale. For Wordsworth, the city fails to impress as sublime. The city is associated with a failed aesthetic: it possesses a false, gaudy representation of a 'true' aesthetic found in nature. The positive side to the city is that the sublime is brought into focus through its very exclusion. This again, has implications for Jackson's theory of the fantastic: 'The fantastic gives utterance to precisely those elements which are known only through their absence within a dominant "realistic" order' (p. 25). Although here Jackson is referring to the fantastic's reliance on absent presences (as in ghosts, for example) this is, nevertheless, similar to Wordsworth's deployment of the sublime. For Wordsworth, 'realism' is equated with a 'truth' present in sublimity. The city potentially threatens this moralistic way of seeing, as it questions its boundaries. In doing so the sublime is strengthened by appearing as an absent presence; it becomes defined and strengthened in relation to what it is not. This is because the sublime offers safety; it enables the poet to escape from the threatening mass and retire to a moralising solitude. In contrast, the structure of class hierarchy in Poe's tale is challenged by the presence of an anomalous element which undermines the narrator's totalising claims to understand the 'real'. This, however, becomes an inverted form of sublimity. The rationale of the narrator is questioned and this opens up the possibility of mystery appearing within what seemed to be a closed, or full, reality. Jackson on fantasy again, 'It is an inverted form of myth. It focuses upon the unknown within the present, discovering emptiness inside an apparently full reality' (p. 158). The man of the crowd represents a gap in interpretation, and his mysterious status is defined by the narrator's inability to locate him within a closed hierarchical system.

The reason why the mystery in 'The Man of the Crowd' takes on sublime dimensions requires some explanation. In this tale the mysterious man confounds all attempts made to interpret his actions. The narrator becomes so caught up within this mystery that he is, quite literally, animated by its presence. The narrator is overwhelmed by the need for an interpretation which he cannot quite reach, although, tantalisingly, there always seems to be one just about to be made, perhaps around the next corner. This compulsive behaviour and the progressive elimination of the narrator's grasp on the mystery echo Kant's notion that the sublime confounds attempts at interpretation. The mystery takes over in both Kant and Poe, and we find that the failure of interpretation means that reason is gestured towards and, as we shall see, Poe will address this notion of reason, in his other mysteries which involve Dupin. For the narrator in 'The Man of the Crowd' the apparently anomalous man represents the 'essence' of crime. What the narrator also attempts to do at the end is to place this man within a system of social types which would reinforce his idea of hierarchy. He 'is the type and the genius of deep crime' (p. 481); when in fact the problem of the man of the crowd is that, 'He refuses to be alone'; he resists (through mere existence), the attempt to place him within any meaningful categorisation. In this way the sublime emerges within a context which appears to be inimical to it.

Poe's tale provides us with a complex reworking of the sublime, one which is always on the edge of neurotic breakdown and therefore one which bears some similarity to Wordsworth's account of the sublime in Book VII of *The Prelude*. It is the unbalanced nature of the sublime in Poe's tale which enables us to see how his version of the sublime looks back to Romanticism and forward to a more properly developed Freudian scene.

In Book VII of *The Prelude* there is a dialectical tension between the city and the sublime. In Poe's tale, the mystery represented by the man of the crowd disturbs the narrator's interpretation, it attacks his system from within, in spatial terms, literally. It is epistemology which is questioned. For Wordsworth, epistemology in the form of the sublime remains intact because it is founded on a 'truth' verified by the state of the lapsed condition of the urban.

The fundamental difference is that for Wordsworth the sublime is strengthened by this exclusion whereas, for Poe's narrator, order is undermined by the existence of the inexplicable. The figure of the man of the crowd also works against Wordsworth's representation of solitariness within the urban condition, as in, for example, Wordsworth's account of the blind beggar. In Poe's tale the man of the crowd appears to be unnatural because he does not coherently belong to the class structure. He is unnatural because he is *too* social, '*He is the man of the crowd*' (p. 481).

It is worth considering whether it is better to see this presence of mystery as a new formulation of the sublime or as one reliant upon older Romantic notions of it, or whether this use of mystery is merely a structural play on sublime mystery. In this way an explanation is required for the possibility that Poe's 'The Man of the Crowd' creates a 'super-reading' of Kant's aesthetic.

An obvious contrast is that whereas in Wordsworth the natural sublime is experienced as plenitude, in Poe's tale the mystery is experienced as loss. In Kant's 'Analytic of the Sublime', as we have seen, the sublime is not tied to any particular object, rather it is made manifest through a set of feelings. It is also manifested through an intimation of reason, of an abstract domain of rationality referred to but which exists beyond the grasp of the subject. All of this suggests that the non-objective status of the sublime means that it is not open to direct (quasi-scientific) perception. Although in Poe's tale sight controls the interpretation of the action (with the narrator as a social commentator) this can be questioned. As suggested earlier, there is a mirroring between the narrator and the man of the crowd. Towards the end the narrator attempts to engineer a confrontation, but instead of this producing a solution, the mystery is maintained:

> as the shades of the second evening came on, I grew wearied unto death, and, stopping fully in front of the wanderer, gazed at him steadfastly in the face. He noticed me not, but resumed his solemn walk, while I, ceasing to follow, remained absorbed in contemplation. (p. 481)

What the narrator notices in the man is the way that he resists his particular mode of classification because he does not occupy any obvious class position. The man of the crowd is the man of the mass, whereas the narrator is positioned in the narrative as having a critical distance from the mass. The man of the crowd recognises mass and not specific individuals, for this reason his following of the crowd takes on the form of a compulsion. For a brief time the crowd disperses until they come across a theatre:

> It was about being closed, and the audience were thronging from the doors. I saw the old man gasp as if for breath while he threw himself amid the crowd; but I thought that the intense agony of his countenance had, in some measure, abated. (p. 480)

Here the man's entrance into the crowd takes on the form of a drug addiction. What I am suggesting in this examination of non-recognition (but a strange mirroring) is that sight has been undermined. 'Pure' sight does not control the gaze, but rather it is a form of social seeing which defines the action. In Kantian terms there is no real, sensuous experience taking place; rather it is reason which has failed. To return to Kant, he writes that

> The sublime may be described in this way: It is an object (of nature) the *representation of which determines the mind to regard the elevation of nature beyond our reach as equivalent to a presentation of ideas.* (p. 119)

In Poe's tale the man of the crowd is on the side of nature because he is not assimilable to a cultural, or class-based, way of seeing. Therefore, there is an equivalence to the Kantian idea that in the sublime moment there is an apprehension of a 'nature' which exists beyond the realm of a determinant reason. Also, for Kant, the apparent triumph of a potential reason is turned into a broader triumph. This is because in the sublime it is imagination which appears to lose out but, in compensation, the ability to reason is placed in accord 'with *ideas* of reason' (p. 104). Here the potential accessiblity of the supersensible realm stimulates certain mental faculties. The failure of rational apprehension, as we saw, 'induce[s] a temper of mind conformable to that which the influence of definite (practical) ideas would produce upon feeling, and in common accord with it' (p. 104). There is thus an apparent synthesis between subject and object. In Poe's tale the failure of reason appears to threaten the narrator's interpretive system with collapse, but this is something he attempts to divert by defining the man of the crowd as the 'essence' of crime. In this, 'pure' crime is defined as ineffable, a secret which cannot be cogently unravelled. As suggested earlier, the man of the crowd appears to be a 'natural' subject at odds with a culturally determined structure; he is an 'essence'.

Poe's tale works through aspects familiar from the Kantian sublime. The man of the crowd appears as a mystery because he cannot be accounted for by understanding. This failure of understanding is compensated by the suggestion that the man possesses an essence which is as yet unknowable but which is potentially available for interpretation. The man is too social, an individual becoming the concept (the crowd), making it problematic to define his individuality. Sensuous perception is put into doubt through this because the narrator's way of seeing is, as is Victor Frankenstein's, culturally positioned. Poe's narrator's grasp on reason is also in doubt. He appears to be a normative presence within the tale and yet his faith in reason seems to be irrational. Poe is thus, paradoxically, challenging systems of reason as much as passing comment on what reason excludes.

Poe's neo-Kantianism: the case of the detective tales

There exists a range of similarities between Poe's detective tales and Kant's version of the subject. The first is that the mystery, the 'crime' to be solved, stimulates reason. In a similar way the sublime stimulates an idea of reason and gestures towards the possibility of a totalising reason; a gesture made manifest in Poe's tales. Also, this reasoning is grounded in an idea of moral conduct. It is a form of reason which helps the community when it becomes a categorical moral imperative to do so; this is to say that Dupin exemplifies a desire to return to the epistemological status quo. Additionally, what is bound up in this is a theory of disinterested pleasure. It is disinterested because this mode of understanding is not employed selfishly by either the Kantian subject or by Poe's detective. There is also a similar reliance on an *a priori* notion of universal laws governing experience. There are two ironies concerning this idea in Poe. One is that Dupin posits a structure of thought (his 'reading' of character) which suggests the knowability of all subjects, only to deny that all subjects have the same knowledge. The other irony is that his theory of the subject, set up at great length at the beginning of 'The Murders in the Rue Morgue', is one which he does not actually use to solve the mystery. A final similarity is that Dupin is not interested in the sense realm as an aspect of logic. This links to the above point, for Dupin deploys theoretical laws pertaining to the subject which are then worked out in an exemplary form.

To properly identify these Kantian reworkings we need to scrutinise Dupin's pronouncements on different types of analytical thought. It is in what Dupin says rather than in what he does that this Kantian presence can be discerned. It is the narrator who gives us a series of portraits of Dupin, ones which describe how the mystery in each tale affects Dupin and, as we shall see, these effects also suggest the presence of Kantian ideas. Poe's detective tales rework the sublime within an urban context, a context which Wordsworth characterised as inimical to sublimity. The sublime is thus used to interpret urban life (or urban mysteries) in the same way that it had earlier been used to understand nature.

Before looking at this sublime presence I first want to highlight how the tales appropriate other Kantian ideas. This enables us to see just how considerable a debt Poe owes to Kant. Poe's use of sublimity is not his only similarity to Kant; there are also echoes which suggest an equivalence to the formal aspects of the detective narratives themselves. In order to grasp this we need to pay attention to how Kant constructs a model of analytical inquiry which is also to be found in Poe's detective tales.

In the 'Critique of Aesthetic Judgement' Kant writes that:

> *Concepts of the understanding* must, as such, always be demonstrable (if, as in anatomy, demonstration is understood in the sense merely of *presentation*). In other words, the object answering to such concepts must always be capable of being given in intuition (pure or empirical); for only in this way can they become cognitions.[10]

It is necessary for intuitions to take on the form of cognitions and this is achieved through demonstration. Kant again refers to the anatomist:

> Where the intuition is *a priori* this is called its construction, but when even the intuition is empirical, we have still got the illustration of the object, by which means objective reality is assured to the concept. Thus an anatomist is said to demonstrate the human eye when he renders the concept, of which he has previously given a discursive exposition, intuitable by means of the dissection of that again. (p. 211)

Here the intuition is granted a physical form and is used to explain an already worked-out narrative (a medical understanding of optics). The connection between this and Poe's detective tales is that they too are based on a recounting of events. Dupin reconstructs the events through a rationalistic discourse which demystifies the mystery. In 'The Murders in the Rue Morgue', for example, the witnesses' confusion over the nationality of the 'murderer' explains other mysteries.[11] The size of the grip on Mademoiselle L'Espanye's neck and the extreme strength and agility of the 'murderer' leads Dupin to deduce that the culprit is an ourang-outang; a conclusion verified in the confused understanding of the ourang-outang's 'accent'. Like the anatomist, Dupin reconstructs the events in a narrative which he has already worked out. This also occurs in 'The Purloined Letter' when Dupin recounts his retrieval of the letter from the Minister D.

Alongside these formal similarities we can also see that there exist points of convergence between Kant's version of reason and Dupin's account of analytical thought. Kant writes (on reason):

> But an adequate reason only exists where their principle, being in no way borrowed from the concept of nature, which is always sensibly conditioned, rests consequently on the supersensible, which the concept of freedom alone makes cognizable by means of its formal laws, and where, therefore, they are morally-practical, i.e. not merely precepts and rules in this or that interest, but laws independent of all antecedent reference to ends or aims. (p. 11)

In this way a form of reasoning which exists independently of the sensuous world can become a form of moral reasoning; for this to occur it requires an idea of freedom so that reason is free from determinate ends. This idea of different forms of mental activity, as in that between understanding and reason, or in a reasoning which is concerned with the object rather than with the supersensible, is echoed in Poe's tales as a clash between Dupin's reasoning and the police's methodology.

Dupin in 'The Purloined Letter' tells the narrator that the police 'have no variation of principle in their investigations; at best, when urged by some unusual emergency – by some extraordinary reward – they extend or exaggerate their old modes of *practice*, without touching their principles'.[12] Poe's detective possesses this scepticism about epistemological abstractions because of the synthetic nature of those abstractions. This false abstract knowledge is something which Dupin associates with axiomatic 'truths'. We can see this in 'The Murders in the Rue Morgue' where a systematic account of logic is given, a logic which differentiates it from the abstract logic of mathematics. We are informed that:

> The faculty of re-solution is possibly much invigorated by mathematical study, especially by that highest branch of it which, unjustly, and merely on account of its retrograde operations, has been called, as if *par excellence*, analysis. Yet to calculate is not in itself to analyse. (p. 141)

Mathematical principles thus create inflexible 'laws'. Dupin uses mathematics in this instance as a trope for all kinds of false mental abstractions. This kind of scepticism can also be found in Kant's 'The Critique of Teleological Judgement' where he discusses mathematics:

> Pure mathematics can never deal with the real existence of things, but only with their possibility, that is to say, with the possibility of an intuition answering to the conceptions of the things. Hence it cannot touch the question of cause and effect, and, consequently, all the finality there observed must always be regarded simply as formal, and never as a physical end.[13]

We can see that Dupin's reasoning fulfils the Kantian dictate concerning freedom because it is not prescriptive. It does not follow the formal procedures evidenced by an abstract logic such as mathematics. Also, it does not copy the formal, calculative logic of police methodology. Dupin moves swiftly from the axiomatic truths of mathematics to the kind of reasoning associated with game-playing, one which makes sense of psychological motivation and so, ultimately, criminal behaviour. Dupin tells the narrator that in a game of draughts:

> to have a retentive memory, and proceed by 'the book' are points commonly regarded as the sum total of good playing. But it is in matters beyond the limits of mere rule that the skill of the analyst is evinced. (p. 142)

Dupin, unlike the police, does not 'proceed by "the book"'. In the place of such formalised practice he favours an intuitive approach. Dupin's logic appears to be intuitive and it is intuition which is linked to the idea of the universal subject. To return to the game of draughts, Dupin advocates winning in the following way:

> Deprived of ordinary resources, the analyst throws himself into the spirit of his opponent, identifies himself therewith, and not infrequently sees thus, at a glance, the sole methods (sometimes indeed

absurdly simple ones) by which he may seduce into error or hurry into miscalculation. (p. 142)

Kant also writes about 'universal laws of nature' that:

judgement is compelled, for its own guidance, to adopt it as an *a priori* principle, that what is for human insight contingent in the particular (empirical) laws of nature contains nevertheless unity of law in the synthesis of its manifold in an intrinsically possible experience – unfathomable though still thinkable, as such unity may, no doubt, be for us. (p. 23)

This is necessary for thought to be turned into an object of cognition for another, in the same way that the anatomist works, or how the detective recounts the solution of the mystery.

Dupin is associated with the workings of the mind. His attempts to form a theory of subjectivity ape Kant's own construction of moral and metaphysical principles. What we can see in such moments from the tales is a reworking of Kant which re-plots his basic conceptual paradigms within an urban context. Poe, however, does not stop there, he also develops this in relation to other thresholds, in particular that between life and death, a notion which is central to the Gothic fascination with different manifestations of the living dead, a point to which I shall shortly return.

Poe's detective tales also rework the Kantian sublime, a reworking which is in part dependent upon the reassessment of the Kantian notion of reason. For Kant the mind is *'set in motion'* by sublime experience, which is echoed in the character of Dupin. Dupin's typical state before the commencement of an investigation is one of inertia. In 'The Murders in the Rue Morgue' the narrator relates that:

Our seclusion was perfect. We admitted no visitors. Indeed the locality of our retirement had been carefully kept a secret from my own former associates; and it had been many years since Dupin had ceased to know or be known in Paris. We existed within ourselves alone. (p. 144)

Seclusion is equated with social inertia. Dupin is inert until 'activated' by the mystery. This position is similarly set up at the beginning of 'The Purloined Letter'. The narrator writes that, 'For one hour at least we had maintained a profound silence; while each, to any casual observer, might have seemed intently and exclusively occupied with the curling eddies of smoke that oppressed the atmosphere of the chamber' (p. 208).

Dupin is typified by inertia, an inertia transcended in the advent of a mystery which animates him. Dupin occupies a position on the mystery which is the same as that of the Kantian subject in the sublime moment. The mysteries appear to defy rationality, but it is the function of rationality which Dupin questions. The mysterious refers the subject to a different order of rationality because the failure of reason gestures towards the supersensible. Dupin is a Kantian subject who is both animated by sublime mysteries and who becomes a mouthpiece for a Kantian philosophy. However, if we explore Dupin's explanations for the mystery we find that his focus is on the status of rationality and how it is used. The narrator observes the sublime effects on Dupin, ones which are ultimately banished, paradoxically, through Dupin's quasi-Kantian reasoning. In one sense Poe's tales differ from Kant's theorising because complete understanding is reached in Poe, whereas for Kant this is not possible with the supersensible; in Poe the supersensible is 'solved'.

I have outlined how Poe's tales work within the parameters of some aspects of Kant's philosophy. The detective's form of reasoning leads to the closure of troubling gaps in knowledge which the mysteries create. It is a universal way of understanding which has the guise of a moral imperative, rather than being an axiomatic truth such as that to be found in mathematics. In its attainment of solutions through pure reasoning it implies a successful grasp of the supersensible. This is something which reveals where a major difference between Kant and Poe emerges, because in the former the supersensible is only apprehended as an idea of unattainable reason.

This process of sublime discovery is worked out in Poe's tales through a link to his critique of mathematics. In 'The Purloined Letter', for example, the Prefect of Police, G, says of the Minister D that he is, 'Not *altogether* a fool ... but then he is a poet, which I take to be only one remove from a fool' (p. 211). The narrator believes the Minister D to be a mathematician rather than a poet, but Dupin enlightens him: 'You are mistaken; I know him well; he is both. As poet *and* mathematician, he would reason well; as mere mathematician, he could not have reasoned at all, and thus would have been at the mercy of the Prefect' (p. 217). Here poetry and mathematics occupy an analogous position to that of reason and understanding in Kant's schema. This idea of reason is linked to the supersensible; here it is the mind's failure at the level of cognition which reveals the possibility of reason rather than its attainment. In the 'Analytic of the Sublime' Kant argues that in the sublime moment the subject is not totally pleased by the sensation but also repulsed, meaning that there is a negative pleasure associated with the sublime. In this sense, what the detective confronts is a mystery which exists at an epistemological level. It highlights the gaps in the police's knowledge, whereby that knowledge equates to, in Kantian terms, a formulation of the understanding, whereas the detective's equates to that of reason. However, in one important sense the supersensible fails to signify at the level of cognition; it is not an object for analysis but an idea of reason.

Poe's detective tales thus incorporate a similar range of registers as are found in Kant. Poe takes these Kantian concepts a stage further by supplying possible answers posed by the mysterious sublime. Poe also develops this issue of a threshold philosophy through an abiding interest in the relationship between life and death. An exploration of this interest reveals how it too is conditioned by a version of sublimity.

Reworking the supersensible in Poe, the case of 'Mesmeric Revelation'

A close reading of Poe's 'Mesmeric Revelation' suggests that it too mirrors aspects of Kant's thought, but in a way different from that of the detective tales. 'Mesmeric Revelation' is a story of a dying man, Van Kirk, who, when put into a mesmeric trance enters another, unworldly, realm. The trance is described as being similar to a near-death experience and so echoes Van Kirk's own precarious physical state. This trance-like state bears a similarity to non-sensuous perception, which in Kant is discovered in the intimation of the supersensible. Van Kirk tells the narrator that in the trance, 'while in this state, the person so impressed employs only with effort, and then feebly, the external organs of sense, yet perceives, with keenly refined perception, and through channels supposed unknown, matters beyond the scope of the physical organs'.[14] Van Kirk sets up a strict opposition between mind and matter, so that the 'true' form of seeing is inward- rather than outward-looking. As he says to the narrator, 'I sent for you tonight ... not so much to administer to my bodily ailment, as to satisfy me concerning certain psychical impressions which, of late, have occasioned me much anxiety and surprise' (pp. 88–9). Van Kirk attempts to codify the existence of the non-sensuous into a universal law, but this idea of a law differs from Dupin's. It is not socially deployed, or ratified, but is inward looking, and grounded in an idea of solipsistic intuition; as Van Kirk tells the narrator, 'I cannot deny that there has always existed, as if in that very soul which I have been denying, a vague half-sentiment of its own existence' (p. 89). Although this way of seeing requires internal ratification, there is still an idea of the fallibility of abstract theorising which can be found in both Kant and Dupin. Van Kirk does this, revealingly, by questioning the very precepts of European philosophy. He tells the narrator:

> I was not long in perceiving that if man is to be intellectually con-
> vinced of his own immortality, he will never be so convinced by the
> mere abstractions which have been so long the fashion of the
> moralists of England, of France, and of Germany. Abstractions may
> amuse and exercise, but take no hold on the mind. Here upon earth,
> at least, philosophy, I am persuaded, will always in vain call upon us
> to look upon qualities as things. The will may assent – the soul – the
> intellect, never. (p. 89)

It is Van Kirk's own intuitive approach (a felt and here only semi-lived experience) which reveals 'immortality'. This becomes apparent when the mind and world appear to co-exist, and it links to Kant's discussion of the pleasure derived from making a judgement, where there is 'the final harmony of an object ... with the mutual relation of the faculties of cognition' (p. 32). This is something Van Kirk is given access to in the mesmeric trance: 'latterly there has been a certain deepening of the feeling, until it has come so nearly to resemble the acquiescence of reason, that I find it difficult to distinguish between the two' (p. 89). Here mind and matter fuse, and it is because of this fusion that reasoning becomes all-encompassing because it combines cause and effect. Van Kirk tells the narrator, 'In sleep-waking, the reasoning and its con-clusion – the cause and its effect – are present together. In my natural state, the cause vanishing, the effect only, and perhaps only partially, remains' (p. 89).

Various binary oppositions become collapsed in the trance: mind/matter (as inner/outer), cause/effect and also a supplementary opposition along a nature/culture axis. This becomes expressed as a dis-trust of the representational efficacy of words (a distrust central to Longinus' and Burke's accounts of the sublime). A question and answer session takes place between the narrator and Van Kirk while Van Kirk is in the trance. The narrator asks a question concerning 'spirit', and the following dialogue takes place:

V. While I was awake I knew what you meant by 'spirit', but now it
   seems only a word – such, for instance, as truth, beauty – a
   quality, I mean.
P. Is not God immaterial?
V. There is no immateriality: it is a mere word. That which is not
   matter, is not at all – unless qualities are things. (p. 90)

Here there is a realm of experience (like the sublime) which exists
outside of any attempt to represent it. As Van Kirk says, 'qualities'
cannot become things (nouns). What is also apparent is a pantheism
missing from both Kant's philosophy and Dupin's logic. What it does,
however, posit is the existence of an ontological signified which is
similar to that of the supersensible. Here a universal spirit is equated
with God and this undermines the mind/body dualism which is collapsed through the process of mental perception. Van Kirk tells the
narrator, 'All created things are but the thoughts of God' (p. 92).
Physical beings are thus mental projections. God is also placed on the
side of matter, but matter has now been collapsed with an idea of
mind, so that: 'God, with all the powers attributed to spirit, is but the
perfection of matter' (p. 92). It is when an idea of the body is sus-
pended that the subject is open to this universal understanding. With
an idea of physicality, 'Thus man is individualised'; however, 'Divested
of corporate investiture, he were God. Now the particular motion of
the incarnated portions of the unparticled matter is the thought of
man; as the motion of the whole is that of God' (p. 93).
    Van Kirk is represented as having experienced a universal ontological
reality. As with Kant on Judgement, objects and understanding co-
incide because, for Van Kirk, those objects have been dematerialised as
thoughts (of God). He tells the narrator that: 'We must not regard it as
a quality, but as a sentiment: – it is the perception, in thinking beings,
of the adaptation of matter to their organization' (p. 95). Thus the
sublime is attained on an emotional and psychological level which
bears comparison with its more formal, intellectual attainment in the
detective tales.

The sublime retains a peculiar presence in Poe's tales. His reworking of
the Kantian sublime places him on a continuum which stretches back
to the eighteenth century and forward to the twentieth. We have
seen how Poe modifies the sublime for an urban context, and this is

apparent in his detective tales which construct an implicit neo-Kantian form of the sublime as an interpretive tool. Sublimity, in Poe's writings, has not fallen out of favour in representations of the city, but has been used by him to understand the city. This is opposed to Wordsworth's understanding of the city in Book VII of *The Prelude*, where the urban fails to match up to sublime expectations in a manner that suggests that the city-scape precludes all possibility of the sublime.

In 'Mesmeric Revelation' a different form of neo-Kantianism is worked out; there the sublime is an internalised ontological force (at odds with an external placing of it in the detective tales). Between Van Kirk and the narrator there exists an implied analyst/analysed relationship and this prefigures an analysis of the Freudian unconscious which I will explore in Chapter 7. The trajectory of the Gothic sublime and its destabilising presence within an emergent scientific discourse which resembles the psychoanalytical, appears towards the end of the nineteenth century. Sex and its discontents informs both science and the sublime and this is best exemplified by a reading of *Dracula*, to which we will now turn.

6
Textuality and Sublimity in *Dracula*

In Chapter 22 we saw how Foucault provided us, coincidentally, with a helpful explanation for the Gothic fascination with constructions of the self, and how this related to notions of modernity. In *The History of Sexuality*, vol. I, Foucault argues that a scientific investigation into a form of sexual self-consciousness takes place in the Victorian period.[1] As we shall see, *Dracula* can be read as a confirmation of Foucault's treatise. However, I will also explore the presence of a sexual sublime in the novel, a version of the sublime which in part unsettles Foucault's account of the attempts made to police, and so contain, desire. This latter reading is not hostile to Foucault's conclusions, but I do want to explore some of the limitations of his history of sexuality and these limitations become apparent when we consider how the sublime recasts some of his conclusions. My aim is to show how this presence of a Gothic sublimity continues to challenge traditional constructions of the self; here in formations of the subject which are to be found within late-nineteenth-century debates concerning science and sexuality.

In the previous chapter we saw how Poe's detective, C. Auguste Dupin, functioned as a cipher for neo-Kantian ideas. In my Foucauldian reading of *Dracula* I focus upon a similar process of detection, arguing that the Count poses a seemingly threatening absence for bourgeois culture, one which is articulated through an apparent clash between feudal and bourgeois knowledge claims. My historicist Foucauldian reading will thus acknowledge class relations in ways which my reading of sublimity does not (or only obliquely so).

From sexuality to textuality: the problem of 'truth' in *Dracula*

> ... not only could sex be affected by its own diseases, it could
> also, if it was not controlled, transmit diseases or create others
> that would afflict future generations. (p. 118)

> ... we belong to a society which has ordered sex's difficult
> knowledge, not according to the transmission of secrets, but
> around the slow surfacing of confidential statements.
> (pp. 62–3)

Foucault's formulation of a *scientia sexualis*, as outlined in these quo-
tations, argues the case that in the nineteenth century bodies were
invested with a sexuality, an examination of which would expose the
'truth' of the subject. That is a 'truth' of the subject's position within
a symbolic order which, for Foucault, has to be encouraged to express
itself in order for it to be translated by a medico-psychological discourse which gauges the 'health' of sexuality. This is opposed to an
ars erotica characterised by a symbolics of blood, which existed at a
time when the notion of possessing a certain type of blood was of
social and economic importance. The aristocrat ensured descent by
virtue of noble blood and as such, blood lines were closely related to
sexuality. For the emerging bourgeoisie the symbolics of blood
became retranslated into theories of sexuality. This means that with
the rise of the professional middle classes possession of a certain kind
of blood no longer ensured group membership; rather it was health
and the possibilities of inherited family wealth which assured economic success.

However, as Foucault points out, the bourgeoisie's sexuality was precarious, subject to infection and susceptible to disease, and thus it was
through 'the slow surfacing of confidential statements' that access to
this vulnerable sexuality was made possible. The bourgeoisie considered its sexuality 'a fragile treasure, a secret that had to be discovered at
all costs' (p. 120), and as such the bourgeoisie were encouraged to
confess their secret desires. The problem of sexuality was therefore
associated with a problem of truth, of its status and function and of
how it was to disclose itself. This process of disclosure, this problem of
sexuality, appears to construct a possible reading of *Dracula* which
reveals an antagonism between a symbolics of blood (the Count) and a
theory of sexuality (the opposing bourgeois group).

One plausible argument is that the Count absorbs members of the latter group by infecting their blood. This infection displaces them from their prescribed subject positions within discourse, and we can observe this through the way that the group's unity is compromised by the use of self-referential forms of writing (diary entries). The type of subject constructed here is associated with a bourgeois individualism which perceives the world in a reified (already given) fashion. Through the circulation of these texts (their diaries) the subject overcomes this reification by adopting subject positions in narration from which they have been excluded.

Initially we will examine Jonathan Harker's opening account, as it is this account whose 'truth' the other texts verify through establishing a relationship between his seemingly outlandish claims and the 'truth' of sexuality. This will lead us into a wider analysis of the relationship between sexuality and textuality in the novel.

The return of the dead and the threat to modernity

Jonathan Harker's journal reveals him to be subject to problems of sexuality and textuality which take on the form of a return of the repressed. He writes of his predicament that, 'It is nineteenth century up-to-date with a vengeance. And yet, unless my senses deceive me, the old centuries had, and have, powers of their own which mere "modernity" cannot kill'.[2] Dead history is brought to life through Dracula who resurrects the past (the history of the Wallachians and Saxons) in order to confirm his aristocratic status: 'in our veins flows the blood of many brave races who fought as the lion fights, for lord-ship' (p. 28). The Count represents the culmination of a feudal history, one from which the bourgeoisie are excluded but from which they emerged. As Chris Baldick puts it, 'Dracula is feudalism's death warmed up' (p. 148).[3]

This historical displacement of the Count and his subsequent clash with the opposing bourgeois group is closely identified in the novel as a clash between bodies, and through a conflict between textuality and non-textuality. The Count's body is an impossible one and this is revealed through its precarious immortality and in his physical actions. Harker seeing the Count leave his room, scaling head downwards down the wall comments, 'What manner of man is this, or what manner of creature is it in the semblance of man?' (p. 34). The Count is thin yet possesses the strength of 'twenty men' (p. 237). His body transgresses these laws of possibility, but is subject to other laws. The crucifix, an inability to cross water unaided, and garlic function as alternative prohibitions upon the vampire's body. These restraints do not reveal, however, the greatest clash between the Count and the bourgeois group, which is in a sexual definition of the body grounded in a symbolics of blood versus a theory of sexuality; or by an *ars erotica* versus a *scientia sexualis*. Foucault writes that *ars erotica* functioned through a process in which:

> the relationship to the master who holds the secrets, is of para-mount importance; and only he, working alone, can transmit this art in an esoteric manner and as the culmination of an initiation in which he guides the disciple's progress with unfailing skill and severity (p. 32).

The Count creates disciples, he propagates his system, by infecting their blood; as Mina recounts her 'seduction' in which the Count says to her, 'you, their best beloved one, are now to me flesh of my flesh; blood of my blood; kin of my kin' (p. 288). Blood becomes politicised because, according to Foucault, in feudalism aristocratic descent was assured by possession of a certain kind of blood, of having noble blood, while with the bourgeoisie, descent is monitored by a theory of sexuality which validates 'health'. The Count, as a representative of an archaic and therefore superseded sexuality, poses problems for a cap-italist culture because he threatens that culture with extinction through absorption. Van Helsing defines the struggle: 'to fail here is not mere life or death. It is that we become as him' (p. 237).

The Count then, becomes irrevocably defined as Other by an his-toricising of his own body: 'What devil or what witch was ever so great as Attila, whose blood is in these veins?' (p. 29). His body is his-torically and physically impossible; his strength, his ability to meta-morphose into a wolf or bat illustrates his 'unnatural' command of nature (or more radically the challenge he presents to Jonathan Harker's assumptions about nature). His sexuality threatens to absorb, and so transform, bourgeois sexuality. Sexuality is therefore directly related in *Dracula* to a notion of the subject; the 'truth' of the subject becomes the truth of its sexuality. The Count becomes a problem of truth for the bourgeois group because 'sex was constituted as a problem of truth' (Foucault, p. 56) in *scientia sexualis*. The Count's subjectivity (sexuality) is expressed in a way different from that of the bourgeois group, and it is in its expression that the status of textuality becomes significant.

The bourgeois group represent the world through their diary extracts. It is a mode of representation in which the world exists as an already given, and so implies that they are passive observers of it. Also, their accounts are personal, secret texts. Francis Barker notes of this type of writing that there is 'the apparent ease of access of its discourse, launched from an inner place to an outer, clarified world; the guilty secrecy not only of its writing but of its sexuality',[4] because in writing, 'the bourgeois subject substitutes for its corporal body the rarefied body of the text' (p. 62). The Count has no text; his desire is only manifested through those it affects. He becomes an object, rather than a subject, of discourse; he does not self-reflect (he does not appear in the mirror).

The most important text in *Dracula* is Jonathan Harker's journal; it is the secrets of Harker's journal that the other texts unravel, so granting it the status of 'truth'. This gives credence to Harker's statement, 'Let me begin with facts – bare, meagre facts, verified by books and figures, and of which there can be no doubt' (p. 30). The Count is 'un-dead', an impossible being, whose status as an object of 'truth' is present as an absence within the scientific discourse of Van Helsing and Dr Seward. This scientific impossibility is identified, paradoxically, as a deficiency that inheres to scientific discourse itself, as Van Helsing puts it, 'it is the fault of our science that it wants to explain all; and if it explains not, then it says there is nothing to explain' (p. 191). It is not, however, solely science which destroys the Count: it is also a circulation of texts which form a joined narration that forces members of the group outside of their narrative positions. This transforms them from being isolated observers (writers) into participants (readers), so that 'truth' is produced communally via the exchange of texts. It is this textuality which is related to the 'truth' of sexuality; Van Helsing says to Mina Harker after reading Jonathan's journal, 'You may sleep without doubt. Strange and terrible as it is, it is *true*!' (p. 186) and Jonathan on hearing this expresses his relief as 'I felt impotent' (p. 188). With truth assured, sexuality is assured. The importance of scrutinising textuality becomes increasingly emphasised. Van Helsing on handing over the collected accounts says to Seward, 'What is here told ... may be the beginning of the end to you and me and many another; or it may sound the knell of the Un-Dead' (pp. 218–19). Their collated texts will reveal this secret. Seward observes that when Mina and Jonathan have collated this material 'they will be able to show a whole connected narrative' (p. 225), a 'connected' or meaningful narrative. Mina writes of this text, 'Whilst they are resting, I shall go over all carefully, and perhaps I may arrive at some conclusion. I shall try to follow the Professor's example, and think without prejudice on the facts before me' (p. 350). The 'facts' before them have surfaced through Van Helsing's encouragement, as he says to Seward, 'Nothing is too small. I counsel you, put down in record even your doubts and surmises' (p. 119). That which appears to be inconsequential is thus given importance, is urged into discourse. Foucault writes that, 'sex became something to say, and to say exhaustively in accordance with deployments that were varied, but all, in their own way compelling' (p. 32). There was a 'polymorphous incitement to discourse' (p. 34). These extracts reveal that this 'incitement to discourse' has taken place, with each diarist keeping an account of personal recollections and doubts.

When Mina is infected by the Count she is hypnotised and forced to disclose her subconscious 'truth'. She is the missing link between the Count's sexuality and the sexuality of the bourgeoisie; like Renfield who mimics the Count's vampirism, she becomes linked to the Count in an 'indexy kind of way' (p. 248). The Count is the 'author of all this our sorrow' (p. 217); he can only be destroyed when 'He is confined within the limitations of his earthly envelope' (p. 292), indicating that anything associated with writing is problematic because writing is perceived as related to health. Van Helsing sees Mina's lack of interest in her diary as indicative of illness: there is 'the silence now often; as so it was with Miss Lucy' (p. 323); and 'She make no entry into her little diary, she who write so faithful at every pause' (p. 363). This reveals the extent of how far her subjectivity is tainted through her connection with the Count, whose own subjectivity is unself-referential and pre-bourgeois. Barker again:

> Pre-bourgeois subjection does not properly involve subjectivity at all, but a condition of dependent membership in which place and articulation are defined not by an interiorized self-recognition – complete or partial, percipient or unknowing ... but by incorporation in the body politic. (p. 31)[5]

Absorption into the 'body' politic defines a political system mediated through a symbolics of blood. The most overt example of this bodily absorption is in the 'seduction' of Lucy Westenra. In her account to Mina of her dream (her seduction) blood plays an important part. It is the taste of the 'something' which is 'very sweet and very bitter' (p. 98) that surrounds her and absorbs her in a sexual fashion, as further referenced in the image of the phallic 'West lighthouse [which] was right under me' (p. 98). Her blood is tested for impurities by Seward; however, 'The qualitative analysis gives a quite normal condition' (p. 111), leading Seward to believe that her problem might be mental rather than physical. Blood becomes defined through a struggle for its ownership. The Count corrupts Lucy by taking her blood and by introducing 'moral' impurities into it. For this to be arrested, Lucy's blood needs to be replaced from a healthy source, so that she is penetrated in a 'healthy' fashion.

The first transfusion is from her fiancée Holmwood, who is 'so young and strong and of blood so pure' (p. 132). When Lucy receives this transfusion she re-enters discourse, writing that 'Arthur feels very, very close to me. I seem to feel his presence warm about me' (p. 126). Lucy's body has collapsed into that which has given her life; from now on her identity is only secured to the extent that she is absorbed by the blood of others. The group have unwittingly become vampiric in 'infecting' Lucy's body, but in a way which makes it pure; it is a healthy form of penetration, a disguised sexual act. The second transfusion is from Seward, who recounts the experience as 'the draining away of one's blood, no matter how willingly it be given, is a terrible feeling' (p. 128). It is not absorption here which is the 'terrible feeling', it is the guilty symbolic penetration of Lucy's body by one who has had his marriage proposal to Lucy rejected. Van Helsing warns Seward not to tell Holmwood of this second transfusion, as it may 'enjealous him' (p. 128). Another transfusion is from Morris, who also had his proposal rejected, and another from Van Helsing. With these transfusions completed, there is a curious transformation in Lucy. Although now infected by the Count's blood, nevertheless with the blood of Holmwood, Seward and Morris in her, Lucy has fulfilled her desire for promiscuity. She had previously told Mina about her three proposals, 'Why can't they let a girl marry three men, or as many as want her ... But this is heresy, and I must not say it' (p. 70). Lucy's death and subsequent transformation into the 'Bloofar Lady' grants her a potential promiscuity because now her 'purity' has changed 'to voluptuous wantonness' (p. 211). But as a vampire, Lucy's unhealthy desire is not overtly sexually expressed, but rather becomes an image of inverted maternal instinct. As the Bloofar Lady she reverses the role of suckling between mother and child.[6] It is Mina who possesses this healthy maternity, one which is defined as an inner power; she writes, 'We women have something of the mother in us that makes us rise above smaller matters when the mother-spirit is invoked' (p. 230).

Lucy is restored to the bourgeois symbolic order through a phallic staking which graphically emphasises her status as a sexualized object. She had 'seemed like a nightmare of Lucy as she lay there, the pointed teeth, the bloodstained, voluptuous mouth – which it made one shudder to see – the whole carnal and unspiritual appearance, seeming like a devilish mockery of Lucy's sweet purity' (p. 214). On a previous visit to Lucy's tomb, Seward describes how from Van Helsing's candle 'the sperm dropped' (p. 197) on to Lucy's coffin. When it comes to the staking of Lucy's body, the task is passed to Holmwood, because it would be by 'the hand of him who loved her best' (p. 215). Inevitably Lucy's staking is described in terms of erotic abandonment:

> The Thing in the coffin writhed; and a hideous, blood-curdling screech came from the opened red lips. The body shook and quivered and twisted in wild contortions; the sharp white teeth champed together till the lips were cut and the mouth was smeared with a crimson foam. But Arthur never faltered. He looked like a figure of Thor as his untrembling arm rose and fell, driving deeper and deeper the mercy-bearing stake, whilst the blood from the pierced heart welled and spurted up around it. His face was set, and high duty seemed to shine through it; the sight of it gave us courage, so that our voices seemed to ring through the little vault. (p. 216)

Lucy's 'opened red lips' and frothing mouth echo vaginal orgasm, with Holmwood 'driving deeper and deeper'. Holmwood is cheered on by the group as Lucy's body is violated in such a fashion as to render it healthy. A natural death (of sorts) is privileged here, removing Lucy from suspension between an unnatural life and death; so that she does not represent the absent presence of a dangerous sexuality which is to be found within the bourgeois group in the first place.

The Count's staking is not described in such overtly sexual terms, his body is violated and he turns to dust, but it is his body (or an idea of it) which is the most striking. His body's incorporeal corporality becomes anchored via physiognomical notions of criminality derived from Lombroso.[7] Leonard Wolf, in *Annotated Dracula*, makes the following juxtapositions between Jonathan Harker on the Count and Lombroso on the criminal:

> Harker: 'His (the Count's) face was ... aquiline, with high bridge of the thin nose and peculiarly arched nostrils ...'

Lombroso: '(The Criminal's) nose on the contrary ... is often aquiline like the beak of a bird of prey.'
Harker: 'His eyebrows were very massive, almost meeting over the nose ... '
Lombroso: 'The eyebrows are bushy and tend to meet across the nose.'
Harker: ' ... his ears were pale and at the tops extremely pointed.'
Lombroso: 'with a protuberance on the upper part of the posterior margin ... a relic of the pointed ear ...'.[8]

Mina says to Van Helsing, 'The Count is a criminal and of criminal type. Nordau and Lombroso would so classify him' (p. 342). The Count is declared a criminal by the state of his body; he has criminality inscribed upon his physiognomy and this can be read out. The Count has no body of text but possesses a body which can be read as a text. His sexuality (his symbolics of blood) exists outside textuality; it is present, made readable, as it becomes manifested through others. This sexuality, however, is linked to the transgression of the 'law' of sexuality. Foucault writes, 'the preoccupation with blood and the law has for nearly two centuries haunted the administration of sexuality' (p. 149). The Count's sexuality as desire, its manifestation of a symbolics of blood, is the inarticulate element in this. However, the possibility of its existence makes him readable as it forces the Count into textuality by introducing a reading practice (a theory of physiognomy) which locates him and decodes him.

The Count can thus be read as irredeemably criminal and this is linked not solely to his corrupting sexuality, but to an idea of primitivism. He is described as possessing a child-like brain; Van Helsing says 'This criminal has not full man-brain' (p. 341) and that 'he be not of man-stature as to brain. He is of child-brain in much' (p. 341). According to this model of evolution the bourgeoisie cannot be bested by what historically preceded them. Yet it is the power of the Count, the strength of his brain, which is related to his physical evolution, 'as his body keep strong and grow and thrive, so his brain grow too' (p. 320). It thus becomes necessary to defeat the Count before he becomes fully mature, before he can become 'the father or furtherer of a new order of beings, whose road must lead through Death, not Life' (p. 302). The child must not be permitted to become 'the father' of a 'new order'. His growth must be thwarted, he has to be condemned to the only permitted form of non-textuality, death. The triumph of the group is thus both the valorisation of its sexuality and the means through which this triumph has been assured, the circulation of its texts.

As we have seen, in *Dracula* there is a play of texts and bodies which implies that they are related. I have used Foucault to suggest that the novel constructs conflict between the feudal and the bourgeois. The bourgeoisie has to locate, read and destroy the troublesome sexuality of the Count because it threatens to destroy them. The sensuality of the Count is the unspoken element and this is decoded by linking him to contemporary accounts of criminality.

Dracula, however, can be read in another way. By introducing the sublime into the analysis an alternative reading of the novel is produced, one which unsettles the claims for scientific certainty towards which the novel appears to gesture. The following reading will thus in part reassess the claims I have made so far in my Foucauldian reading of the novel. It also gives testimony to the continuing troubling tendencies associated with the sublime.

The place of writing

In *Dracula* the sublime takes on the status of being a troubling presence, a presence referred to in the specific functions accorded to different types of writing. By exploring how writing is used in the novel we can highlight its peculiar fear of non-linguistic experience, one which reveals the existence of the sublime. Earlier I explored the link between sexuality and textuality; however, the use of textuality is not necessarily an 'even' one in *Dracula* because writing means different things at different times. There are three forms of writing in the novel which I want to briefly explore: they are those which represent self-therapy, those moments when writing seems to obscure the 'action' in the novel and one explicit reference which links writing to economics.

Writing in *Dracula* is the site of knowledge and the site of therapy. This latter is apparent in, for example, Harker's opening journal when he writes 'I turn to my diary for repose. The habit of entering accurately must help to soothe me' (p. 36). Mina later similarly writes 'I am anxious, and it soothes me to express myself here; it is like whispering to one's self and listening at the same time' (p. 71). Later, Jonathan Harker writes 'I must keep writing at every chance, for I dare not stop to think' (p. 289). Writing is therefore a means by which the subject externalises internal anxiety. Anxiety when turned into text becomes distanced from the subject and this is partly due to the social fashion in which writing is deployed throughout the novel. The reason for this is because the written text has implied readers within the novel, so that on a textual level the subject overcomes fears felt in isolation in order to transmit those fears at a communal level (an issue which we focused on in Chapter 4). It is a way of reintegrating the isolated subject into the 'conversation' of the novel.

Writing is also defined as problematic. This is because writing obscures the action. Jonathan Harker's opening text ends with him seemingly locked up in Castle Dracula with no obvious means of escape. He hears the workmen removing the Count's coffins. Harker believes that when the men leave he will be killed by the three female vampires he had erotically encountered earlier. However, instead of Harker taking action he prefers to write about his predicament:

As I write there is in the passage below a sound of many tramping feet and the crash of weights being set down heavily, doubtless the boxes, with their freight of earth. There is a sound of hammering; it is the box being nailed down. Now I can hear the heavy feet tramping along the hall, with many other idle feet coming behind them. (p. 52)

Harker becomes a listener (Harker)/writer, and the reader is never informed of his means of escape. The implication in such a scene is that text is more important than lived 'reality'. This is echoed later in the novel when Dr Seward is informed that Renfield has had a serious accident. This is how he responds to the crisis:

The attendant came bursting into my room and told me that Renfield had somehow met with some accident. He had heard him yell; and when he went to him found him lying on his face on the floor, all covered with blood. I must go at once ... (p. 274)

Seward does not 'go at once', first he writes it down. The implication is that experience has to be textually mediated in order for that experience to become 'truth'. There is thus a fear, expressed in the journalist's account of the arrival of the Demeter, that experience might take 'place more quickly than it takes to write these words' (p. 78). This means that another fear is a temporal one, of actions happening more quickly than they can be expressed. Therefore, what fails to coincide with writing is another threat to the group. It is this anxiety which reveals the presence of an unrepresentable sublimity. As we shall see, the sublime, as it is reworked into the unconscious, becomes the new source of terror for a culture defined by its need for both scientific 'truth' and textual expression.

Earlier I stressed that the link between textuality and sexuality via a *scientia sexualis* was, historically, a bourgeois formation. If *Dracula* works through this formation then it is not surprising to see a link made, overtly, between writing and money. This occurs in Seward's account of Renfield prior to Renfield's fatal 'accident', where money and writing are explicitly linked in a fashion which has echoes with *Robinson Crusoe*. Seward writes of Renfield that:

> He has evidently some deep problem in his mind, for he keeps a little note-book in which he is always jotting down something. Whole pages of it are filled with masses of figures, generally single numbers added up in batches, and then the totals added in batches again, as though he were 'focusing' some account, as the auditors put it. (p. 69)

Seward conflates this idea of money with religion. Writing after the rejection of his marriage proposal to Lucy, he writes of Renfield that:

> He has closed the account most accurately, and to-day began a new record. How many of us begin a new record with each day of our lives? To me it seems only yesterday that my whole life ended with my new hope, and that truly I began a new record. So it will be until the Great Recorder sums me up and closes my ledger account with a balance to profit or loss. (p. 71)

Writing then, is linked to both money and ethics (religion) and due to this connection there appears to exist no space for the sublime, because the sublime implies a dematerialised moment in which the subject is extricated from social relations. However, it is in the other forms of writing that the sublime becomes anxiously expressed. Seward's attempt to define life (and indeed death) through an economic metaphor is a fragile attempt at holding on to a form of certainty which grants the bourgeoisie its economic status. An exploration of this fragility opens up the sublime for our analysis.

The unconscious sublime

So far in this history we have observed how the internalisation of the sublime is matched by a Gothic reworking of that internalisation. In the latter part of the nineteenth century it is in the troublesome function of the unconscious that the problematic workings of the sublime are to be found. This unconsciousness is also associated with a form of the uncanny in that it is characterised by a series of uneasy recognitions: the bourgeois subject finds in vampirism something which is inherent in their own suppressed model of desire. Additionally the return of the dead is one of the defining features of the uncanny and this is referenced in the novel through the 'un-dead' presence of the vampires.

The sublime is a discrete presence in the novel because the unconscious, although identified as *the* place where true identity is to be found, is not explicitly analysed. This is because the novel expels desire through a demonisation of what vampirism effects, without acknowledging what those effects are. *Dracula* is, in part, composed from a range of erotic images none of which are perceived as such by the characters themselves. The novel represents a failure to contain an explicitly sexual sublimity, one which it manages through a curious silence, and it is this discrete sexual sublime which is so intimately linked with the unconscious. What we ultimately find is that the unconscious in *Dracula* resists scientific explorations of it. The novel, as Ken Gelder has pointed out, develops images of the scientist who appears to anticipate Freud but who fails to make the connection between sexuality and the unconscious.[9] This failure to account for the unconscious represents a failure to understand its sublime provenance, and it is for this reason that unconscious states in *Dracula* tend to resemble the plight of the subject when confronted with the sublime. The specifically sexual sublime found in *Dracula* has been characterised by Peter De Bolla in these terms:

> I am thinking here of the evident links that pertain between sublime sensation and the 'rapture' or 'transport' of sexual union. This is not only because the presumed 'bliss' arising from that union is the only physical analogue that approaches the extreme sensation of the sublime. It is also because the discourse on the sublime produces and examines subjectivity in gender-specific terms, thereby signalling its participation within the larger set of discourses determining sexuality for the period.[10]

The idea that a sexual sublime helps us identify something about the periodisation of gender construction parallels readings of *Dracula* which have related it to the *fin-de-siècle*.[11] However an examination of this sexual sublime also enables us to consider how, and why, the unconscious becomes the site where sublime transformations take place. One reason is that it is the unconscious which provides the Count with the means of entry into 'human' subjectivity. Lucy, for example, writes of the Count's visitations:

> I have a dim half-remembrance of long, anxious times of waiting and fearing; darkness in which there was not even the pain of hope to make present distress more poignant; and then long spells of oblivion, and the rising back to life as a diver coming up through a great press of water. (p. 135)

It thus becomes necessary to make conscious the unconscious. A similar sense of anxiety and doubt surrounds Jonathan Harker's opening journal. Mina writes, 'It may be that it is the doubt which haunts him; that when the doubt is removed, no matter which – waking or dreaming – may prove the truth, he will be more satisfied and better able to bear the shock' (p. 181). The truth exists at an unconscious (sublime, or uncanny) level, a 'truth' which has to be verified by text. Arriving at the truth is, however, problematised by the function of the dream because in *Dracula* the dream bridges the conscious/unconscious divide, but in a way which seems to unsettle both. Mina notes on waking:

> I think that it took me an effort and a little time to realise where I was, and that it was Jonathan who was bending over me. My dream was very peculiar, and was almost typical of the way that waking thoughts become merged in, or continued in, dreams. (p. 258)

These blurrings have to be clarified in order for 'truth' to appear and it is Van Helsing who is the chief instigator of a social policy which is introduced to try to impose this clarification. Christopher Craft writes of Van Helsing that

> His largest purpose is to reinscribe the dualities that Dracula would muddle and confuse. Dualities require demarcations, inexorable and ineradicable lines of separation, but Dracula, as a border being who abrogates demarcations, makes such distinctions impossible. He is *Nosferatu*, neither dead nor alive but somehow both, mobile frequenter of the grave and boudoir, easeful communicant of exclusive realms, and as such he toys with the separation of the living and the dead, a distinction critical to physician, lawyer, and priest alike.[12]

What is also implicit in this rejection of mergers and blurrings is a rejection of the sublime. In the Kantian sublime, although no object is necessarily required (the sublime as pure idealism), there does exist the notion that entering into a sublime state is liberating. In this moment the subject's capacity for reason is questioned, but this 'anxiety' on the part of the subject is compensated by an apprehension of a noumenal presence which creates positive feelings of transcendence. In relation to sexuality in *Dracula*, it is significant that when these mergings take place the subject feels lost or erotically abandoned. This leads Seward to wonder, 'Is it possible that love is all subjective, or objective?' (p. 201). It is Van Helsing who tries to impose a model of health in order to clarify what are politically necessary demarcations. It is the separation of the unconscious from the conscious which is important; as Van Helsing tells Seward of Lucy, 'She is dying. It will not be long now. It will be much difference, mark me, whether she dies conscious or in her sleep' (p. 160). It is the unconscious as the site of the sublime which we now need to consider historically.

A thoroughly modern vampire

Peter De Bolla's *The Discourse of the Sublime* helps to open up the novel to an alternative reading.[13] It is his identification of two types of discourse concerning the sublime which enables us to reconsider the relationship between science and desire in Stoker's novel. The important issue here is epistemological authority and the way that the novel, analysed through De Bolla's reading of the sublime, reverses the historical relationship between the feudal Count and the modern bourgeoisie. To understand this we need to explore what De Bolla means by two sublime discourses.

De Bolla differentiates between those accounts which are *on* the sublime and writing which self-consciously creates sublimity and which is therefore *of* the sublime. De Bolla's notion of a discourse *on* the sublime would include a secondary text such as Burke's *Enquiry*, whereas the *of* form is a more literary manifestation of the sublime, such as that to be found in Romanticism or the early Gothic novel. De Bolla's two categories of the sublime, those works *on* the sublime and those *of* the sublime, are reversed in *Dracula* and the paradoxical effect of this is to grant the Count a peculiarly modern status. The reason for this lies in the historical explanation which De Bolla gives for the emergence of these two sublime discourses.[14]

According to De Bolla, in the history of the sublime, discourses *on* the sublime become replaced by discourses *of* the sublime. He charts this development through 'ethics via rhetoric and empirical psychology to political economy' (p. 34), so that 'the discourse on the sublime transforms from an ethico-aesthetic enquiry into a psychology of the individual' (p. 42). De Bolla sees this development as a natural progression, because for the discourse on the sublime:

> once it had begun to describe how an experience is sublime and what caused it, it began to create a discourse which not only explained the effect or demonstrated the mechanism by which it is produced, but also created the experiential possibility for sublime sensations. There is, then, a natural tendency for the discourse on the sublime to produce the conditions necessary for the construction of the discourse of the sublime, a discourse which produces from within itself sublime experience. (p. 12)

We can see that this is represented in *Dracula* in the opposing bourgeois group's attempt to effect a decisive rupture with a past from which they were produced. If the bourgeoisie can be associated with the controlling (putatively scientific) discourse *on* the sublime then it is the Count who can be linked to the *of* form.

De Bolla writes of the discourse of the sublime that, 'it is self-reflexive in the first instance, making reference to itself as discourse in its explanatory procedures rather than to adjacent or prior discourses, objects in the world of human subjectivity' (p. 34). The Count functions in this broadly self-validating fashion and this is also revealed in the way that dependent membership defines the Count's order of vampirism. As he says to the group, 'Your girls that you all love are mine already; and through them you and others shall yet be mine – my creatures, to do my bidding and to be my jackals when I want to feed' (p. 306). The Count represents a world which is beyond bourgeois explanations of apparently 'deviant' behaviour. Rather the attempt to control vampirism through science is largely unsuccessful; what proves to be more useful is an older, paganistic knowledge of folklore. The Count's irreducibility to bourgeois claims for scientific practice is also representative of a sublimity which can only be apprehended (through dreams, through desire) but not understood by empirical analysis. The Count may not literally self-reflect but he is associated with a dangerous spontaneity which marks him out as a peculiarly Romantic figure, one who, paradoxically, illustrates something about an aspect of the modern bourgeois unconscious.

The opposing group function through an apparently objective, absolute knowledge; in reality through a pseudo-scientific knowledge embodied by Van Helsing and Dr Seward. De Bolla writes about the discourse on the sublime in a way which reflects on this: 'The discourse on the sublime places external authority as the control for its analyses and descriptions, as the reference point that authenticates its findings' (p. 34). This, crucially, means that it is possible to read *Dracula* the other way around and, revealingly, it is the Count who initiates reversals. Early on he says to Harker about his proposed trip to England:

> When I go there I shall be all alone, and my friend Harker Jonathan – nay, pardon me, I fall into my country's habit of putting your patronymic first – my friend Jonathan Harker will not be by my side to correct and aid me. (p. 22)

This reverses the cultural order at the level of personal identity. The Count's project is also an attempt to return to the past in order to freeze history by reducing it to a process of endless repetition.

To refer to De Bolla's definition of the discourse *on* the sublime, it is Van Helsing who supplies both an ethical (quasi-Catholic) platform and a pseudo-scientific explanation. Their project thus bears a similarity to what De Bolla sees as characterising the discourse on the sublime, a discourse which is prior to the *of* form:

> The discourse on the sublime, in a move that is becoming familiar in our discussion of early eighteenth-century works on aesthetics, is held in check by a prior and unexamined discourse of ethics thereby defusing its potential power to the sublime, and its mutation into a discourse of the sublime. (pp. 79–80)

In *Dracula* this is worked out at the level of sexuality. It is sexuality, as a displaced form of the sublime, which is 'held in check by a prior and unexamined discourse of ethics'; in doing so, the 'potential power of the sublime', or the troublesome sexuality manifested by the vampire, has only an implicit presence. The Count's apparent 'otherness' then, is a disguised 'sameness'; the Count is linked to the group because he expresses, and exposes, their sexual desires. This means that the Count is an internal rather than an external 'enemy'. This is briefly acknowledged by Van Helsing when he says of the Count that

There have been from the loins of this very one great men and good women, and their graves make sacred the earth where alone this foulness can dwell. For it is not the least of its terrors that this evil thing is rooted deep in all good; in soil barren of holy memories it cannot rest. (p. 241)

Here it is not solely that 'evil' is judged in comparison to what is 'good', but that the two are intimately related. For this reason there is a series of disquieting mergings between 'good' and 'evil' which gloss the relationship between conscious and unconscious states. As Van Helsing says about Lucy, 'In trance she died, and in trance she is Un-Dead, too. So it is that she differ from all other' (p. 201). Lucy has entered into, and is now defined by, a form of the unconscious which is typified by desire. An additional danger is that it is the unconscious which erases social distinctions and this threatens the social (class) identity of the group. It is therefore necessary to overcome egoism and this is apparent in a comment made by Seward concerning Renfield: 'His attitude to me was the same as that to the attendant; in his sublime self-feeling the difference between myself and attendant seemed to him as nothing' (p. 100). In the sublime, social distinctions become obviated; social distinctions which have to be maintained in the struggle against the Count, precisely because he also threatens those social distinctions. It is when Renfield is in a 'sane' mood that these distinctions appear. He subsequently addresses the group as 'You gentlemen, who by nationality, by heredity, or by the possession of natural gifts, are fitted to hold your respective places in the moving world' (p. 244).

The sublime thus not only threatens the sexuality but also the social, class distinctions through which the bourgeoisie institutes its authority. Yet it is the pressure of the sublime which is internally generated and which is located within the psyche. Richard Wasson, writing on the use of science in *Dracula*, comes to the conclusion that:

These themes add up to the idea that technological progress having cut humanity off from the old superstitious, dark knowledge, makes itself increasingly vulnerable to the demonic powers like the vampire, for, having written them off as unreal, civilised man (sic) has no defense against them. Since only doctors of the mind, Seward and Van Helsing, can cope with such monsters the novel carries the implication that demonish forces have been unloosed in the human psyche by technological and political progress.[15]

In this sense the sublime is fully internalised in a way akin to Burke's idea of sublime terror. It also bears a similarity to the potential over-whelming of the subject suggested by Schiller; here:

> The sublime object is of a dual sort. We refer it either to our *power of apprehension* and are defeated in the attempt to form an image of its concept; or we refer it to our *vital power* and view it as a power against which our own dwindles to nothing. (p. 198)[16]

The sublime generates a sense of terror in *Dracula* because it implies a loss of control on the part of the subject.

What is at issue is the attempt to expel desire. The novel, for all its modish referencing to Nordau and Lombroso, fails to explicitly develop a means of expression through which desire can be repre-sented. Rather what we find is a fascination with the corporal marks of degeneracy which is at the expense of an analysis of the unconscious. The failure of science runs through *Dracula*, a failure which gives due testimony to the continuing presence of a sublimity which is encrypted into an unconscious state that science cannot properly decode: ultimately Count Dracula is a metaphysical, not just a phys-ical, threat to the bourgeoisie.

In *Dracula*, the sublime inheres to the subject. If De Bolla's identification of two forms of discourse concerning the sublime is correct then they can be seen as historically reversed in Stoker's novel. The implication is that the discourse of the sublime, which is self-reflexive and self-legislating, has emerged from the externally ratified discourse on the sublime. It means that the Count is produced by what comes after him and, although this unsettles the historical clash between the bourgeois and the feudal, this is a process akin to what Harold Bloom in *The Anxiety of Influence* identifies as 'Apophrades', where: 'the uncanny effect is that the new poem's achievement makes it seem to us, not as though the precursor were writing it, but as though the later poet himself had written the precursor's characteristic work'.[17] This is significant because Bloom uses the idea of Apophrades to suggest the return of the dead. A return which, reading the novel through De Bolla's account of discourses and the sublime, is a neces-sary one because the discourse *on* the sublime 'naturally' produces a discourse *of* the sublime. The sublime has now become, not a redun-dant and superseded metaphysics, but a troubling presence which has to be exorcised from within by 'doctors of the mind' who anticipate the work of Freud and who battle against the living dead.

7
Freud's Uncanny Sublime

Throughout, we have explored how the Gothic provides a critique of both the sublime and the Freudian notion of the unconscious. So far our argument has largely been centred on an analysis of the sublime, but I will now explore how the Gothic critically reconstructs the Freudian subject. First, however, we need to spend some time looking at the profound debt which Freud owes to Kant. My reading of Freud is one which reveals the continuing presence of the sublime within the heart of his putative scientific practice.

My concluding reading of Stevenson's *The Strange Case of Dr Jekyll and Mr Hyde* reveals how the sublime, in the guise of the uncanny, is worked out in fantasy. The argument, as throughout this book, is that it is in the irrational that the sublime appears as an 'excess' in fantasy. Fantasy thus offers an alternative to a philosophical understanding of the sublime and a psychoanalytical account of the uncanny. It is similar to, but critically distanced from both.

The uncanniness of 'The Uncanny'

Freud begins 'The Uncanny' with an analysis of aesthetics: 'when aesthetics is understood to mean not merely the theory of beauty but the theory of the qualities of feeling' (p. 339). Aesthetics does not solely (or 'merely') provide a 'theory of beauty' but is linked to 'the qualities of feeling'. This account of aesthetics is important for us to consider as it places Freud's essay in the same terrain as Kant's reading of the aesthetic and its relationship to the sublime. Freud struggles with the significance of aesthetics, revealing a concern about whether the aesthetic is related to 'feeling' or 'beauty' or both. What we find is that Freud, in an attempt to clarify the terms of his confused account of aesthetics, restates the confusion. He writes that he is concerned with: 'treatises on aesthetics, which in general prefer to concern themselves with what is beautiful, attractive and sublime – that is, with feelings of a positive nature' (p. 339). The aesthetic becomes partly associated with sublimity. In one way this will later make sense in Freud's essay because the sublime, in its guise of the uncanny, maintains its universalising tendencies. However, this idea of positive feelings in the sublime appears to differentiate 'The Uncanny' from Kant's 'Analytic of the Sublime'. As we have seen, for Kant the sublime takes on a negative quality because it dramatises the subject's failure to comprehend the sublime moment, a failure compensated at the level of the supersensible. Also, for Kant, beauty is defined through a process of subjective aesthetic apprehension; it individualises in ways precluded from sublimity.

Freud's formulation of beauty and sublimity is not clearly referenced to 'treatises on aesthetics'. It is not that Freud offers an alternative account of the sublime (from Kant's) but rather a muddled version of it. This becomes clear in Freud's discussion of the subject's feelings. His confused account also appears to offer a negative version of the sublime, because it is associated with 'unpleasure', which is similar to Burke's understanding of sublime terror. Freud writes that: 'It is undoubtedly related to what is frightening – to what arouses dread and horror' (p. 339). As if aware that this is an unsatisfactory account of the 'uncanny', Freud writes of the need to: 'start by translating himself into that state of feeling, by awakening in himself the possibility of experiencing it' (p. 340). In effect he argues for a position which is analogous to that of Poe's detective, Dupin, who can enter into the mind of the 'criminal' through an act of mental projection. What is of interest is that Freud suggests the possibility of purposefully entering a state of uncanniness rather than simply encountering it. As if conscious of this theoretical indecisiveness, Freud switches from constructing a programmatic outline of the uncanny in favour of becoming a more subtle reader of it. He moves from writer to reader in order to search for a textual authority with which to anchor his opening remarks. Paradoxically, in doing so, he discovers an authority in Jentsch whose meandering account of the uncanny is echoed in Freud's muddled opening account of aesthetics, the sublime and the uncanny. He writes that Jentsch relates: 'uncanniness to intellectual uncertainty; so that the uncanny would always, as it were, be something one does not know one's way about in' (p. 341). Freud comments 'that this definition is incomplete' (p. 341), before attempting to explain the uncanny through dictionary definitions.

In his account of the uncanny then, after his problematic description of aesthetics, Freud offers a view of the subject who can enter the required 'state of feeling' which wills the uncanny into being. This conundrum, of the subject who discovers a feeling of uncanniness but who can nevertheless create that feeling from within, is never fully resolved. Moreover, this problematic relationship between the internal and the external is in part manifested in the conflation of his terms *heimlich* and *unheimlich*, a point which I will develop below. What we find is that Freud's discussion of Jentsch's construction of the uncanny echoes Freud's own inchoate position. This regression in Freud's account moves from a definition of theory, to a reading of theory, to a new position which attempts to establish the (for Freud, psychic) etymology of words. This is a movement which is mirrored in how he defines the uncanny, because one of the defining characteristics of the uncanny is repetition. He writes that the uncanny is associated with 'that class of the frightening which leads back to what is known of old and long familiar' (p. 340). This is also echoed in his account of *heimlich* and *unheimlich*, or homely and unhomely, as being 'old and long familiar', and because there is a repetition (the two terms coming, as we shall see, to mean the same thing) there is also a doubling. In this way, Freud's reading practice mirrors what it is attempting to define. We can clearly see this in the conflation of *heimlich* with *unheimlich*; my argument is that here there is a doubling between what Freud sees as characteristic of the uncanny, and the strategies (theoretical, textual, lexicographical) which he employs to account for it. This is not to say that Freud's review of the existing literature on the uncanny means that his repetition of those accounts is uncanny. Rather my suggestion is that Freud's text becomes uncanny because his attempts to define the uncanny begin to collapse in a strangely uncanny way. We can see this in the relationship between *heimlich* and *unheimlich*.

Freud's initial definition of *heimlich* suggests that it is a term split along a culture/nature axis. *Heimlich* is firstly associated with culture; it is: '(a) (Obsolete) belonging to the house or the family, or regarded as so belonging ... the members of the household' (p. 342). It is secondly defined as on the side of nature: '(b) Of animals: tame, companionable to man. As opposed to wild' (p. 342). The second definition refers to a tamed nature, of nature becoming culture; in this way both definitions complement each other because they collapse into each other. The obsolete domesticity apparent in 'the family' is carried over into the taming of animals for domestic purposes (presumably for the family).

Freud then develops a definition of *unheimlich* which relates it to *heimlich*. After a lengthy dictionary account of these terms, he writes that: 'What interests us most in this long extract (from the dictionary) is to find that among its different shades of meaning the word "*heimlich*" exhibits one which is identified with its opposite, "*unheimlich*"' (p. 345). The one meaning is that of secrecy, of what is kept hidden: 'withdrawn from knowledge, unconscious' (p. 346). What is significant in this collapse (or repetition) of *heimlich* with *unheimlich* is the fashion in which the uncanny can only be problematically contained within its referencing. The uncanny has become uncanny because it is neither specifically *heimlich* nor specifically *unheimlich*, but both. In this doubling between *heimlich* and *unheimlich* a repetition of meaning takes place which is precisely what Freud sees as one characteristic of the uncanny in the first place.

This problematic conditions his discussion of Hoffmann's 'The Sandman' where Freud writes explicitly about the double. In Hoffmann's tale:

> we have characters who are to be considered identical because they look alike. This relation is accentuated by mental processes leaping from one of these characters to another – by what we should call telepathy so that the one possesses knowledge, feelings and experience in common with the other. (p. 356)

There is uncanniness here because of repetition; in a way a repetition of the terms of Freud's argument which conflate *heimlich* and *unheimlich*. These terms of reference, homely and unhomely, are later superseded in Freud's account of death as a version (or source) of the uncanny. It is the subject's relation to the idea of death that evokes the double as that which 'was originally an insurance against the destruction of the ego' (p. 356). However, for Freud, once narcissism is overcome, the double takes on a more sinister aspect: 'From having been an assurance of immortality, it becomes the uncanny harbinger of death' (p. 357). This idea of the double, which assures immortality and then promises death, is unstable. In keeping with the way that other forms of doubling have been set up by Freud, they cancel each other out. However, whereas with *heimlich* and *unheimlich* there is a collapse, in the case of the immortal or murderous portent of the double there is a dialectical resolution. Freud writes of the ego's development with the double that:

A special agency is slowly formed there, which is able to stand over against the rest of the ego, which has the function of observing and criticizing the self and of exercising a censorship within the mind, and which we become aware of as our 'conscience'. (p. 357)

The double is now both a stifling and a protective agent in its relationship to the ego. Stifling, because the conscience operates as a censor and so enables Freud to resurrect the terms *heimlich* and *unheimlich* in an account of repression. As if having clarified the collapse between the two terms, he writes that:

we can understand why linguistic usage has extended *das Heimliche* ['homely'] into its opposite, *das Unheimliche*; for this uncanny is in reality nothing new or alien, but something which is familiar and old-established in the mind and which has become alienated from it only through the process of repression. (pp. 363–4)

The two terms are now subsumed under Freud's category of repetition as that which characterises the uncanny. What is not addressed, however, is the fashion in which two linguistic (dictionary) terms structure that which is defined by Freud as non-linguistic. Freud thus evades a debate about how figurative language functions in all of this. Rather the two terms repeat each other because they are in essence the same. The uncanny is now ubiquitous, pervading the very terms employed to describe it. Neil Hertz writes of the absence of an account of figurative language in Freud's essay, that: 'The wishfulness inherent in the model is not simply in its isolating the *forces* of repetition from their representations, but in its seeking to isolate the *question* of repetition from the question of figurative language itself.'[1] For Hertz, what is uncanny is the process of repetition, not what is repeated.

In Freud's account of the uncanny, then, repetition is divorced from figurative language; in a sense it motivates all forms of repetition. What is revealed in this is that it is controlled by an idea of the same. Meaning returns to its site of departure in a way which does not unsettle that meaning (as it does in the account of *heimlich/unheimlich*) but which instead constructs a circularity that excludes any possibility of an 'objective' analysis. Thus potentially everything can get pulled into the uncanny; even, for Freud, psychoanalysis itself: 'Indeed, I should not be surprised to hear that psychoanalysis, which is concerned with laying bare these hidden forces, has itself become uncanny to many people' (p. 366). This is not solely because it lays 'bare ... hidden forces', but implicitly because it is associated with repetition (doubling). As Freud writes: 'These last examples of the uncanny are to be referred to the principle which I have called "omnipotence of thoughts", taking the name from an expression used by one of my patients' (p. 362). This reference to the Rat Man implies a doubling between the analyst and the analysed. As with *heimlich* and *unheimlich*, where the two become confused, what is uncanny is narcissistic repetition. Here the Rat Man's comment captures the essence of neurotic behaviour for the psychoanalyst and in so doing the meta-discourse of psychoanalysis becomes caught up in a movement of infinite regress. Everything can get pulled into the uncanny, so that meaning is seen to reside in a point of origin (birth, the patient's childhood, etymological origins); or as Freud puts it:

> It often happens that neurotic men declare that they feel there is something uncanny about the female genital organs. This *unheimlich* place, however, is the entrance to the former *Heim* (home) of all human beings, to the place where each one of us lived once upon a time and in the beginning. (p. 368)

Here, neurotic men have a problem with origins, with the fairy-tale place where 'once upon a time' 'each of us lived'. In this way meaning becomes associated with the return of an unattainable origin.

So then, what we find in 'The Uncanny' is that there is an initial movement going from an attempt at theorising to an act of reading (Jentsch), followed by an extensive concentration on dictionary definitions. The paradoxical result is that the controlling terms of the uncanny, *heimlich* and *unheimlich*, become uncanny themselves. Freud then interprets Hoffmann's 'The Sandman' as expressive of a castration anxiety; an anxiety mediated through the motif of the double. Freud then discusses the varying significances of the double, seeing it as representing a return of the same (as happens in *heimlich/unheimlich*) and in this way everything becomes potentially uncanny because everything is potentially repeatable. It is in this process that meaning becomes lost because the possibility of an 'outside', allegedly objective, critical discourse is negated, for (as in the example of the Rat Man) it too can be doubled. The only uncanny area not assimilable to repetition is the notion of a point of origin; rather there exists an original creativity which can be strived after, in a Platonic sense, but which cannot be attained.

We now need to link these arguments to Romanticism through a re-exploration of the Kantian subject. What we will find is that the apparent differences between Kant and Freud, the differences between a conception of a unified transcendental subject versus a fragmented psyche are, in fact, disguised similarities.

Kant, Freud, and the subject

David E. Pettigrew in 'The Question of the Relation of Philosophy and Psychoanalysis: the Case of Kant and Freud' sets out three fundamental areas of disparity between Kant and Freud.[2] The first is that whereas Freud is concerned with the possibility of the unconscious, Kant is concerned with how the subject is able to think. The second is that Freud's notion of the unconscious views the mind as informed by various memories and desires; whereas for Kant the mind is essentially blank, or 'without contents' (p. 70). The third difference is that for Freud the psyche is characterised by its strange ruptures and desires, whereas in Kant there are no such divisions because he is reliant upon an idea of unity inherent in transcendental experience.

However, these seemingly disparate positions are ones which Pettigrew replaces with 'three points of probable convergence' (p. 83). These are replies to these three differences. First, Freud sees experience as governed by the unconscious which, for Pettigrew, echoes Kant's notion that the mind possesses an *a priori* structure without which it would not be able to reflect on its own experience of thought. Second, in Freud there is a search for an original unity which is located within the subject. In Kant there is a similar search for unity, which as in Freud's investigation, ironically implies the presence of a now fragmented identity. Pettigrew perceives two movements made towards unity in Kant. The first is in an attempt to discover how it is possible for the subject to 'know the world as we say we know it' (p. 83). Whereas, in the second movement, reason is 'in conflict with itself seeking the *unconditioned unity* of its experience' (p. 83), so that 'The *a priori* ... as *unifying* is at the same a division' (p. 83). Thus the subject is split because it does not necessarily know itself through self-reflexive thought, or as Pettigrew puts it; 'Kant's work *calls* forth the paradox of the subject that knows itself as it appears to itself and not as it is in itself' (p. 83), therefore the transcendental unity of apperception is unconscious. This is also in part a reply to the third disparity between Kant and Freud found in the idea of a subject decentred by neurosis.

It is this third reply which suggests how it is possible to tie in the unconscious with Kant's philosophy. Pettigrew writes that Kant's idea of consciousness is characterised by a fundamental absence, or by an abyssal scene. Here the link with Freud is that: 'The unity is abyssal as the inorganic and quiescent state of death itself. The unconscious, and the drive to unification seem both foundational and inaccessible in a way that is analogous to Kant's ideas of pure reason' (p. 84).

In this way Pettigrew links Kant with Freud without collapsing one into the other. These similarities are important because they make possible a reading of Weiskel's *The Romantic Sublime* which accounts for what Weiskel sees as a structural failure in the negative sublime. We will explore this 'failure', which I touched on in Chapter 1, in greater depth further on.

However, we will now turn to Freud's *The Interpretation of Dreams*.[3] When looking at 'The Uncanny', our argument was that the uncanny became uncanny itself because it could not be contained within its form of referencing. We will now see how *Dreams* restates many of the problematics which can be found in 'The Uncanny'. Such a reworking also means that, to follow Pettigrew, the Kantian subject ghosts *Dreams*.

The interpretation of Freud's *Dreams*

The term homely, or *heimlich*, appears in a flippant fashion in *Dreams* when Freud quotes from a letter to Wilhelm Fliess, dated 12 June 1899. On a visit to Bellevue Freud had the dream which initiated his investigation into dreams. Freud suggests (half-heartedly) that a plaque should be put on the house in Bellevue, which would read:

> In This House, on July 24th, 1895
> the Secret of Dreams was Revealed
> to Dr Sigm. Freud.

> (p. 199)

If it is possible to see the 'home' as a point of origin for Freud, then such a comment takes on greater significance. The precision recorded in this facsimile of a plaque can be read as the record of the birth of *Dreams*. His claim made for hero-status is similar to 'the omnipotence of thoughts' Freud found (or rather had 'revealed' to him) by the Rat Man. Freud also states that the secret of dreams was revealed to him, rather than discovered. In this way the revelation itself takes on uncanny characteristics, and this links to the way dreams operate, at a manifest level, to partially conceal their latent content. In 'The Uncanny', Freud had written of *heimlich*, or home, that: 'on the one hand it means what is familiar and agreeable, and on the other, what is concealed and kept out of sight' (p. 345). Thus at uncanny moments that which has been 'concealed and kept out of sight' is revealed. It is thus not fortuitous that Freud links his initiation into dream interpretation to the place where its inauguration took place. The house is both the source of origin and the point of departure for a de-familiarisation of experience.

After this letter to Fliess there immediately follows another letter to him (6 August 1899) which outlines Freud's intended construction for *Dreams*. He writes that:

> The whole thing is planned on the model of an imaginary walk. First comes the dark wood of the authorities (who cannot see the trees), where there is no clear view and it is easy to go astray. Then there is a cavernous defile through which I lead my readers – my specimen dream with its peculiarities, its details, its indiscretions and its bad jokes – and then, all at once, the high ground and the open prospect and the question: 'which way do you want to go?' (p. 200)

Freud leaves open the possibilities for interpretation in an implicit reference to the way absolute meaning (as absolute regress) is elided in 'The Uncanny'. There the uncanny becomes ubiquitous, collapsing the terms which try to define it. Here Freud abandons the reader at the 'open prospect', with a question rather than an answer. However, for Freud this open question is only possible because he sees dreams as being overdetermined so that no absolute truth can be reached. Freud writes that 'Even if the solution seems satisfactory and without gaps, the possibility always remains that the dream may have yet another meaning. Strictly speaking, then, it is impossible to determine the amount of condensation' (p. 383). This is because 'each of the elements of the dream's content turns out to have been "overdetermined" – to have been represented in the dream-thoughts many times over' (pp. 388–9). Here the uncanny returns (is repeated) because the problem for interpretation is compounded by repetition. So, because the dream's content is 'represented in the dream-thoughts many times over', the attempt to locate meaning becomes problematic. It is a similar repetition-compulsion which characterises the uncanny. This links to Hertz's contention that what is important in the uncanny is not what is repeated, but the act of repetition itself. Freud reaches a similar conclusion with dreams: 'What appears in dreams, we might suppose, is not what is *important* in the dream-thoughts but what occurs in them several times over' (p. 416).

Repetition, as a mode of emphasis, determines what is significant. This means that the dream has now become the site where repetition takes place. It is the site which has to be explored in order to secure meaning. Freud now sees a way in which the dream can be opened up and its meaning exposed through an analogy to reading:

> Yet, in spite of all this ambiguity, it is fair to say that the productions of the dream-work, which, it must be remembered, *are not made with the intention of being understood*, present no greater difficulties to their translators than do the ancient hieroglyphic scripts to those who seek to read them. (p. 457)

Thus the dream can be translated into the type of narrative which appears to ensure the possibility of meaning. This would appear to differ from the abyssal realm in Kant's idea of the perceiving mind. Rather here, for Freud, the subject can be unified through an act of interpretation. However, Freud abandons any sense of a total interpretation of any one dream. This is because of the existence of what he terms the 'dream's navel'; he writes that

> There is often a passage in even the most thoroughly interpreted dream which has to be left obscure; this is because we become aware during the work of interpretation that at that point there is a tangle of dream-thoughts which cannot be unravelled and which moreover adds nothing to our knowledge of the content of the dream. This is the dream's navel, the spot where it reaches down into the unknown. (p. 671)

The irony is that that which resists interpretation is for Freud the least significant. What is important is that it is yet another gesture towards a point of unattainable origin; a return to the umbilical, echoing the point of origin referred to in 'The Uncanny', a point also unavailable for interpretation.

We can see that the similarities between 'The Uncanny' and *Dreams* largely reside in the importance attached to repetition. In both cases it is repetition which is a defining factor. In 'The Uncanny' meaning itself becomes problematic because a return to absolute origins is impossible, and this is restated in *Dreams*. The idea of the home (as that to which one returns) is the site of absence, in the sense that for Freud the 'navel' is a meaningless tangle. However, this idea that the navel 'adds nothing to our knowledge of the content of the dream' revises his earlier view on its significance, where he had written that 'There is at least one spot in every dream at which it is unplumbable – a navel, as it were, that is its point of contact with the unknown' (p. 186), which does not necessarily make it meaningless. The unknown by definition resists interpretation and this is similar to Kant's abyssal construction of the mind.

One irony in all of this is the claim that Freud makes for the scientific significance of psychoanalysis in its search after origins: 'psycho-analysis may claim a high place among the sciences which are concerned with the reconstruction of the earliest and most obscure periods of the beginnings of the human race' (p. 700). Psychoanalysis thus has a privileged position in analysing the past because it identifies the transhistorical psyche in a, paradoxically, archaeological fashion. In this way it claims that it can excavate the past from the position of the present. The possession of an original meaning thus becomes possible; in this way the past is preserved, but this view can itself become an example of the uncanny because it partially fulfils the description of a return of the dead with which it is associated. Freud writes of the uncanny that 'Many people experience the feeling in the highest degree in relation to death and dead bodies, to the return of the dead, and to spirits and ghosts' (p. 364). This also occurs when such (imaginary) feelings are made manifest, 'when something that we have hitherto regarded as imaginary appears before us in reality, or when a symbol takes over the full functions of the thing it symbolizes, and so on' (p. 367).

In *Dreams* the notion that the past lives on in the present would be a possible source of the uncanny if this were literally (corporally) true, as it is, for example, in both *Frankenstein* and *Dracula*. However, the uncanny as a secret come to light, the uncanniness of psychoanalytic practice, pervades *Dreams* as an account of invisible laws on which Freud writes that: 'The most that we can conclude from this is that it proves that *the most complicated achievements of thought are possible without the assistance of consciousness*' (p. 751).

What we have seen is that the uncanny is a pervasive (uncanny) presence in *Dreams*, the term becoming associated with a possible access to primary, or absolute, meaning. The uncanny is analogous to what Freud terms the dream's navel; it is that which appears to resist interpretation. A point of origin is psychically reclaimable in the unconscious, but if manifested would become uncanny. These ideas of meaning, origins and the nature of the unconscious enable us to return to Weiskel's *The Romantic Sublime*.

Weiskel's sublime

Weiskel regards the relationship which the poet has to poetic legacy as, following Harold Bloom, an Oedipal one.[4] This is expressed by the poet through his/her handling of the sublime. Weiskel writes that:

> The poet is uniquely vulnerable to the hypsos of past masters, but his counteroffensive of identification or mimesis can make the power of hypsos his own. In its Romantic transposition, this identification exhibits the precise features of an oedipal crisis, as we shall see. These shifting confrontations, the turns and reversals of literary power, are what seem to be the timeless elements of the sublime, requiring only some kind of auxiliary idealism for their local support. (p. 5)

Weiskel is as much concerned with origins as Freud; it is the poet's identification with, and subsequent movement from (or within), a literary tradition which controls the trajectory of poetic discourse. The sublime is the emotional register of this process, becoming a focal point for both anxiety and liberation. It also defends 'against the fact of origins' (p. 10) and indicates 'the obscure guilt which is the surest signal of those origins' (p. 10). The sublime therefore is situated at the point where psychoanalytic practice can intervene because the sublime functions as a psychology: 'the sublime comes to be associated both with the failure of clear thought and with matters beyond determinate perception. It is not a radical alternative but a necessary complement to a psychology that stressed its limits' (p. 17).

The sublime is thus as much controlled by the function of invisible laws as the Freudian unconscious is. There is here a movement which internalises the observing eye in the sublime, and this is staged in the collapse of external, or outward-looking, modes of perception,[5] so that 'Any excess on the part of the object cancels the representational efficacy of the mind which can only turn, for its new object, to itself' (p. 24). Weiskel explores this in greater depth when discussing Kant, where he writes that: 'the sublime moment offers to reason an occasion for self-recognition' (p. 42). This is problematised, however, because in Kant's theory of the mind there is an alternative *a priori* basis for the mind, one which we looked at earlier when discussing Pettigrew. In Pettigrew's reading of Kant, reason is problematised when it attempts to think through its status as an '*unconditioned unity* of ... experience'. Reason is in conflict with itself because it is not possible for reason to think through its function as reason. There thus exists a logical division between how reason works, and how its processes are to be understood. So what the sublime offers to the Kantian realm of reason exists in the collapse of perceptual understanding when the presence of an unattainable noumenal realm is intimated. However, Weiskel takes the view that this moment of crisis for the Kantian subject suggests repression because the imagination is overwhelmed (repressed) by the presence of reason. It would, however, logically seem that the sublime liberates because phenomenal restrictions are elided and entry into a higher realm is made possible. Ironically this is implied in Weiskel's discussion of a division between imagination and reason, a division which suggests the presence of alienation but which also suggests that a dialectical resolution is possible.

So then, unity could be reached through the synthesis of imagination with reason. However, the relationship between the two is not a balanced one, as it resists a Freudian psychic economy, because greater importance is placed by Kant on one term over the other. The subject does not feel alienated (internally) in the collapse of the imagination but is rather granted a privileged position in relation to the noumenal. Thus a dialectical construction between phenomenal/noumenal is problematic because they are different from, rather than radically opposed to, each other.

As we saw in Chapter 1, it is in Weiskel's account of the negative sublime that he discusses alienation. Here it is the case that:

> The negative sublime apparently exhibits some features of a response to superego anxiety, for in the suddenness of the sublime moment the conscious ego rejects its attachment to sensible objects and turns rather fearfully toward an ideal of totality and power which it participates or internalizes. (p. 83)

The sublime thus becomes an indicator of Oedipal development. It reveals the way that the poet both identifies with a poetic tradition and affects a repudiation of it. However, Weiskel later comes to view this as problematic when applied to the negative sublime. He concludes that the negative sublime is not constructed in a way which bears relation to an Oedipal drama because, as we saw, there is only a structural similarity between the two.

Freud's central arguments can be brought into a discussion of the sublime because the Kantian phenomenal/noumenal is represented in terms of a conscious/unconscious doubling. However, as implied in the Kantian model, this is a unity which is not dialectically resolved. The unconscious only becomes discerned via its mediation through consciousness, meaning that the unconscious becomes displayed in an already partially censored form. It is as a result of this that Weiskel's line of argument fails. It is not because of a 'mere' structural play on the Oedipus complex, but because the functions of the sublime are analogous to the relationship between the conscious and the unconscious and as such they are too close to Freudian practice to be easily explored by it. There is thus a strange, uncanny doubling between Kant and Freud. This is replicated in Weiskel's argument about alienation where 'dualism is legitimated and intensified' because 'the sublime splits consciousness into alienated halves' (p. 48). However, such a doubling implies the uncanny because it is dependent upon the terms of strangeness, secrecy and the eventual disclosure of the hidden which characterise it; an idea which, as suggested earlier, is carried over into *Dreams*. Thus the negative sublime does not reveal Oedipal anxiety, but rather dramatises the relationship between conscious/unconscious as a displaced version of phenomenal/noumenal. The Romantic sublime as it is formulated by Kant therefore has ramifications for a Freudian investigation of it, and this is partly due to the way that the sublime represents a nascent form of the uncanny. This is apparent, for example, in the first part of *The Critique of Judgement*, where Kant discusses the mind in terms of the inner, mental possibilities of the subject. This is because:

> on account of this inner possibility in the Subject, and on account of the external possibility of a nature harmonizing therewith, it finds a reference in itself to something in the Subject itself and outside it, and which is not nature, nor yet freedom, but still is connected with the ground of the latter, i.e. the supersensible – a something in which the theoretical faculty gets bound up into unity with the practical in an intimate and obscure manner. (p. 224)

What is uncanny here is the subject's relationship to the supersensible. Like the sublime it is a 'something' which is 'obscure' and yet 'intimate', it is 'not nature, nor yet freedom'; it is a precursor of the unconscious because it offers a potentially attainable unity.

We will explore how these themes of conscious and unconscious, meaning and interpretation, and phenomenal and noumenal relate to *The Psychopathology of Everyday Life*.[6] In *Psychopathology* Freud extends his account of the conscious/unconscious relationship in order to embrace non-neurotic behaviour, or rather he sees in the 'everyday' the 'abnormal' processes of a seemingly functional psychology.

The Psychopathology of Everyday Life

Earlier we saw how in 'The Uncanny' and *Dreams* Freud makes reference to an original moment which secures absolute meaning. In 'The Uncanny' it is through an unattainable return to the womb, whereas in *Dreams* it is via the possibility of a trans-historical notion of the unconscious. In *Psychopathology* it is an investigation of childhood neurosis which offers this return; although one which is problematised by the existence of what Freud terms 'screen memories'. In this:

> One is ... forced by various considerations to suspect that in so-called earliest childhood memories we possess not the genuine memory-trace but a later revision of it, a revision which may have been subjected to the influences of a variety of later psychical forces. Thus the 'childhood memories' of individuals come in general to acquire the significance of 'screen memories' and in doing so offer a remarkable analogy with the childhood memories that a nation preserves in its store of legends and myths. (p. 88)

Freud makes a leap towards the end of this passage when he refers to folklore as the receptacle of a culture's 'childhood memories'. Why it is that Freud equates screen memories to folklore seems to be unclear. However, in this account of the subject, the return to a point of origin, of childhood, represents a difficulty for Freud which seems less problematic in his final comments concerning the 'nation'. This can be clarified by a return to 'The Uncanny' where Freud discusses the status of the literary text for psychoanalytic discourse. As we saw in our discussion in Chapter 3, literature becomes a version of the uncanny because it has the potential to represent a fictive excess. It offers a possible return to origins which is represented by folklore in *Psychopathology*, and which is uncanny because, 'an uncanny effect is often and easily produced when the distinction between the imagination and reality is effaced' (p. 367). Thus Freud's account of folklore becomes clear; it offers a fictive understanding of a point of origin which is problematic for the subject due to the interference of screen memories. However, as it is fiction it lacks a certain veracity because it is somehow 'more' than real. This again means that the attempt to negotiate a return to origins leads back to the ubiquitous uncanny. In *Psychopathology* Freud writes that: 'In the field of symptomatic acts, too, psychoanalytic observation must concede priority to imaginative writers' (p. 271). This is partly because Freud regards imaginative writing as a sublimation of drives rather than as a direct (transparent) expression of an inherently sexual urge.

Mary Ann Doane's account of sublimation in *Femmes Fatales* links the sublime to sublimation and so bears relevance to our argument.[7] Doane writes of a separation between the sexual drive manifested through symptomology, and a drive represented by sublimation. She writes that: 'Sublimation ... has as its product the highest manifestations of human culture, that which constitutes, most exactly, the sublime' (p. 249). This is because it is works of the imagination (cultural works) which produce an excess that suggests a sublime presence. Also, Doane notes that sublimation cannot be reversed: 'Within the Freudian schema, "desublimation" is either impossible or extremely difficult; it is as though the "raising," "lifting," or "elevating" effects associated with the etymological roots of sublimation could not be undone' (p. 250). Thus there is no possible return to origins. It is the imaginative (or folklore) text which appears to contain a culture's history, but in its narrative excess it is able to 'transport' the reader into the sublime. However, because it is excessive, it obliterates origins and makes sublimation irreversible. Therefore a point of absolute origin becomes doubly effaced.

This process is also evidenced in the subject's relationship to fantasy. It is precisely in fantasy that the subject loses a sense of subject-hood, because: 'what the most intense fantasy ultimately effects is the loss of the very distinction between subject and object' (p. 253). This is similar to the experience of the Kantian subject. In Kant's schema no object is necessarily present (physically) for a sublime sensation to occur. However, an idea of such an object can result in the collapse of the imagination and so the distinction between the subject and the supersensible becomes blurred. These blurrings between what appear to be mutually exclusive realms also underpin a Freudian account of sublimation and the connection that it has with sexuality. Again, origins are both present and unattainable. Doane writes that: 'while the source or origin of sublimation is sexuality, sublimation is sublimation by virtue of a radical disjunction between the two, a gap which is unbridgeable – the displacement is irreversible' (p. 254). Thus sublimation corresponds to how screen memories function in relation to childhood memories, and this is also apparent in the associations Freud makes in his peculiar account of folklore.

Freud tries to get around this problem of diminishing origins in *Psychopathology* by attempting to reintroduce, from *Dreams*, a notion of transtemporality. He writes that:

> The unconscious is quite timeless. The most important as well as the strangest characteristic of psychical fixation is that all impressions are preserved, not only in the same form in which they were first received, but also in all the forms which they have adopted in their further developments. This is a state of affairs which cannot be illustrated by comparison with another sphere. Theoretically every earlier state of mnemic content could thus be restored to memory again, even if its elements have long ago exchanged all their original for more recent ones. (p. 339)

This is, however, only a theoretical solution to the problem of disruptive screen memories, and it is in the notion of screen memories that sublimation is analogously worked out. It is the idea of a profound perplexity which here links the sublime with the uncanny. Doane, for example, writes of sublimation that:

> Laplanche, Lacan, and Montrelay share a certain nervousness with respect to a concept which emerges in Freud's discourse, which Freud in fact produces, but which remains somehow free-floating, without proper metapsychological grounding, lacking the rigorous systematicity usually associated with Freud's work. (p. 258)

This is because Freud's argument on the uncanny cannot sustain the terms used to describe it; his argument thus replicates, at an analytical level, the terms of his debate. Doane sees this as an example of psychoanalysis searching for a ground of meaning which is outside its own field, one which is perhaps more properly identifiable with the sublime. She writes on Freud's account of sublimation:

> What are the terms which Freud is attempting so desperately to keep apart, insuring that one is not contaminated by the other? It

would seem that this is psychoanalysis striving to think its own
limits, to situate something beyond the grasp of its own methodology. (pp. 258–9)

What is beyond its grasp, what I am stressing here, is the Romantic
sublime, and it is for this reason that Weiskel's account of the synthetic negative sublime becomes undermined. This is because the
sublime in Freud is that which, necessarily, has yet to be fully defined.
Weiskel appropriates the wrong Freudian model (the Oedipus complex)
to apply to the sublime, because it is the sublime itself which functions
as a spectral presence in Freud's texts.

Doane's conclusion is that Freud wished to grant the sublime a free
space so that he could grant culture (or a 'high' version of it) a
privileged position. She writes that

> What Freud experienced and attempted to deny was a certain histor-
> ical assault on the sublime. Aesthetics and aesthetic activity held an
> important place for Freud, sometimes a quasi-sacred one. This
> inevitably motivated his constantly failing attempt to safeguard an
> area of culture from his own interpretive psychoanalytic techniques,
> in particular, symptomatic reading. (pp. 265–6)

However, I take issue with Doane's reading of the aesthetic object.
What we can see is that a special place is accorded to literature by
Freud, not because of its aesthetic status, but because of what goes on
within it. When in 'The Uncanny', for example, Freud interprets
Hoffmann's 'The Sandman', he does not discuss Hoffmann's text in
terms of aesthetic accomplishment, but instead sees it as representing a
particular neurosis, the castration complex, which he links to the
uncanny through the tale's doubling of characters. For Freud, the literary text represents the reality of psychic life in symbolic terms
(although literature also retains a dimension which transcends reality).
In this way the literary is an example of the uncanny because it 'realis-
tically' creates the imaginary. It offers a possible return to origins
which screen memories camouflage. Therefore, in relation to sublimation, Freud's valorisation of the cultural (or fictional) is not couched
in terms linking it to aesthetic contemplation, but is rather the site
where the uncanny (as the sublime) is deployed. It becomes the space
beyond which psychoanalysis cannot progress. It is similar to Freud's
inability to explain one of the mechanisms he sees as governing slips
of the tongue, and which also implies the inherent sociability of

sublime apprehension. Freud writes that: 'Now slips of the tongue are in a high degree contagious, like the forgetting of names ... I cannot suggest any reason for this psychical contagiousness' (p. 104). This follows an invisible rule concerning contagion, but because of its invisibility it is only possible to describe it rather than account for it.

One of the central premises of our argument is that in the Gothic there is a construction of a parallel version of the Romantic sublime. It is thus not fortuitous that Freud discusses the uncanny in relation to a Gothic text. The Gothic version of the sublime is a parallel one because in its use of 'fantastic' elements it offers a potentially excessive form of it. To see how the ideas in this chapter are rehearsed in the Gothic we will explore how they apply to Stevenson's *Jekyll and Hyde*. I have selected this text rather than 'The Sandman' in order to show how widely the sublime has entered the Gothic discourse. In particular, we need to attend to how the uncanny is worked through in Stevenson's novella with specific reference to how its deployment of the double suggests the terms of Freud's argument.

Jekyll and Hyde

Towards the end of Stevenson's tale, in the account attributed to Henry Jekyll, the idea of the double is explicitly discussed. Here the separation between 'good' and 'evil', a separation explicitly organised by the foregoing action, is collapsed. Jekyll expresses the view that:

> Though so profound a double-dealer, I was in no sense a hypocrite: both sides of me were in dead earnest; I was no more myself when I laid aside restraint and plunged in shame, than when I laboured, in the eye of day, at the furtherance of knowledge or the relief of sorrow and suffering.[8]

Here the notion of public morals is conflated with an idea of a philosophy of morals as a 'science' of the subject. In effect the origin of 'ethical' behaviour is external and abstract, whereas the subject's own behaviour is personal and innate. However, this idea of the innate is not biologically conditioned but is associated with consciousness and desire. It is thus similar to Freud's construction of the relationship between consciousness and unconsciousness in which both become dependent upon each other, in *Psychopathology*, through the mediating function of parapraxis. In a similar way, Hyde is screened through Jekyll because it is in the latter's account that Hyde is discussed. This is, however, problematic because of the ambiguity about authorial control in Jekyll's narrative, a point which we will explore later.

We can see that in the above quotation the subject bears a similarity to how Freud collapses the controlling references of *heimlich* and *unheimlich* in 'The Uncanny'. The view ascribed to Jekyll is that:

> I learned to recognise the thorough and primitive duality of man; I saw that, of the two natures that contended in the field of my consciousness, even if I could rightly be said to be either, it was only because I was radically both ... (p. 82)

In this way Jekyll/Hyde is the authentic site of subjectivity, and this authority is guaranteed through self-knowledge, by a 'Jekyll (who was a composite) now' (p. 89). Thus the two elements which constitute the subject, Jekyll and Hyde, although the domain of some 'authenticity', are unable to contain that authenticity. This is because the subject is either Jekyll or Hyde at any one time and can never be both. In this way it dramatises Freud's attempt to separate *heimlich* from *unheimlich*. The terms of Freud's debate collapse in a way which echoes with the conflation between Jekyll/Hyde, both containing aspects of the same self, the one homely, the other sinister. The unity of the subject is not guaranteed, as the construction of Hyde is built on a misconception concerning the accessibility of the self. Jekyll sees this as his inability (or the inability of contemporary 'science') to go beyond a mere doubling:

> man is not truly one, but truly two. I say two, because the state of my own knowledge does not pass beyond that point. Others will follow, others will outstrip me on the same lines; and I hazard the guess that man will be ultimately known for a mere polity of multifarious, incongruous and independent denizens. (p. 82)

This is both a mandate for a future science and an admission of failure. As suggested earlier, Jekyll/Hyde bears a similarity to Freud's *heimlich–unheimlich*. The Jekyll/Hyde matrix cannot contain subjectivity in the same way that *heimlich–unheimlich* cannot contain the uncanny or the sublime. Thus Jekyll/Hyde cannot be properly separated because the two terms are essential for the understanding of each other.

It is the idea of separation which leads Jekyll into a discussion of origins, in a manner similar to Freud's search for an originating moment. Jekyll writes of 'Good' and 'Evil' that 'It was the curse of mankind that these incongruous faggots were thus bound together – that in the organised womb of consciousness these polar twins should be continuously struggling. How, then, were they dissociated?' (p. 82). This question is left unanswered because those origins are unattainable. This notion of origins is translated into the appearance of Hyde who represents, the story suggests, a primitive (original) desire. However, because origins are unattainable his presence is problematic. He is both physically present and figuratively absent and this is a view which inheres to all the characters who encounter him. In the beginning of the tale Enfield attempts to describe Hyde to Utterson:

> He is not easy to describe. There is something wrong with his appearance; something displeasing, something downright detestable. I never saw a man I so disliked, and yet I scarce know why. He must be deformed somewhere; he gives a strong feeling of deformity, although I couldn't specify the point. He's an extraordinary-looking man, and yet I really can name nothing out of the way. No sir; I can make no hand of it; I can't describe him. And it's not want of memory; for I declare that I can see him this moment. (p. 34)

Hyde remains hidden because the vocabulary does not exist to describe him. This is something made explicit in Utterson's description of Hyde:

> he spoke with a husky, whispering and somewhat broken voice, – all these were points against him; but not all of these together could explain the hitherto unknown disgust, loathing and fear with which Mr Utterson regarded him. 'There must be something else,' said the perplexed gentleman. 'There *is* something more, if I could find a name for it.' (p. 40)

In *Jekyll and Hyde* subjectivity is fragmented and this relates to Freud's idea of the subject split upon a conscious/unconscious divide. The tale replicates the terms *heimlich* and *unheimlich* and collapses them into the Jekyll/Hyde relationship. It is Hyde who poses a problem for representation because he represents in part an unattainable, primitive origin. This is also echoed in 'The Uncanny', *Dreams* and *Psychopathology*. Again, because Hyde exemplifies the existence of primitive origins he poses a problem for representation because origins have become effaced.

A description of the social space between Jekyll and Hyde in part accounts for the revulsion in which Hyde is held. Hyde becomes associated with a specific fear of the working class. In the tale, high culture is represented by 'Henry Jekyll, M.D., D.C.L., LL.D., F.R.S., &c' (p. 35), whereas Hyde occupies a social position where there are: 'many ragged children huddled in the doorways, and many ragged women of different nationalities passing out, key in hand, to have a morning glass' (p. 48). Hyde thus represents the invisibility of working-class culture, a culture which is effaced by a middle-class discourse which seeks to banish such experiences from all social practice. The area of Soho occupied by Hyde appears to Utterson to be 'like a district of some city in a nightmare' (p. 48).

Hyde is therefore separated from Jekyll along a social scale as well as a 'moral' one. Hyde thus in part becomes an object of fear because his very existence suggests that the class hierarchy can be collapsed because it is reversible. However, this is not the only distance between Jekyll and Hyde, there is also a 'moral' one which becomes conflated with physicality. This other gap is dramatised in the tale through the way that Hyde is seen as internally generated, so that: 'Jekyll had more than a father's interest; Hyde had more than a son's indifference' (p. 89). In this way the uneven relationship between the two is physically dramatised: 'The evil side of my nature, to which I had now transferred the stamping efficacy, was less robust and less developed than the good which I had just deposed' (p. 84). There is thus a fear of degeneration which David Punter sees as characterising *Jekyll and Hyde* as well as *The Island of Dr Moreau*, *The Picture of Dorian Gray* and *Dracula*,[9] a fear that the evolutionary model (and the class hierarchy) could be reversed, as witnessed by Hyde's 'ape-like fury' (p. 47) when he murders Sir Danvers Carew and when Jekyll laments Hyde's 'ape-like tricks that he would play me' (p. 96). However, as in our discussion on Kant concerning the phenomenal and the noumenal, there is no dialectical resolution between Jekyll and Hyde. This is because one side is 'stronger' than the other and because they are doubled.

At one level they are defined by mutual dependence rather than antagonism. Although antagonisms between the two do later emerge, these are positioned in the tale as 'natural' antagonisms, as being warring factions within the self. There is, however, a suggestion that the relation of Jekyll to Hyde is arbitrary because it depends upon a chemical contingent, and therefore the relationship between the two is not necessarily a natural one. This problematises Jekyll's idea of the innate existence of Hyde. This becomes clear in Jekyll's account of his experimentation. He writes of his first transformation that:

> That night I had come to the fatal cross roads. Had I approached my discovery in a more noble spirit, had I risked the experiment while under the empire of generous or pious aspirations, all must have been otherwise, and from these agonies of death and birth I had come forth an angel instead of a fiend. The drug had no discriminating action; it was neither diabolical nor divine. ... (p. 85)

Thus, subjectivity in the Jekyll/Hyde relationship is unstable, and this is caused by a chemical process which 'controlled and shook the very fortress of identity' (p. 83). Hyde is socially other to Jekyll, and yet he is the same because he represents Jekyll's tabooed desires. The subject is split and this is dramatised both socially and physically. The psychic unification which Jekyll seeks through Hyde is thus necessarily disrupted. Hyde appears as the uncanny, which is similar to what Freud saw as the imaginary becoming real. Also, because Hyde is uncanny he takes on characteristics which inhere to the sublime. His appearance causes a reaction which confounds the imagination's ability to represent him, and this is true for all subjects who encounter Hyde. But there does exist the possibility that Hyde can be recuperated for reason; what is required is a 'name for it'. Hyde has also been produced through a scientific discourse which links the tale to *Frankenstein*. Jekyll's experiments take place in what was an anatomy theatre but 'his own tastes being chemical rather than anatomical' (p. 51), he has turned it into a laboratory; the tale thus obliquely gestures towards, and affects a break with, Frankenstein's own production of the double. Hyde is also an uncanny element to the extent that he exemplifies an originating moment of pre-social (located in the tale as un-social) desire, which accounts for 'the odd, subjective disturbance caused by his neighbourhood' (p. 77). Jekyll perceives a psychic origin in Hyde, but only in terms of an inadequate duality and it is because this duality is an inadequate one that it becomes precarious. It is because identity is neither Jekyll nor Hyde but both, that identity is made unstable and this is reflected in Jekyll's document; there Jekyll loses a sense of an 'I' which is controlling the narrative, so that he writes about himself in the third person. As in, for example, 'Jekyll was now my city of refuge' (pp. 91–2), and 'The powers of Hyde seemed to have grown with the sickliness of Jekyll' (p. 95). It is through writing that Jekyll attempts to maintain his identity because: 'I remembered that of my original character, one part remained to me: I could write my own hand' (p. 93). However this is an inadequate anchor for identity because the 'hand' of Jekyll is also that of Hyde. Jekyll writes of Hyde's 'ape-like tricks that he would play me, scrawling in my own hand blasphemies on the pages of my books, burning the letters and destroying the portrait of my father' (p. 96). Here Hyde again effaces the idea of origins by destroying the portrait of Jekyll's father. This is because Hyde defines the identity of Jekyll and not family ties. Therefore, although identity is controlled by the referencing between Jekyll and Hyde it is not contained within it. This is made explicit both in Jekyll's use of third-person narration and in the final struggle between Jekyll and Hyde.

The death of Jekyll/Hyde occurs in secret; it is a part of the hidden of both Hyde and the uncanny, so that it remains unclear whether Jekyll has killed Hyde or Hyde killed Jekyll. When Utterson finds the body (of Hyde) he 'knew that he was looking on the body of a self-destroyer' (p. 70). But at this point because identity has become confused it is ambiguous which side of Jekyll/Hyde was responsible. Jekyll's account finishes with the equally ambiguous: 'Here, then, as I lay down the pen, and proceed to seal up my confession, I bring the life of that unhappy Henry Jekyll to an end' (p. 97), which is a comment which could have been made by Hyde. The story thus resists a closed reading by suggesting the impossibility of a full interpretation: thus the uncanny is maintained throughout.

Jekyll and Hyde works through many of the features which characterise both the Romantic sublime and Freud's idea of the uncanny. The sublime functions in Stevenson's novella to confound understanding. Hyde has a precarious status as an absent presence. He is perceived as both part of humanity and as something excessive, as in part inhuman(e). In a Kantian sense this failure to represent Hyde figuratively is compensated by an idea of reason furnished by Jekyll's philosophy of the subject and by the pseudo-scientific discourse which has produced him. Jekyll has attempted to construct a subject who can expand the function of the self because he regarded the subject as non-unified, and therefore unconstrained by the pressures of some undefined bourgeois ideology. However, this formulation of the subject is inadequate for Jekyll, because it only admits of a duality which reflects the state of modern science.

Thus the attempt to anchor Hyde takes place via a theorising of the subject and through a valorisation of scientific procedure. It is in this way that a Kantian idea of reason becomes evoked. This is because neither Jekyll's philosophy nor his science can effectively anchor the subjectivity of Hyde, so that an idea of reason rather than its attainment is implied. Hyde, however, does not solely take on the guise of the sublime, he also becomes representative of the uncanny. This is apparent in the use of doubling within Stevenson's tale. In 'The Uncanny', Freud had written of the double that 'From having been an assurance of immortality, it becomes the uncanny harbinger of death' (p. 357). Later Freud anecdotally discusses an uncanny apprehension of the double when he recounts how he caught sight of, but failed to recognise, himself in a mirror: 'I can still recollect that I thoroughly disliked his appearance' (p. 371). Hyde is similarly uncanny for Jekyll because he fails at certain points to fully recognise himself in Hyde: 'Henry Jekyll stood at times aghast before the acts of Edward Hyde' (p. 87). Hyde also operates as an uncanny presence for the other characters by appearing as a primitive element within their 'civilised' world. This is not to say that *Jekyll and Hyde* either anticipates Freud in any explicit way, nor to suggest that the tale is unproblematically assimilable to Freud's theory. It offers a parallel version of both the Romantic sublime and the uncanny but cannot be collapsed into either. Rather it is the fantastic excesses of the tale which express similar concerns, but in an imaginary form. Also, in the sublime and the uncanny an idea of the subject is set up which is experiential whereas in the Gothic the subject is handled in 'irrational' or impossible ways. In this way it offers an alternative understanding of the sublime and the uncanny by exposing their irrationality. This is particularly significant in relation to the uncanny's function as a version of the sublime. Stevenson's story highlights the problem of anchoring identity within a split form of referencing, and this can be read back into the uncanny in order to reveal how such a problematic (re)occurs.

Two basic conclusions can be drawn from these arguments. First, that there exists a similarity between Kant and Freud and that this is revealed by the presence of the sublime in the uncanny. Both the sublime and the uncanny represent the potential sites where interpretation collapses. In Freud there is a pervasive sense of the uncanny which both defines an idea of an unattainable origin, and a formulation of the double. Second, in *Jekyll and Hyde* a similar idea of the double is entertained, and the tale's representation of the irrational can be read back into Freud. Such a reading would reveal where, and how, the controlling registers of the uncanny are prone to becoming uncanny themselves because in Stevenson's novella the loss of control is characterised by this creeping 'I'. In this way Stevenson's tale dramatises the transmutation of the sublime into the uncanny, but in such a manner that the irrational, and arbitrary, aspects of the uncanny are made explicit.

Afterword

Implicit in this study of the Gothic sublime has been a reconsideration of the relationship of the Romantics to the Victorians. Such periods of literary history are inevitably sites of contestation, but it is usual to see these two periods as possessing distinct characteristics. It is unusual to suggest that the sublime still plays a role in our understanding of Victorian culture, but this is principally because of its comparatively discrete presence in the late nineteenth century. That the sublime still retains a significance for the Victorians is, I hope, clear. The transformation of the sublime into the incoherent images associated with the unconscious suggests the presence of a new structure of sublimity in the Victorian era. Gone is a sense of passive reverence before the numinous and in its place we find a more rigorous, quasi-scientific investigation into its perceived sexual provenance. However, the science does not quite seem to work.

In *Dracula* it is a superior knowledge of folklore which ultimately helps the vampire-hunter. The (failed) blood-transfusions inflicted on Lucy Westenra do not work because they are not particularly scientific. Even Van Helsing's use of hypnotism is more a matter of blind faith than the product of analytical science. Henry Jekyll's own chemical experiments are contaminated by a cultural limitation imposed upon subjectivity: the real horror seems to be that Jekyll could, socially, stoop so low. The reason for these scientific shortcomings is because the Gothic does not use science as science, but rather as a trope for a range of issues concerning sublimity, sexuality and epistemology. Mary Shelley uses science in *Frankenstein*, for example, in order to critique Romantic abstractions. It is the failure of Victor's science which provokes his confessional narrative; one which emphasises that communication, and the social bonding which this implies, are more important than any selfish aspirations.

Poe, as we have seen, also uses images of scientific analysis in the figure of Dupin. It is Dupin who, through a complex exploration of cause and effect, solves the mysterious. Poe's tales also dwell on the status and function of reason by placing an emphasis on the presence of a universal psychology which identifies the limits of thought itself. Again, this is not using science as science but rather traces how the analytical possibilities of thought provide a solution to what are social and political ills (such as in, for example, the game of courtly intrigue played out in 'The Purloined Letter'). Additionally, Poe develops a range of Kantian ideas in order to explore how Kant's concept of reason can be modified to explain specifically urban mysteries. Poe's debt to Kant is not confined to a reworking of the sublime. Poe also develops Kantian ideas concerning the efficacy of various, apparently analytical, discourses (including science and mathematics). What unites Poe and Kant is a shared fascination with reason and the structures of thought with which it is associated. It is the possibility of analytical thought which points (historically speaking) towards Freud and which Poe develops into a model of the mind that is adapted from Kant's idea of phenomenal/noumenal realms (as in 'Mesmeric Revelation') and which anticipates Freud's distinction between the conscious and unconscious mind. However, analytical thought for Poe is both related to social and political problems and to the fantastical (such as in Van Kirk's strange half-life) and thus science is used in order to discuss a variety of non-scientific issues.

To some degree, Freud is the culmination of these peculiar pseudo-scientific rationalities. We can see this in how the continuing destabilising tendencies of the sublime inform his analyses. Instead of objectivity we find evasion, confusion and incomplete analyses and it is these moments which represent a failure to account for the sublime. It is these failed readings of sublimity which are to be found, as failures, within the Gothic discourse. Freud comes so close to analysing this discourse in 'The Uncanny' only to shy away from it by developing an alternative investigation of repetition-compulsion, an investigation which, like Poe's man of the crowd, goes nowhere, although like Poe's man it does so with an air of studied purpose. Psychoanalysis does not touch the sublime because to do so requires a self-exploration that it is unable to make. This is caught in Freud's uneasy, horrified but narcissistic moment of delayed self-recognition in 'The Uncanny' when he writes of catching sight of himself in a train-door mirror. It is Weiskel who comes closest to some kind of acknowledgement of the inability to psychoanalyse the sublime, but he too fails to perceive that the sublime continues on into other means and so overlooks how the sublime inheres to Freudian practice.

The sublime is itself a concept which is compromised, specifically by problems of referencing, problems which also help to plot Freud in a continuum which stretches back to Burke. This is because one common thread which runs through accounts of the sublime, its later Freudian variant, and the Gothic discourse which rewrites this history, is language. The failure of language to coherently designate absolutes unravels the claims for certainty made by Longinus, Burke, Kant and latterly Freud. At the heart of this failure lies the essential paradox of a sublime presence which is *meant* to evade representation. The sublime is a fictive structure (although no more so, I believe, than the Freudian model of the unconscious) which marks out the limit of what is representable (in Kant's terms, the thinkable). That both Kant and Freud suggest that there exists something beyond this world of representability acknowledges that rational deductions of the world and the 'lived' experience of it are not always in accord. This is infinitely debatable but it indicates to us that science, at least in its Freudian guise, posits the existence of something which exists beyond its interpretive strategies. That Freud struggles with this is evidenced by the confusions in his essay on the uncanny. Freud searches for the uncanny in a variety of places only to find that it evades his attempts to capture and investigate both the alleged experience itself and its proper provenance. This paradox of the sublime, that it exists beyond conscious thought but requires a scientific scrutiny, is also echoed in the Freudian model of the unconscious.

It is a different notion of the unconscious which I have explored here, one which cannot be reduced to either a psychoanalytical enquiry nor made to conform to an analysis of ideology. If any theorist ghosts this study then it is Foucault, whose model of history (if it can be so schematically identified) emphasises that change is produced through discontinuities and resistances to power. It is this resistance to power which indicates the radicalism of the Gothic discourse in my argument. What we also find is that the Gothic bears relevance to Foucault's plotting of the rise of the human sciences in the nineteenth century. Foucault helpfully explains the epistemic changes which refocused attention on a model of subjectivity which is relevant both to *Frankenstein* and 'The Uncanny'.

Historically we find that the Gothic discourse unwittingly incorporates within itself a remodelled version of the sublime, because it was the sublime which supplied it with its model of terror in the first place.

This is more apparent in some texts than others. *Frankenstein,* for example, is more overtly predicated on discourses of sublimity than *Dracula,* but then this is because the latter retranslates the sublime into a form barely recognisable in Kant's chaste philosophising.

This, of course, is only one particular Gothic history and it is not necessarily hostile to those readings of the Gothic which explore the form's more overt political gestures and affiliations. Such is the complexity of the Gothic discourse that its radical reworking of the idealist tradition is often at odds with its more reactionary representations. *Dracula,* for example, might illustrate the presence of a peculiarly Gothic sexual sublimity, one which tells us something about the limitations of science, but it also makes reactionary points about class, the status of women, gender and allegedly dangerous foreigners. The novel, for example, seems to evidence a specific horror of female (heterosexual) desire. The overtly phallic staking of Lucy provides a corrective to such apparently transgressive desires. This endorsement of the potency of a male culture which celebrates its communality is witnessed in the cheers which accompany Holmwood's violation of Lucy. The novel as a whole seems to celebrate a world of bourgeois professionals who consign feudalism, in the guise of the Count, to the past. At another level, however, the novel is also saying something about the failure of science to comprehend the sublime. The multi-vocal structure of Stoker's novel almost becomes an analogy for the range of disparate political, cultural and historical voices which motivate it. Almost an analogy, because these voices do not, as they do in the novel, work together. That the Gothic sublime can be detached from such political messages reveals to us just how inherent it has become in the Gothic discourse itself. In part this is because the sublime is hidden within the Gothic's modality of the terrifying: Burke and Kant are never far away from the Gothic, although their ideas become rewritten by the Gothic along the way.

Throughout I have accorded a special privilege to the Gothic by arguing that it is a counter-cultural form, and implicitly suggesting that this rebellious tendency transcends any overt political message. I have argued that the Gothic is not necessarily in control of its own image-making; the sublime influences Gothic discourse in a way which is beyond the conscious control of individual writers. What I want to stress is that the Gothic offers us an alternative version of events from that found in more orthodox histories. In this instance I have emphasised how the Gothic provides a critical revision of an idealist tradition of thought. The Gothic is both reliant on this tradition and usurps it.

To this end I have compared a range of writers who are not usually discussed in such close proximity. That I have been able to do so tells us that the sublime, in all its modifications, is present.

I want to finish on a brief summary note concerning psychoanalytical readings of the Gothic. Such psychoanalytical readings have been popular because they perceive something in the Gothic which seems to correspond with certain analytical models. To look at the Gothic like this is to ignore its history. Once we start to explore historically these representations of fragmented subjectivity and tabooed desire a different story emerges. The Gothic self, with all its instabilities and apparent neurosis, is in reality little more than the sublime's instabilities, personified and made flesh but for all that no more available for psychoanalysis than the sublime itself.

Notes

Introduction

1. Angela Leighton, *Shelley and the Sublime* (Cambridge: Cambridge University Press, 1984) p. 18. Also see Rosemary Jackson, *Fantasy: the Literature of Subversion* (London: Methuen, 1981) p. 24. All subsequent references are to this edition, and are given in the text.
2. See for example, Marie Bonaparte's classic Freudian study of Edgar Allan Poe, *The Life and Works of Edgar Allan Poe: a Psycho-Analytic Interpretation* (1933) trans. J. Rodker (London: Imago, 1949). See also Christine Brooke-Rose, *The Rhetoric of the Unreal* (Cambridge: Cambridge University Press, 1981) for an early study which uses Lacanian ideas.
3. Terry Castle, *The Female Thermometer: Eighteenth-Century Culture and the Invention of the Uncanny* (Oxford: Oxford University Press, 1995). All subsequent references are to this edition, and are given in the text.
4. Vijay Mishra, *The Gothic Sublime* (New York: State University of New York Press, 1994). All subsequent references are to this edition, and are given in the text.
5. David B. Morris, 'Gothic Sublimity', *New Literary History* 16, 2 (1985) 299–319, 302. All subsequent references are to this edition, and are given in the text.
6. Clive Bloom, *Reading Poe Reading Freud: the Romantic Imagination in Crisis* (London: Macmillan, 1988) p. 8.

1   The Gothic and the Sublime

1. Sigmund Freud, 'The Uncanny' (1919) in *Art and Literature: Jensen's Gradiva, Leonardo Da Vinci and Other Works*, trans. J. Strachey, ed. A. Dickson (Harmondsworth: Penguin, 1985) pp. 339–76. All subsequent references are to this edition, and are given in the text.
2. See Jackson, *Fantasy: the Literature of Subversion* pp. 49–53. Her arguments concerning the relationship between I/not-I are drawn from Tzvetan Todorov's, *The Fantastic: a Structural Approach to a Literary Genre*, trans. R. Howard (Ithaca: Cornell University Press, 1975).
3. Cassius Longinus, *Longinus on Sublimity* (c.1st 2nd century AD) trans. D.A. Russell (Oxford: Clarendon, 1965) p. 46. All subsequent references are to this edition, and are given in the text.
4. Thomas Weiskel, *The Romantic Sublime: Studies in the Structure and Psychology of Transcendence* (Baltimore: Johns Hopkins University Press, 1986) p. 24. All subsequent references are to this edition, and are given in the text.
5. Edmund Burke, *A Philosophical Enquiry into the Origin of Our Ideas of the Sublime and Beautiful* (1759) ed. James T. Boulton (Oxford: Blackwell, 1987). This is the edition which includes Burke's preamble on Taste which is relevant to our argument and so is the edition referred to. It also includes the 1757 text. All subsequent references are to this edition, and are given in the text.

6. Immanuel Kant, 'The Analytic of the Sublime' in *The Critique of Judgement*, Part 1 (1790) trans. James C. Meredith (Oxford: Clarendon, 1986) pp. 90–203. All subsequent references are to this edition, and are given in the text.

2 *Frankenstein*: Sublimity Reconsidered, Foucault and Kristeva

1. Mary Shelley, *Frankenstein: or the Modern Prometheus* (1831) (Harmondsworth: Penguin, 1985) p. 103. All subsequent references are to this edition, and are given in the text.
2. See Andrew Griffin, 'Fire and Ice in *Frankenstein*' in *The Endurance of Frankenstein*, eds. G. Levine and V.C. Knoepflmacher (London: California University Press, 1979) pp. 49–73, p. 50.
3. Chris Baldick, *In Frankenstein's Shadow: Myth, Monstrosity, and Nineteenth-Century Writing* (Oxford: Clarendon, 1990) p. 45. All subsequent references are to this edition, and are given in the text.
4. Stephen Knapp, *Personification and the Sublime* (Cambridge, Mass.: Harvard University Press, 1985) p. 73.
5. David E. Musselwhite, *Partings Welded Together: Politics and Desire in the Nineteenth-Century English Novel* (London: Methuen, 1987) p. 69. All subsequent references are to this edition, and are given in the text.
6. Michel Foucault, *The Order of Things: an Archaeology of the Human Sciences* (1970) (London: Tavistock, 1982). All subsequent references are to this edition, and are given in the text.
7. See Foucault, *The Order of Things* p. 304.
8. Musselwhite argues that the creature moves from an understanding that language is classifactory to an understanding that the social function of language can be learned, see *Partings Welded Together* pp. 55–6.
9. Mary Poovey, *The Proper Lady and the Woman Writer: Ideology as Style in the Works of Mary Wollstonecraft, Mary Shelley, and Jane Austen* (London: Chicago University Press, 1984) p. 126.
10. Kristeva, *Revolution in Poetic Language*, trans. Margaret Waller (New York: Columbia University Press, 1984) p. 24. All subsequent references are to this edition, and are given in the text.
11. David Ketterer, *Frankenstein's Creation: the Book, the Monster, and Human Reality* (Victoria: Victoria University Press, 1979). All subsequent references are to this edition, and are given in the text.
12. See also Musselwhite, *Partings Welded Together*, p. 64.
13. Kristeva, *Freud and Love: Treatment and its Discontents* in *The Kristeva Reader*, ed. Toril Moi (Oxford: Blackwell, 1987) pp. 238–71, p. 259. All subsequent references are to this edition, and are given in the text.

3 History and the Sublime

1. Walter Jackson Bate, *The Burden of the Past and the English Poet* (London: Chatto & Windus, 1971). All subsequent references are to this edition, and are given in the text.

2. David Hume, 'Of the Rise and the Progress of the Arts and Sciences' in *Of the Standard of Taste and Other Essays*, ed. John W. Lenz (Indiana: Bobbs-Merrill, 1965) pp. 70–94, p. 70.
3. Velleius Paterculus, *The History of Rome* (*c.*AD 4) trans. and intro. Frederich W. Shipley (London: Heinemann, 1890) p. ix.
4. Mary Shelley, 'Valerius: the Reanimated Roman' in *Mary Shelley: Collected Tales and Stories*, ed. Charles E. Robinson (Baltimore: Johns Hopkins University Press, 1976) pp. 332–44. All subsequent references are to this edition, and are given in the text.
5. Marcus Antoninus Aurelius, *The Meditations of the Emperor Marcus Antoninus* (*c.*AD 170) trans. A.S.L. Farquharson (Oxford: Clarendon, 1944) pp. 292–3.
6. Mary Shelley, 'The Mortal Immortal: a Tale' in *Mary Shelley: Collected Tales and Stories*, ed. Charles E. Robinson (Baltimore: Johns Hopkins University Press, 1976) pp. 219–30, p. 220. All subsequent references are to this edition, and are given in the text.
7. See Friedrich Schiller, 'On the Sublime', in *On the Sublime & Naive and Sentimental Poetry* (1793–95), trans. J.A. Elias (New York: Ungar, 1975) pp. 191–212. All subsequent references are to this edition, and are given in the text.
8. This might appear to confuse the chronology but my argument is that Mary Shelley is reassessing an aspect of Romanticism which Kant's philosophy makes possible.

4 Sublime Utterance: Gothic Voyages, Going Public with the Private

1. As we saw in Chapter 1, Burke also attacks the idea of solitude in *The Philosophical Enquiry*, p. 43.
2. Peter Brooks, '"Godlike Science/Unhallowed Arts": Language, Nature and Monstrosity' in *The Endurance of Frankenstein*, eds. G. Levine and V.C. Knoepflmacher (London: California University Press, 1979) pp. 205–20, p. 210.
3. Raymond Williams, 'The Metropolis and the Emergence of Modernism' in *Unreal City: Urban Experience in Modern European Literature and Art*, ed. E. Tims and D. Kelley (Manchester: Manchester University Press, 1985) pp. 13–24, p. 22.
4. Carl Woodring, 'The Mariner's Return' in *Studies in Romanticism*, vol. II, No. 3 (1972) 375–380, 377.
5. Samuel Taylor Coleridge, 'The Rime of the Ancient Mariner' in *The Complete Poetical Works of Samuel Taylor Coleridge* (1912), Vol. 1, ed. E.H. Coleridge (Oxford: Clarendon, 1975) pp. 186–208. All subsequent references are to this edition, and are given in the text.
6. J.G. Lockhart, *Blackwood's Edinburgh Magazine*, VI (October 1819), cited in *Coleridge–The Ancient Mariner and Other Poems*, eds A.R. Jones and W. Tydeman (London: Macmillan, 1973) pp. 76–80, p. 77.
7. Richard Haven, *Patterns of Consciousness: an Essay on Coleridge* (Massachusetts: Massachusetts University Press, 1969) p. 18.

8. Jean-Pierre Mileur, *Vision and Revision: Coleridge's Art of Immanence* (London: California University Press, 1982) p. 68.
9. Katherine M. Wheeler, *The Creative Mind in Coleridge's Poetry* (London: Heinemann, 1981) p. 46. All subsequent references are to this edition, and are given in the text.
10. Jerome J. McGann, *The Beauty of Inflections: Literary Investigations in Historical Method and Theory* (Oxford: Clarendon, 1988) p. 151.
11. Edward E. Bostetter, 'The Nightmare World of "The Ancient Mariner"' in *Coleridge–The Ancient Mariner and Other Poems*, eds. A.R. Jones and W. Tydeman (London: Macmillan, 1973) pp. 184–99, p. 184.
12. David Aers, Jonathan Cook and David Punter, *Romanticism and Ideology: Studies in English Writing* (London: Routledge, 1981) p. 95.
13. Mary Shelley, letter to Maria Gisborne 22 January 1819, in *The Letters of Mary Wollstonecraft Shelley*, Vol. 1, ed. Betty T. Bennett (Baltimore: Johns Hopkins University Press, 1980) pp. 85–6.
14. Karl Kroeber, *Romantic Fantasy and Science Fiction* (London: Yale University Press, 1988) p. 7. All subsequent references are to this edition, and are given in the text.
15. Sigmund Freud, *Jokes and their Relation to the Unconscious* (1905) trans. J. Strachey and A. Richards (Harmondsworth: Penguin, 1991). All subsequent references are to this edition, and are given in the text.
16. Edgar Allan Poe, *The Narrative of A. Gordon Pym* in *The Complete Tales and Poems of Edgar Allan Poe* (Harmondsworth: Penguin, 1982) pp. 748–883. All subsequent references are to this edition, and are given in the text.

5   The Urban Sublime: Kant and Poe

1. For a specific account of the relationship between Poe and Freudian analysis see Clive Bloom's *Reading Poe, Reading Freud: the Romantic Imagination in Crisis* (London: Macmillan, 1988).
2. Additionally we will note that Poe modifies the Kantian sublime rather than provides a trenchant criticism of it as Shelley does with the Burkean sublime in *Frankenstein*.
3. William Wordsworth, *The Prelude: or Growth of a Poet's Mind* (1805) ed. Ernest De Selincourt (Oxford: Oxford University Press, 1984). All subsequent references are to this edition, and are given in the text.
4. Max Byrd, *London Transformed: Images of the City in the Eighteenth Century* (London: Yale University Press, 1978) p. 139.
5. Mary Jacobus, *Romanticism, Writing and Sexual Difference: Essays on 'The Prelude'* (Oxford: Clarendon, 1989) p. 211.
6. Thomas Weiskel, *The Romantic Sublime*.
7. Marquis de Sade, 'Florville and Courval or the Works of Fate' in *The One Hundred and Twenty Days of Sodom and Other Writings* (1788) trans. A. Wainhouse and R. Seaver (London: Arrow, 1991) pp. 133–82. All subsequent references are to this edition, and are given in the text.
8. Ann Radcliffe, *The Italian, or The Confessional of the Black Penitents. A Romance* (1797) ed. Frederick Garber (Oxford: Oxford University Press, 1992) p. 34. All subsequent references are to this edition and, are given in the text.

9. Edgar Allan Poe, 'The Man of the Crowd' in *The Complete Tales and Poems of Edgar Allan Poe* (Harmondsworth: Penguin, 1982) pp. 475–81. All subsequent references are to this edition, and are given in the text.
10. Immanuel Kant, 'Critique of Aesthetic Judgement' in *The Critique of Judgement* Part 1, trans. James C. Meredith (Oxford: Clarendon, 1986) p. 210.
11. Edgar Allan Poe, 'The Murders in the Rue Morgue' in *The Complete Tales and Poems of Edgar Allan Poe* (Harmondsworth: Penguin, 1982) pp. 141–68. All subsequent references are to this edition, and are given in the text.
12. Edgar Allan Poe, 'The Purloined Letter' in *The Complete Tales and Poems of Edgar Allan Poe* (Harmondsworth: Penguin, 1982) pp. 208–22, p. 216. All subsequent references are to this edition, and are given in the text.
13. Immanuel Kant, 'The Critique of Teleological Judgement' in *The Critique of Judgement* Part 2, trans. James C. Meredith (Oxford: Clarendon, 1986) pp. 12–13.
14. Edgar Allan Poe, 'Mesmeric Revelation' in *The Complete Tales and Poems of Edgar Allan Poe* (Harmondsworth: Penguin, 1982) pp. 88–96, p. 88. All subsequent references are to this edition, and are given in the text.

6 Textuality and Sublimity in *Dracula*

1. Michel Foucault, *The History of Sexuality* (1976) Vol. 1, trans. R. Hurley (Harmondsworth: Penguin, 1990). All subsequent references are to this edition, and are given in the text.
2. Bram Stoker, *Dracula*, intro. Maud Ellman, (Oxford: Oxford University Press, 1996) p. 36. All subsequent references are to this edition, and are given in the text.
3. Chris Baldick, *In Frankenstein's Shadow*.
4. Francis Barker, *The Tremulous Private Body: Essays on Subjection* (London: Methuen, 1984) p. 11. All subsequent references are to this edition, and are given in the text.
5. An argument could be made that this also applies to bourgeois subjectivity as well because this is a model of subjectivity which is available to, but denied by, a bourgeois culture which emphasises individuality.
6. See Rosemary Jackson, *Fantasy: the Literature of Subversion* pp. 120–1, where she gives an interesting Lacanian reading of Lucy's transformation. See also Phyllis A. Roth, 'Suddenly Sexual Women in Bram Stoker's *Dracula*' in *Dracula*, ed. Glennis Byron (London: Macmillan, 1999) pp. 30–42: see p. 37 where Roth discusses Lucy's 'Bloofar Lady' transformation as an inversion of motherhood. Roth's article was originally published in *Literature and Psychology* 27, 3 (1977) 113–21.
7. Cesare Lombroso, *Criminal Man* (1875) (London: G.P. Putnam's Sons, 1911).
8. Leonard Wolf, *Annotated Dracula* (London: N. Potter, 1975) p. 300.
9. Ken Gelder, *Reading the Vampire* (London: Routledge, 1994) p. 66
10. Peter De Bolla, *The Discourse of the Sublime: Readings in History, Aesthetics and the Subject* (Oxford: Blackwell, 1989) p. 56. All subsequent references are to this edition, and are given in the text.

11. See for example, Bram Dijkstra, *Idols of Perversity: Fantasies of Feminine Evil in Fin-de-Siècle Culture* (Oxford: Oxford University Press, 1986) pp. 341–8. Articles which give some focus to the idea of the New Woman include Anne Cranny-Francis, 'Sexual Politics and Political Repression in Bram Stoker's *Dracula*', in *Nineteenth Century Suspense: from Poe to Conan Doyle*, eds. C. Bloom *et al.* (London: Macmillan, 1988) pp. 64–79 and Rebecca Pope, 'Writing and Biting in *Dracula*', *Literature, Interpretation, Theory* 1 (1990) 199–216. Pope also applies an interesting Bakhtinian approach to textuality in the novel.

12. Christopher Craft, '"Kiss me with those red lips": Gender and Inversion in Bram Stoker's *Dracula*' in *The Vampire and the Critics* ed. Margaret L. Carter (London: UMI Research Press, 1988) pp. 167–94, p. 177. Originally published in *Representations* 8 (1984) 107–33.

13. Peter De Bolla, *The Discourse of the Sublime: Readings in History, Aesthetics and the Subject*. Although De Bolla's focus is principally on the eighteenth century it still bears relevance to our argument.

14. The reason why Stoker can reverse these discourses and so rework historical precedence is, of course, because at the end of the nineteenth century both of them are available for him to do so. This is not necessarily to suggest that Stoker consciously set out with this specific reversal in mind.

15. Richard Wasson, 'The Politics of *Dracula*', *English Literature in Transition* (1966) 24–7, 25.

16. Friedrich Schiller, 'On the Sublime'.

17. Harold Bloom, *The Anxiety of Influence* (1973) (Oxford: Oxford University Press, 1975) p. 16. Bloom's study is, of course, a Freudian one, but I am using him here in order to illustrate how the Freudian moment, accidentally, tells us something about history.

7   Freud's Uncanny Sublime

1. Neil Hertz, *The End of the Line: Essays on Psychoanalysis and the Sublime* (New York, Columbia University Press, 1985) p. 121.

2. David E. Pettigrew, 'The Question of the Relation of Philosophy and Psychoanalysis: the Case of Kant and Freud' in *Metaphilosophy*, ed. T.W. Bynum, 21, 1 & 2, (Jan/April 1990), 67–88.

3. Sigmund Freud, *The Interpretation of Dreams* (1900), trans. and ed. J. Strachey, Vol. 4 (Harmondsworth: Penguin, 1986). All subsequent references are to this edition, and are given in the text. Further references in the text are shortened to *Dreams*.

4. The reference is to Bloom's central argument in *The Anxiety of Influence*.

5. For a more in-depth historical account of this, see Angela Leighton, *Shelley and the Sublime* (Cambridge: Cambridge University Press, 1984) pp. 18–23.

6. Sigmund Freud, *The Psychopathology of Everyday Life* (1901), trans. A. Tyson, ed. J. Strachey (Harmondsworth: Penguin, 1987). All subsequent references are to this edition, and are given in the text. Further reference is shortened to *Psychopathology*.

7. Mary Ann Doane, *Femme Fatales: Feminism, Film Theory, and Psychoanalysis* (London: Routledge, 1991). All subsequent references are to this edition, and are given in the text.

8. R.L. Stevenson, *The Strange Case of Dr Jekyll and Mr Hyde* (1886) in *The Strange Case of Dr Jekyll and Mr Hyde and Other Stories* ed. Jenni Calder (Harmondsworth: Penguin, 1984) pp. 27–97. All subsequent references are to this edition, and are given in the text.
9. David Punter, *The Literature of Terror: the Modern Gothic* (London: Longman, 1996), Vol. 2, pp. 1–26.

Index